LEBANON

In a time of great political change and unrest in the Middle East, this highly topical text offers a succinct account of the contemporary political environment in Lebanon. Tom Najem provides both a developed understanding of the pre-civil war system and an analysis of how circumstances resulting from the civil war combined with essential pre-war elements to define politics in Lebanon.

Systematically exploring Lebanon's history, society and politics, the author stresses the importance of the crucial role of external actors in the Lebanese system. The analysis encompasses:

- the formation of the state
- weaknesses and dynamics of the Lebanese state
- the civil war
- post-war government and change
- the Lebanese economy
- foreign policy

Written in a clear and accessible manner, this book fills a conspicuous gap in the existing academic literature on Lebanon. It will be of interest not only to students of international politics and Middle East studies, but also to anyone travelling in, or wanting to learn more about, the region.

Tom Najem is Associate Professor and the Head of the Department of Political Science, University of Windsor, Canada. He teaches in the areas of International Relations and Comparative Politics (Developing World), with a regional specialisation in the Middle East.

LEBANON

The politics of a penetrated society

Tom Najem

LONDON AND NEW YORK

First published 2012
by Routledge
2 Park Square, Milton Park, Abingdon, Oxon OX14 4RN

Simultaneously published in the USA and Canada
by Routledge
711 Third Avenue, New York, NY 10017

Routledge is an imprint of the Taylor & Francis Group, an Informa business

© 2012 Tom Najem

British Library Cataloguing in Publication Data
A catalogue record for this book is available from the British Library

Library of Congress Cataloging in Publication Data
Najem, Tom.
Lebanon : the politics of a penetrated society / Tom Najem.
p. cm. -- (The contemporary Middle East)
Includes bibliographical references and index.
ISBN 978-0-415-27428-9 (hardback) -- ISBN 978-0-415-45747-7 (pbk.) --
ISBN 978-0-203-50508-3 (ebk.) 1. Lebanon--History--1946-
2. Lebanon--Politics and government--1946- I. Title.
DS80.95.N35 2011
956.9204--dc23
2011019614

ISBN: 978-0-415-27428-9 (hbk)
ISBN: 978-0-415-45747-7 (pbk)
ISBN: 978-0-203-50508-3 (ebk)

Typeset in Bembo
by Taylor & Francis Books

CONTENTS

CHRONOLOGY OF LEBANON

The formation of the modern Lebanese state

1860 – Druze–Christian sectarian conflict in Mount Lebanon and neighbouring Syria kills thousands. French troops intervene to end conflict and, with other European powers, establish an autonomous political entity in Mount Lebanon dominated by Maronite Christians.

1918 – The Ottoman Empire collapses, ending centuries of Ottoman control of the Middle East.

1920 – The League of Nations grants France a mandate for Lebanon. At the behest of Lebanon's Christians, the State of Greater Lebanon is proclaimed. It includes the former autonomous province of Mount Lebanon, plus the provinces of North Lebanon, South Lebanon and the Biqa Valley, historically part of Syria. The move is highly unpopular with the Muslim inhabitants of the annexed areas.

1926 – A Lebanese Constitution (modelled after the French one) is drawn up and a new Lebanese Republic announced.

1940 – Lebanon comes under the control of Vichy France.

1941 – Following liberation by Free French and British troops in June 1941, independence is declared on November 26.

1943 – The foundations of the state are laid out in an unwritten National Covenant (the National Pact), which lays out a formula of power-sharing among the different sectarian communities and establishes the basis of Lebanese foreign policy for the post-war period.

The post-Second World War Lebanese state, 1943–75

1943 – France agrees to the transfer of power to the Lebanese government.

1946 – The last of French troops leave Lebanon.

1957 – President Camille Chamoun accepts the Eisenhower Doctrine, which offers US economic and military aid to Middle Eastern countries to counteract Soviet influence in the region. The move is unpopular with large segments of the Lebanese population, who increasingly identify with the pan-Arabism of Nasser's Egypt.

1958 – Lebanese civil war erupts; reasons for the conflict are largely related to domestic political strife, though the interference of Egypt in Lebanese domestic affairs contributes to the conflict.

– At the request of President Chamoun, the United States sends troops to Lebanon to re-establish order. Political crisis ends when Chamoun steps down and is replaced by General Fouad Chehab.

1968 – Palestinian guerrilla organisations use Lebanon as a base for their conflict with Israel. In retaliation for an attack by two members of the Popular Front for the Liberation of Palestine (PFLP) on an Israeli aeroplane in Athens, Israel raids Beirut airport, destroying thirteen civilian planes.

1969 – The Cairo Agreement. Army Commander-in-Chief Emile Bustani and Palestine Liberation Organization (PLO) Chairman Yasser Arafat sign an agreement in Cairo, which aims to control Palestinian guerrilla activities in Lebanon. Many critics argue that the Cairo Agreement legitimised an armed Palestinian presence in Lebanon and created an autonomous zone of operations for Palestinian fighters. This situation increased tensions in Lebanon considerably, and contributed to the collapse of the Lebanese state and the ensuing civil war.

1970 – Evicted from Jordan, the PLO relocates its headquarters and main theatre of operations against Israel to Lebanon.

1970–75 – Over the next five years, the various guerrilla organisations of the PLO increase their raids into Israel, leading to significant Israeli military retaliation against Palestinian and Lebanese targets in Lebanon. The situation increases tensions between Lebanese supporters and opponents of the Palestinian presence in Lebanon, leading to numerous armed clashes. All major groups, including Christian Rightist parties and Leftist organisations, arm themselves. The Lebanese state loses its monopoly over coercive power.

The collapse of the Lebanese state and civil war, 1975–90 (five phases)

Phase I (1975–76)

Fighting erupts between Christian forces and Lebanese Leftists/Palestinians, and Syria enters the conflict.

1975–76 – Heavy fighting takes place between Christian militias and Palestinian guerillas and their Lebanese Leftist allies. These clashes mark the start of the civil war.

1976 – At the behest of Lebanese President Suleiman Franjieh, Syrian troops enter Lebanon to restore peace.

– Following Arab summit meetings in Riyadh and Cairo, a ceasefire is arranged and a predominantly Syrian Arab Deterrent Force (ADF) is established to maintain it. Critics argue that the force legitimised Syria's military presence in Lebanon. Syria came to dominate Lebanese politics from this point until its troops withdrew from Lebanon twenty-nine years later, in the spring of 2005.

Phase II (1976–82)

Sectarian entrenchment and shifting alliances. Sectarian militias and foreign armies carve up Lebanese territory as the Lebanese government fails to re-establish authority or control.

1978 – In reprisal for a Palestinian attack into its territory, Israel launches a major invasion of Lebanon, occupying land as far north as the Litani River.

– UN Security Council (UNSC) passes Resolution 425, which calls on Israel to withdraw from all Lebanese territory, and establishes the UN Interim Force in Lebanon (UNIFIL) to confirm the Israeli withdrawal, restore peace and help the Lebanese government re-establish its authority in the area.

– Israel hands over territory in Southern Lebanon not to UNIFIL, but to a proxy Lebanese militia it set up known as the South Lebanon Army, led by Major Saad Haddad. Israel and its ally the South Lebanon Army (SLA) would come to control this strip of land in South Lebanon for twenty-two years, until Israeli forces withdraw in 2000.

Phase III (1982–85)

The Israeli invasion. Israel invades Lebanon in an attempt to defeat its enemies – Palestinians and Syrians – and establish a pro-Israeli government in Beirut under the control of its right-wing Christian allies led by Bashir Gemayel.

1982 – Israel launches in June a full-scale invasion of Lebanon, which it refers to as "Operation Peace for Galilee".

– Israeli ally and President-elect Bashir Gemayel is assassinated. The following day, Israeli forces occupy West Beirut, and their allies the Phalangist militia kill Palestinians in Sabra and Shatila refugee camps.

– Basher's elder brother, Amin Gemayel, is elected President.

– The first contingent of a mainly US, French and Italian peacekeeping force, requested by Lebanon, arrives in Beirut.

1983 – Israel and Lebanon sign an agreement on Israeli withdrawal, ending hostilities and establishing a security region in Southern Lebanon.

– 241 US marines and fifty-six French paratroopers are killed in two bomb explosions in Beirut, responsibility for which is claimed by militant Shiite groups. Western peacekeeping troops leave Lebanon, dealing a blow to the Gemayel government.

Phase IV (1985–88)

Militia rule. Gemayel government fails to establish control over the country, which is divided into cantons dominated by sectarian militias, in particular Maronite (Lebanese Forces and Phalangist) and Shiite (Amal and Hizbollah), and the reassertion of Syrian influence. Parts of Lebanon become havens for militant groups, and abductions of Westerners become endemic.

1985 – Most Israeli troops withdraw, but some remain to support the SLA, which operates in an Israeli "security zone" in Southern Lebanon.

1987 – Lebanon abrogates the 1969 Cairo Agreement with the PLO as well as officially cancelling the May 17 1983 agreement with Israel.

– After Prime Minister Rashid Karami is killed, Salim Hoss becomes acting Prime Minister.

Phase V (1988–90)

"Dual government" and the end of the civil war. General Michel Aoun's wars of liberation led to wide-scale destruction, and were the impetus for international consensus led by Arab states and the West to end the conflict.

1988 – When no candidate is elected to succeed him, outgoing President Amin Gemayel appoints a six-member interim military government, composed of three Christians and three Muslims, though the latter refuse to serve. Lebanon now has two governments – one mainly Muslim in West Beirut, headed by Hoss and backed by Syria; the other Christian in East Beirut, led by the Maronite Commander-in-Chief of the Army, General Michel Aoun.

1989 – Aoun declares a "war of liberation" against the Syrian presence in Lebanon. Syria and its Lebanese Muslim allies strike at Aoun's forces in East Beirut, leaving widespread destruction.

– Under international support, Lebanese parliamentarians meet in Ta'if, Saudi Arabia, to endorse a Charter of National Reconciliation. A plan, later known as the Ta'if Accord, is conceived to reconfigure the political system so as to give Muslims equal powers to Christians. For example, Parliament would have an equal number of Christian and Muslim members instead of the previous six-to-five ratio in favour of Christians.

– General Michel Aoun refuses to accept the Ta'if Accord, purportedly because it refuses to lay out a clear timetable for Syrian withdrawal from the country.

– President-elect Rene Mu'awwad is assassinated on November 22 and succeeded by Elias Hrawi on November 24. The following day, Salim Hoss becomes Prime Minister; on November 28, Gen Emile Lahoud replaces Michael Aoun as Commander-in-Chief of the Army.

1990 – Syrian Air Force attacks the Presidential Palace at Baabda, where Michael Aoun is based. Aoun takes refuge in the French Embassy. The Syrian move is supported by the USA and Europe, in part in return for Syrian support of American actions against Iraq. This date marks the end of the civil war.

Post-civil war Lebanon, 1990–2005

The period is defined by the reassertion of Lebanese state control over Lebanese territory and the rebuilding of Lebanon following fifteen years of war. However, this was done under the heavy tutelage of the Syrian military. Critics claim Syria's control (political and military) over Lebanon during this period amounted to an occupation, and Lebanon's very sovereignty was questionable. South Lebanon was the scene of a number of conflicts between Hizbollah and Israel.

1990 – Omar Karami heads a Government of National Reconciliation.

1991 – National Assembly orders the dissolution of all militias by April 30, but Hizbollah is allowed to keep its arms and remain active, ostensibly to liberate South Lebanon from Israeli control. Hizbollah is the only militia to retain its arms post-civil war (which remains true at the time of writing in 2010). Although the SLA also refuses to disband, it dissolved following Israel's withdrawal from Lebanon in 2000.

– A Treaty of Brotherhood, Cooperation and Coordination is signed in Damascus by Lebanon and Syria and a Higher Council, co-chaired by the two Presidents, is established. Critics view this document as evidence of Damascus's political control or even "annexation" of Lebanon.

– National Assembly grants an amnesty for all crimes committed during the civil war, 1975–90. Michel Aoun receives a presidential pardon and is allowed to leave for France.

1992 – Sheikh Abbas al-Musawi, Secretary-General of Hizbollah, is killed when Israeli helicopter gunships attack his motorcade on a road southeast of Sidon.

– By June 17, all Western hostages held in Lebanon have been released, ending a dark chapter in Lebanon's history that began in the early 1980s.

– Parliamentary elections held in Lebanon, the first since 1972. Christians largely boycott the elections because of Syrian control over the process. Nabih Berri, Secretary-General of the Shiite militia and now political party Amal, becomes Speaker of the National Assembly. He is widely viewed as Syria's closest ally.

– Rafiq Hariri, a billionaire businessman with close ties to Saudi Arabia and Western leaders, becomes Prime Minister, heading a cabinet of technocrats. His mandate is to rebuild the Lebanese economy decimated by years of war. Syria's acquiescence to his appointment reflects its concerns that popular discontent over the economic situation may spill over to anti-Syrian activities. Hariri became the most powerful post-war Lebanese politician, until his assassination in 2005.

1993 – Israel attempts to end the threat from Hizbollah and others in Southern Lebanon by launching "Operation Accountability", the heaviest attack against Lebanese soil since 1982.

1996 – Israel launches "Operation Grapes of Wrath", bombing Hizbollah bases in Southern Lebanon, the Southern district of Beirut and the Biqa Valley.

– USA negotiates a truce and "understanding" under which Hizbollah and Palestinian guerrillas agree not to attack civilians in Northern Israel, and which recognises Israel's right to self-defence but also Hizbollah's right to resist the Israeli occupation of Southern Lebanon. Lebanon and Syria do not sign the "understanding", but the Israel–Lebanon Monitoring Group (ILMG), with representatives from the USA, France, Israel, Lebanon and Syria, is established to monitor the truce.

1998 – Israel's inner cabinet votes to accept UNSC Resolution 425 of 1978 if Lebanon guarantees the security of Israel's northern border. Both Lebanon and Syria reject this condition.

– Army Commander-in-Chief Emile Lahoud is sworn in as President, succeeding Elias Hrawi. Lahoud is seen as being close to Damascus.

– Salim Hoss becomes Prime Minister, heading a cabinet that includes no militia leaders and only two ministers from the previous administration.

2000 – Israeli cabinet votes for the unilateral withdrawal of Israeli troops from Southern Lebanon by July 2000.

– After the collapse of the SLA and the rapid advance of Hizbollah forces, Israel withdraws its troops from Southern Lebanon, more than six weeks before its stated deadline of 7 July.

– 25 May declared an annual public holiday, called "Resistance and Liberation Day".

– Rafiq Hariri takes office as Prime Minister in October for the second time.

2003 – The Syria Accountability and Lebanese Sovereignty Restoration Act (SALSRA) is a bill of the US Congress passed in December, which calls on Syria to end its presence in Lebanon.

2004 – In a highly controversial move, and under Syrian pressure, Parliament votes to extend pro-Syrian President Emile Lahoud's term by three years. This is the first time in Lebanon's modern history that a president's term has been extended. The move is deeply unpopular, and strongly opposed by Prime Minister Rafiq Hariri and his allies.

– Four ministers step down to protest against the constitutional change that facilitated the presidential term extension.

– UNSC adopts Resolution 1559, calling upon all foreign forces (including Syria) to withdraw from Lebanon, as well as for the disbanding and disarmament of all Lebanese and non-Lebanese militias. The Resolution is co-sponsored by France and the United States.

– Prime Minister Rafiq Hariri and his cabinet resign and state they will not run for re-election.

– President Emil Lahoud appoints Omar Karami as the new Prime Minister.

– Hundreds of thousands of pro-Syrian protestors gather in Beirut to voice their support for a Syrian presence in the country and their opposition to UN resolution 1559, which calls for Syrian withdrawal from Lebanon.

Post-civil war Lebanon and the end of Syrian military control, 2005–11

The equivalent of a political earthquake occurs in Lebanon when the powerful Lebanese politician and father of Lebanon's reconstruction, Rafiq Hariri, is assassinated. The event eventually leads to Syria's spectacular military withdrawal from Lebanon. The period also witnesses heightened sectarianism, increased violence, and an overall deterioration of the security situation in a country where political stalemate has dominated. The third major war takes place between Hizbollah and Israel since the Lebanese war ended in 1990.

February 2005 – The Assassination of Rafiq Hariri. Former Prime Minister Rafiq Hariri and eight others are killed on February 14 by car bomb in Beirut. Syria is widely blamed for carrying out the assassination, a charge it strongly denies.

– Hariri's funeral is held in downtown Beirut and is the site of large anti-Syrian protests. Thousands protest against Syrian influence in Lebanon. Prime Minister Omar Karami resigns along with his cabinet.

March 2005 – Anti- and pro-Syrian rallies dominate the month, leading to the departure of Syrian troops from Lebanon. Hundreds of thousands of pro-Syrian protesters gather, at the urging of Hizbollah, to denounce "Western influence" in Lebanon. The date of the protest, March 8, lends its name to a political alliance of pro-Syrian groups led by Hizbollah.

– President Emile Lahoud re-appoints Prime Minister Karami.

– Hundreds of thousands of pro-Syrian protestors gather in the Southern city of Nabatiyya.

– Hundreds of thousands of anti-Syrian protestors gather in Beirut. The date of the protest, March 14, lends its name to a political alliance of pro-Western anti-Syrian groups led by the former Prime Minister Hariri's Future Movement and Christian allies.

– Under enormous international and domestic pressure, Lebanon agrees to cooperate with the UN investigation into the killing of former Prime Minister Hariri.

– In a surprise move, but as a consequence of significant international pressure, the last of Syrian troops leave Lebanon after a nearly thirty-year presence in the country.

April 2005 – Initial UN report is inconclusive as to who is responsible for the killing of Hariri, but finds Syria responsible for the tensions in Lebanon.

– Prime Minister Karami steps down after failing to form a government.

– Prime Minister-designate Najib Mikati forms a new government made up of fourteen pro-Syrian ministers.

May 2005 – Parliamentary elections, the first held outside Syrian control.

– Opposition leader General Michel Aoun returns from exile in France, after the departure of Syrian troops a month prior.

– The first round of parliamentary elections begins to take place. Anti-Syrian bloc led by Rafiq Hariri's son, Saad Hariri, sweeps all nineteen seats in Beirut.

June 2005 – Anti-Syrian journalist and professor Samir Kassir is killed in his car in a Christian neighbourhood of Beirut.

– Saad Hariri's anti-Syrian coalition secures a majority of the seats in Parliament, the first time since the end of the civil war that an anti-Syrian government will rule the country.

– Anti-Syrian candidate and close political ally of the Hariris, Fouad Siniora, nominated as Prime Minister-designate.

July 2005 – The first government is formed since the end of the civil war that is free of Syrian influence and is considered pro-Western.

– US Secretary of State Condoleezza Rice visits Beirut, the highest-level US visit since Syrian troops left the country.

August 2005 – Four pro-Syrian security chiefs are arrested at the urging of the UN investigation into the death of Rafiq Hariri for complicity in the assassination.

December 2005 – Anti-Syrian MP Gibran Tueni is killed in Beirut, the fourth critic of Syria since February to be killed.

– Tens of thousands attend his funeral, which turns into a protest against continuing Syrian interference in the country.

January 2006 – Thousands of pro-Syrian protestors gather in front of the US Embassy to protest against American influence on the Lebanese government.

February 2006 – Hundreds of thousands of Lebanese gather in Beirut to mark the one-year anniversary of the death of Rafiq Hariri.

March 2006 – The so-called "National Dialogue" talks between the leaders of Sunni, Shiite and Christian communities take place to discuss the fate of the nation, the first time such talks have been held since the end of the civil war.

July 2006 – The Israel–Hizbollah War. Hizbollah captures two Israeli soldiers and kills an additional seven in a cross-border raid. In response, Israel launches air strikes and a naval bombardment targeting Hizbollah strongholds and infrastructure. Israel also moves troops into Southern Lebanon for the first time since their withdrawal in 2000. Hizbollah responds by launching rockets into Israel.

August 2006 – UNSC Resolution 1701 calls for a termination of hostilities.

September 2006 – First major deployment of UN forces lands in Lebanon.

– Israeli air and naval blockade of Lebanon is lifted.

November 2006 – Three Hizbollah ministers and two ministers from the Amal movement resign from the Lebanese cabinet in protest when talks concerning greater opposition representation in the cabinet break down.

– Lebanese cabinet approves the establishment of a tribunal to bring to justice those responsible for the assassination of Rafiq Hariri. The UNSC will oversee the trial.

– Lebanese Industry Minister and Christian leader Pierre Gemayel is shot dead in a Beirut suburb.

– An anti-Hizbollah/anti-Syria demonstration takes place in Beirut's Martyrs' Square, emerging from the funeral procession of Pierre Gemayel.

– President Emile Lahoud announces that he will not approve the international tribunal to investigate the killing of Rafiq Hariri, arguing that due to lack of Shiite representation in cabinet, the decision was void.

December 2006 – Hizbollah organises a mass rally, estimated at 800,000, to protest against the "unconstitutional government".

January 2007 – Hizbollah-led opposition pressures the government to resign by calling for general strikes.

– Aid conference in Paris pledges $7.6 billion to Lebanon.

May 2007 – Lebanese Army siege of the Palestinian refugee camp, Nahr al-Bared, which is controlled by militant Islamic group.

– Security Council votes to set up Special Tribunal for Lebanon (STL) to try suspects in the assassination of Hariri.

June 2007 – MP Walid Eido (member of the governing anti-Syrian bloc) and five others killed by a car bomb.

September 2007 – Lebanese military seizes control of the Nahr al-Bared from the Fatah al-Islam militants, ending almost five months of fighting. More than 400 people die, including 168 soldiers, and 40,000 are displaced before the army takes control.

– MP Antoine Ghanim (member of the governing anti-Syrian bloc) and seven others are killed by a car bomb.

November 2007 – President Emile Lahoud finishes his term and leaves the presidential palace without a successor. Prime Minister Fouad Siniora says his cabinet will assume executive powers until a successor is found.

December 2007 – Speaker of the House Nabih Berri says leaders have agreed on General Michel Suleiman to be next Lebanese President. Disagreements over share of positions in the new cabinet prevent his election.

– Brigadier General Francois al-Hajj and a bodyguard are killed by a car bomb.

January 2008 – Lebanese presidential vote is delayed.

– Car bomb, aimed at American diplomatic vehicle in Christian area of Beirut, kills three and wounds sixteen others.

– Blast in east Beirut kills six people, including Wisam Eid from the Lebanese Police Intelligence Unit.

February 2008 – Hizbollah holds mass funeral for its assassinated commander Imad Moughniyah in Beirut. He was killed in Damascus the day before by a bomb blast. Israel is widely considered to have carried out the assassination.

April 2008 – Two officials from the Phalange Party (and members of March 14 Alliance) are killed.

– Lebanese Parliament fails to hold a session to elect a new president for the eighteenth time.

May 2008 – Hizbollah flexes its military muscle in showdown with Lebanese government. The Lebanese government bans a fixed-line communication network used by Hizbollah and fires the head of airport security, also a Hizbollah ally. Hizbollah gunmen clash with government supporters and the capital is paralysed as Hizbollah blocks main roads.

– Hassan Nasrallah, leader of Hizbollah, says that the government has declared open war on the group.

– Several die in gun battles in Beirut, while an offer by Saad Hariri to refer the issue to the army is rejected by Hizbollah.

– Opposition forces led by Hizbollah seize control of West Beirut.

– Hizbollah and other members of the opposition begin to withdraw fighters from the streets while the army takes over in a security role. The army also overturns the measures that sparked the fighting.

– Leaders of the government and the opposition meet in Doha for crisis talks. Government and opposition reach power-sharing agreement in Doha, referred to as the Doha Agreement. The opposition wins a greater share of seats in the cabinet, officially giving them a veto over executive decisions.

– Former Lebanese General Michel Suleiman is elected Lebanon's new President.

June 2008 – Three are killed and four wounded between clashing pro- and anti-government forces in Biqa Valley.

– Heavy sectarian fighting erupts in Tripoli, nine are dead and numerous are injured. Army is deployed to end fighting.

July 2008 – Unity government is formed as agreed under Doha deal.

August 2008 – Bomb kills fifteen, including ten soldiers in Tripoli. No claims of responsibility. The area has been the scene of numerous conflicts between militant groups and the Lebanese authorities, as well between Lebanese factions.

September 2008 – Sunni and Alawite leaders in Tripoli sign a reconciliation deal, ending the fighting that has taken place since June.

October 2008 – Lebanon and Syria begin diplomatic relations for the first time since independence from France in the 1940s. Syria has previously refused to do so, leaving its critics to accuse it of not recognising Lebanese sovereignty.

January 2009 – Syria approves Lebanon's first Ambassador to Syria.

March 2009 – STL officially begins.

April 2009 – Syrian Mohammed Zuhair al-Siddiq, a former Syrian intelligence officer, is arrested in connection with the killing of Rafiq Hariri. Subsequently, four pro-Syrian Lebanese generals are freed after the UN court rules that there is not enough evidence to convict them.

May 2009 – American Vice-President Joseph Biden visits Lebanon prior to the country's June parliamentary elections. This is the first time an American Vice-President has visited the country in twenty-six years, leading a top Hizbollah leader to accuse the USA of meddling in Lebanese affairs.

– An article in German newspaper *Der Spiegel* hints at Hizbollah's role in Hariri assassination.

June 2009 – Second parliamentary elections since Syrian withdrawal from Lebanon. Turnout for elections reportedly close to 55 per cent, with pro-Western March 14 Alliance taking seventy-one seats and Hizbollah-led March 8 Alliance securing fifty-seven. About 50,000 security personnel are deployed to prevent violence. Despite the March 14 victory, opposition demands role in government, including a number of cabinet seats which would give them veto powers over key government decisions.

July 2009 – Lebanese Army breaks up a cell of Islamic militants who had allegedly planned to attack UN peacekeepers in the south of the country. The group is allegedly tied to Al-Qaeda.

September 2009 – Prime Minister-designate Saad Hariri presents his cabinet to the opposition parties, and it is promptly rejected.

– Hariri announces that he is stepping down after failing to form a unity government.

– Hariri reinstated as Prime Minister-designate and given a second chance to form a government.

November 2009 – Six months after winning the parliamentary elections, Prime Minister Saad Hariri forms a new thirty-member coalition government with the opposition, including fifteen members from Hariri's majority March 14 alliance, ten from the Hizbollah-led March 8 opposition, and five chosen by President

Michel Suleiman. Despite winning the June parliamentary elections, a coalition or unity government with the opposition is deemed necessary. Agreement on the make-up of the unity government takes place after intense negotiations between the various Lebanese factions and their regional and international patrons, including Syria and Saudi Arabia (reflecting the influence external powers continue to wield over key Lebanese groups).

December 2009 – Prime Minister Saad Hariri meets with Syrian President Bashar Assad in Damascus to discuss bilateral relations. Many analysts see the meeting as recognition of Syria's influence and importance in Lebanon, despite its withdrawal from the country in April 2005.

February 2010 – Thousands gather in Beirut to mark the fifth anniversary of the assassination of Rafiq Hariri. The gathering has been held annually since his assassination in February 2005.

– A clash between the Asbat al-Ansar militia and Fatah gunmen in the Ein el-Hilweh Palestinian refugee camp results in at least two deaths. Control over Palestinian refugee camps remains of significant concern to the Lebanese government because of the presence of a number of militant Islamic groups who have clashed with Lebanese authorities on numerous occasions.

March 2010 – The leader of Lebanon's Druze community, Walid Jumblatt, meets with the Syrian president for the first time since the assassination of former Prime Minister Rafiq Hariri. The meeting marks Jumblatt's decision to move away from the anti-Syrian March 14 movement. Some analysts see this move as recognition of the growing influence of Syria's Lebanese allies in the March 8 movement and the general reassertion of Syrian influence in Lebanese politics.

– Hizbollah's Secretary General, Nasrallah, confirms that members of Hizbollah were questioned by the STL, and that he believes indictments implicating the movement are forthcoming.

April 2010 – Israeli officials claim that Syria delivered to Hizbollah long-range Scud missiles capable of hitting large Israeli cities, including Tel Aviv. UNIFIL later responds to these assertions, claiming that Southern Lebanon is a Scud-free zone.

– Hundreds of young Lebanese march for secularism in the country. This represents the first serious public demonstration for secularism in a country where sectarianism remains entrenched in the political and social fabric of society, and where sectarian tensions remain high.

May 2010 – Lebanese municipal elections take place throughout the month amid increasing tension and violence between contending political movements and alliances. The results confirm the stark divisions among the Lebanese population, with both the March 14 and March 8 alliances maintaining control in regions considered to fall within their respective traditional strongholds.

– The President of the STL suggests indictments could be issued before the end of the year.

June 2010 – Lebanese and Syrian Presidents meet in Damascus to discuss a host of bilateral issues, including working toward demarcating their maritime and land borders as soon as possible.

July 2010 – Grand Ayatollah Mohammed Hussein Fudlallah, key in founding of Hizbollah, dies.

– Syrian President and Saudi King visit Beirut, the first visit of the Syrian President to Lebanon since the country's army was forced out of Lebanon in 2005.

– Hizbollah's leader publicly criticises and discredits the STL by linking its evidence to Israeli intelligence services.

– Hizbollah's leader states that Saad Hariri had told him the STL would implicate Hizbollah members.

August 2010 – Israeli and Lebanese soldiers exchange fire along the border. By the end of the border conflict, two Lebanese soldiers, a senior Israeli officer and a journalist are killed.

– STL calls for the submission of all material held by Hizbollah, which claims its data implicates Israel in the killing of Rafiq Hariri.

– Lebanese security officials have shot and killed leader of Sunni militant group "Fatah al-Islam".

September 2010 – Hizbollah MP Hassan Fadlallah states that the STL should be abandoned when a parliamentary Finance and Budget Commission falls apart after pro-Hizbollah MPs demand members vote on a 2010 state budget clause related to STL funding.

– Prime Minister Saad Hariri vows to stay committed to the STL despite rising political tensions.

– Prime Minister Saad Hariri withdraws his earlier charge that Syria was behind his father's assassination.

October 2010 – Among rising sectarian tensions, Iranian President Ahmadinejad visits Lebanon, including the South, where he is given a hero's welcome in Hizbollah strongholds.

– Three members of the STL are attacked in Beirut by a large group of people.

November 2010 – US government announces it will transfer an additional $10 million dollars to the STL.

– Canadian Broadcasting Corporation reports that phone records suggest Hizbollah officials communicated with the owners of the cell phones allegedly used to coordinate the bombing.

December 2010 – Hizbollah MP says the STL lacks legal basis, stating that "the mechanism by which the international tribunal was set up has transcended the Lebanese government and its Constitution" [*The Daily Star* (Beirut, Lebanon) December 9, 2010].

– The cabinet reconvenes to discuss the STL and the issue of so-called "false witnesses", which pro-Hizbollah members of cabinet want investigated and tried in Lebanon's highest court.

– Wikileaks report states that in 2008 Saudi Arabia urged an Arab-led military force to destroy Hizbollah.

January 2011 – Lebanon's Unity Government collapses. Members of Hizbollah and their allies in the March 8 Alliance bring down the government after resigning from Prime Minister Saad Hariri's cabinet over the government's refusal to distance itself from the STL.

– UN prosecutors issue a sealed indictment expected to indict Hizbollah members in the assassination of the former Prime Minister.

– Lebanese Druze leader Walid Jumblatt announces that he will back Hizbollah's efforts to form a new government.

– Protests begin to break out, largely by supporters of Saad Hariri, who are protesting against Hizbollah's attempts to form a new government.

– Saudi Arabia announces that it has abandoned mediation efforts ongoing with Syria over the fate of the STL.

– Hizbollah-backed Najib Mikati is appointed Prime Minister, despite large protests in Tripoli dubbed "day of rage"; protests also take place in Beirut and Sidon.

February 2011 – Lebanon's highest Shiite religious authority slams the UN-backed STL as a political tool designed to target Hizbollah and calls on the Lebanese government not to cooperate with it.

– Saad Hariri announces that he will not join a unity government and will instead lead the opposition to what he claims will be a Hizbollah-dominated government.

– Prime Minister Mikati continues to try to put together a government.

MAP OF LEBANON

INTRODUCTION

Background

Lebanon is located along the eastern Mediterranean and borders both Syria and Israel, a fact that was to weigh particularly heavily on Lebanese politics during the second half of the twentieth century. At 10,452 km², it is geographically smaller than every US state except Delaware and Rhode Island. Lebanon currently has 4 million people (plus an additional Palestinian refugee population of approximately 300,000), and with nineteen officially recognised sectarian communities, is one of the most diverse countries in the Middle East. Sectarian identity is an essential and deeply ingrained aspect of Lebanese society, and is a crucial, if not defining, feature of the Lebanese political system to this day.

As an independent political entity, Lebanon is a relatively recent creation, tracing its origins to three distinct historical periods – the 1860s and the establishment of an autonomous Mount Lebanon within the confines of the Ottoman Empire; the 1920s and the creation of Greater Lebanon under French Mandate rule; and the establishment of an independent Lebanese state during the 1940s.

From 1943 until 1974, Lebanon was a prosperous and stable country, with a political and economic system that was the envy of many. Indeed, the political system was even held out by some scholars as a model of governing for other deeply divided societies. The Lebanese political system was an example of a consociational model of democratic governance, a concept coined by the political theorist Arend Lijphart in the 1960s. Consociational democracy is defined as "government by elite cartel designed to turn a democracy with a fragmented political culture into a stable democracy".[1] Lebanon had its own unique version of a consociational system, fusing elements of a liberal democratic system with those of a traditional confessional and neo-patrimonial one. Some, however, may argue that, precisely for these reasons, the Lebanese system was not democratic, a point that is examined in considerable length in Chapter 1.

Whether democratic or not, the system worked relatively well for thirty years, and provided Lebanon with a sustained period of political stability and economic prosperity. In popular terms, Lebanon was even referred to as the Switzerland of the Middle East, and Beirut as the Paris of the Middle East. The situation in Lebanon during this period could also be contrasted with that of its Arab neighbours, all of whom were led by authoritarian regimes of either the traditional monarchical or socialist one-party variety.

However, by 1975 the situation could not have been more different. The Lebanese political system collapsed spectacularly, and the country entered a sustained period of "civil war", which ended only in 1990, some sixteen years later. The civil war cost the lives of well over 100,000 people, displaced hundreds of thousands more, and cost billions of dollars in damage to the country's infrastructure. By the 1980s, the Lebanese government's authority had dissipated and the country had broken down into various cantons dominated by sectarian militias, or foreign armies that had entered Lebanon at various stages of the conflict. In contrast to a more peaceful period, Lebanon became synonymous with lawlessness, international terrorism and Islamic radicalism. And with the taking of Western hostages by radical elements, the country became a global pariah.

In 1990, the civil war finally came to an end. The Lebanese began the long process of rebuilding their political and economic systems. This required dealing with the remnants of the civil war, including the continuing presence of armed militias such as the radical Shiite party Hizbollah, as well as the presence of foreign forces on Lebanese soil.

Outline of the book

The aim of this book is to provide a succinct account of the contemporary political environment in Lebanon. It is written with both the general reader and first-time student of Lebanese politics in mind, although seasoned students will also benefit from the analysis offered.

The material in this book encompasses: 1) a developed understanding of the pre-civil war system in Lebanon – the circumstances of its formation, its unique characteristics, its underlying dynamics, and the weaknesses that led to its collapse; and 2) an analysis of how circumstances resulting from the war, combined with essential elements of the pre-war system, came to define the contemporary political process in Lebanon.

As the title *The Politics of a Penetrated Society* suggests, a major theme of this book is the crucial role of external actors in the Lebanese system. Prior to the civil war, the penetration was a result of pan-Arabism and the Arab–Israeli conflict. Indeed, in the early 1970s, Lebanon became heavily penetrated by the Palestine Liberation Organization (PLO). This fact would contribute considerably to the outbreak of the civil war. During the course of the sixteen-year conflict, the country was further penetrated by a number of regional and international actors. One of these actors, Syria, established the basis for a long-term penetration that made it the dominant force in Lebanese politics during the 1990–2005 period. Syria's control over the Lebanese system was so extensive that the existence of Lebanon as an independent sovereign entity was legitimately questioned during this period.

Although Syria's stranglehold over the political system ended once its military withdrew from the country in 2005, its influence continues to be felt through its extensive patron–client network with a number of important Lebanese groups. Further, Iran's influence over the Lebanese political process has increased substantially after 2005, as its main client, Hizbollah (created by Iran in 1982), has become arguably the most powerful actor within the Lebanese political system. The role of external actors, combined with deep sectarian divisions, has left the political system vulnerable to developments within the wider Middle East regional system, including the dynamics of the current Israeli–Iranian rivalry.

The book consists of five chapters. Chapter 1 serves two basic functions. First, it provides necessary historical background on important developments prior to the civil war period. Second, and more importantly, it explains the nature and workings of the pre-war political system, and considers the reasons for its ultimate failure. It examines the origins of the Lebanese nation state, explains the function of the Lebanese political system from 1943 to 1975, and considers the key political and social factors that caused the civil war.

The aim of Chapter 2 is to provide a relatively brief analytical account of the civil war that explains the transition from the pre-war political system to the post-war system. It summarises the major developments during the civil war period and proceeds to consider the lasting systemic implications of the war that have figured very significantly in post-war Lebanese politics.

Chapter 3 examines the post-war political system in some detail, and is divided into two parts. Part I examines the main features of the post-war political system until 2005, the year that the so-called "cedar revolution" forced the Syrian military to quitthe country. Part II examines the implications of Syria's unexpected military withdrawal for the post-war political system.

The purpose of Chapter 4 is to examine and evaluate the economic policies pursued by successive Lebanese governments since autumn 1992. The primary focus will be on "Horizon 2000", the major reconstruction programme of the 1990s that was the centrepiece of Prime Minister Rafiq Hariri's attempts to repair Lebanon's economy after the devastation of the civil war period. I feel that it is important to focus on this period as it established the general framework for the post-civil war economy. Chapter 4 then proceeds to examine the main economic issues faced by subsequent Lebanese governments.

Finally, Chapter 5 considers contemporary Lebanese foreign policy. The chapter is divided into two parts. Part I deals with Lebanese foreign policy during Syria's occupation (1990–2005). Part II focuses on the period following Syria's withdrawal (2005–2010).

The book argues that the Lebanese political system continues to suffer from the three systemic weaknesses that led to its collapse in 1975: 1) sectarian tensions, which continue to permeate nearly all facets of Lebanese society; 2) external penetration, which has continued to tie the fortunes of the country to regional and international conflicts and dynamics; and 3) the weakness of the Lebanese state, which continues to lack even the basic coercive capacity to assert its authority.

Indeed, these three systemic weaknesses are now worse than at any time in Lebanon's modern history, a fact that may not bode well for Lebanon's political future.

1

THE FORMATION OF THE MODERN LEBANESE STATE

Many of the state institutions that continue to characterise the Lebanese political system to this day actually date back to the nineteenth and early twentieth centuries. However, most scholars would agree that the key event in the formation of the modern system took place in 1943, when leaders from two of Lebanon's major sectarian communities, the Maronite Christians and the Sunni Muslims, agreed to a political arrangement that became known as the National Pact. This agreement essentially established a framework for power-sharing and cooperation that would make it possible for the country's many and deeply divided sectarian groups to govern collectively. From the end of the First World War, the country had effectively been governed by the French, but developments during the Second World War set the stage for Lebanese independence and prompted the major sectarian leaders to prepare for self-government. As events developed, the framework established by the National Pact would become the fundamental blueprint for the independent Lebanese state, and would continue to function until 1975. By that time, a combination of internal and external pressures had made the system unsustainable, and a long and disastrous civil war ensued.

This chapter serves two basic functions. First, it provides necessary historical background on important developments prior to the civil war period. Second, and more importantly, it explains the nature and workings of the pre-war political system and considers the reasons for its ultimate failure. The chapter is organised along chronological and thematic lines, and is divided into three main sections.

In the first section, I examine the origins of the Lebanese nation state, beginning with the Ottoman period (prior to 1860), proceeding through the establishment of an autonomous Lebanese entity, the *mutasarrifiyya* (1860–1918), and concluding with the French mandate period (1919–46). I then look at the National Pact in some detail, focusing on the underlying issues and divisions it was intended to address.

In the second section, I examine the function of the Lebanese political system from 1943 to 1975. First, I look at the main features of the political order, particularly its unique blend of confessionalism and neo-patrimonialism and the workings of its "consociational democracy". I then provide a chronological overview of the major political and economic developments during this period.

Finally, in the third section, I consider the factors that brought about the collapse of the Lebanese system and led to the civil war. I begin by presenting an overview of the different schools of thought concerning this issue, and then present my own analysis concerning the key causal factors.

1.1 The birth of the Lebanese state

The seeds of modern Lebanon (up to 1860)

Prior to the First World War, the territories that make up present-day Lebanon had long been part of the once-mighty Ottoman Empire (1288–1923), which, at the height of its power, stretched across the Middle East, Asia and parts of Southern and Eastern Europe. The empire was ethnically and religiously diverse, and used a range of methods to govern the territories under its control. In Lebanon, the Ottomans relied, for the most part, on local feudal leaders and powerful families to rule the area. In return for providing both allegiance and taxes to the Ottomans, these elements were permitted some autonomy in local matters. This was particularly the case in remote mountainous regions. These were of limited strategic interest in any case, and the Ottomans would have found it difficult to control them otherwise. Tensions between the central authorities and local leaders occurred often, as each would use opportunities to increase their own power at the expense of the other. For example, local leaders were often able to exercise considerable autonomy during periods of Ottoman weakness.

Another feature of Ottoman administration that was particularly significant with respect to Lebanon was the so-called "millet system", which governed legal relations between the majority (Sunni Muslim) and minority religious groups. Effectively, the millet system accorded the religious minorities a relatively autonomous legal and cultural status. For example, Christians and other minority sects were entitled to make their own arrangements with respect to religious practice, marriage and family law, inheritance, education, and so on. Lebanon, due to the Crusades and other historical and geographical circumstances, had a much higher concentration of minority sects than most parts of the empire. There were large numbers of Christians, including Maronite Catholics, Greek Catholics and Greek Orthodox, as well as other non-Muslim and Muslim minorities such as Druze, Jews and Shiites. Thus, over time, some sectarian communities gradually developed their own sense of cultural, and ultimately political, identity within the broader Ottoman framework.

By the middle of the eighteenth century, and throughout the nineteenth century, the influence of the Ottoman Empire declined significantly in comparison with the emerging European colonial powers. Due largely to the growing importance of international trade, the decentralised nature of Ottoman administration, and the growing aspirations of ethnic and religious minority groups, the empire's relative weakness in the international sphere had grave internal implications.

For one thing, beginning in 1569, successive Ottoman governments negotiated a series of treaties with European powers known as "capitulations". These treaties gave European merchants, traders and diplomats ever-increasing freedom to operate within Ottoman borders, to the extent that, by the eighteenth century, such elements were able to operate almost completely outside the bounds of normal Ottoman laws. This, along with the growing volume and importance of trade, provided an important lever that the European states were able to use to undermine Ottoman central authority to their own advantage.

The decentralised nature of Ottoman administration also contributed to growing European influence within the empire, as autonomous local leaders in the Ottoman provinces were largely free to negotiate their own trade and diplomatic agreements with foreign governments. For their part, the Europeans were able to use such agreements to advance their own political, strategic and economic objectives in Ottoman regions. In addition, the local leaders and the ethnic, cultural and religious interests they represented were able to use the agreements to increase their autonomy from central government control.

The Ottoman central authorities made a number of attempts to reform the empire as it became more and more susceptible to the external and internal pressures that these developments were generating. However, for various reasons, they were unable to prevent European penetration and halt their own, ultimately terminal, decline. Thus, during the course of the 1800s and 1900s, the Ottomans lost *de facto* and/or *de jure* control of many of their provinces in North Africa and Eastern Europe. Significant occurrences in Lebanon at this time were part of a general and intensifying trend.[1]

Throughout the early and mid-nineteenth century, internal tensions were on the increase in the Ottoman provinces that make up present-day Lebanon and Syria, particularly in the region of Mount Lebanon. What may have started as class-related disputes between peasants and landowners ultimately took on a sectarian character, with the result that the Druze and Maronite communities became increasingly hostile to each other. By 1860, the situation became a fully fledged war that spread throughout the surrounding provinces and involved the local sects in a wider Christian–Muslim conflict. This naturally prompted action from the Ottoman central authorities and also attracted significant attention and concern in Europe, particularly in France, which had by this time cultivated close relations with the Maronite community. Indeed, the French dispatched an expeditionary military force to the region to protect the Christian element. After the conclusion of the conflict, the European powers, essentially at the behest of the Maronites, induced the Ottomans to allow for the creation of an autonomous political entity in Mount Lebanon. This entity, known as the *mutasarrifiyya*, was overwhelmingly Christian, and its security was guaranteed by the five great European powers (France, Britain, Prussia, Russia and Austria-Hungary).[2]

The mutasarrifiyya *(1860–1918)*

From 1860 until the end of the First World War, the *mutasarrifiyya* began to lay the foundations of a Lebanese national consciousness, albeit one strongly influenced by

European penetration and dominated by the Christian worldview and Christian political, economic and cultural priorities. Although the *mutasarrifiyya* continued to contain a diverse mix of sects, the Christians, and particularly the Maronites, made up a considerable majority of the population during this period.

From a political perspective, Mount Lebanon ostensibly continued to function as part of the broader Ottoman Empire. In practice, however, the influence of the central Ottoman authorities was very limited. The region was administered by a Christian governor (*mutasarrif*) from outside the entity, with a sort of consultative council including representatives from all of the sectarian groups. It maintained a strong European orientation with particularly visible economic, cultural and diplomatic ties to France. At the same time, largely as a consequence of this orientation, the Ottoman and Muslim character of the region became somewhat muted.

Economically, the *mutasarrifiyya* forged increasing links with the emerging capitalist economies of the West throughout this period. Naturally, the Christians were able to use their strong European and New World ties to begin to exercise a decisive advantage over the other sects. This advantage was intensified by the ability and willingness of the Christians to establish emigrant communities throughout the Western world.

From the cultural standpoint, the education system was heavily influenced by the French model, and by French language and culture more generally. The emerging Lebanese press and publishing houses were also heavily influenced by European models and standards. Religious links with the Catholic European states, especially France and Italy, also increased. It is also worth noting that the political influence of the Maronite Church began to increase significantly after 1860.[3]

The French mandate period (1919–46)

The conclusion of the First World War saw the final dissolution of the Ottoman Empire. While what remained of the Ottoman central government formed the basis of the modern Turkish state, the vast majority of Ottoman territory was divided into regions with different types of official political standing. Some parts of the empire, such as the Arabian peninsula, were granted independence immediately. Other parts were classified as European colonies. However, most of the territory was placed under the control of the victorious European states through legal "mandates" initially issued at the San Remo Conference in 1920 and formally ratified by the new League of Nations organisation in 1922. Ostensibly, the function of the mandatory authorities was to prepare the territories for full independence. However, the duration of the mandates was never specified, and, in practice, they were granted to the European powers that already exercised military control on the ground in the respective territories. There was no mechanism to establish when a territory would be deemed ready for independence, and for the most part, the European powers continued to rule until the Second World War redefined geo-political realities to make the mandate system unsustainable.

The creation of Le Grand Liban

The mandate for Syria and Lebanon was granted to France. As part of this arrangement, the autonomous Lebanese entity was significantly expanded to *Le Grand Liban*, a territory that basically included the whole of present-day Lebanon. In short, the mandate established the borders of the modern state.

The creation of *Le Grand Liban* was extremely controversial. It was primarily a Maronite initiative, but it was ultimately supported by the French in the League of Nations and thereby gained international sanction. The Maronite community had been gaining increasing political influence since the creation of the *mutasarrifiyya* in 1860. As the most natural and reliable allies of the French within the mandated territories, they were in a good position to advance their long-term interests. By this point in time, these had come to include greater territorial, economic and political aspirations.

The underlying logic of the territorial expansion plan was that, if there were to be an independent state of Lebanon at all, it must be constructed as an economically viable entity with a port, an agricultural base and established territorial and infra-structural links to surrounding states. While this was undeniably a valid argument, it did not take account of some very significant potential obstacles. The first of these was that the majority of the people in the territory who were directly affected, Sunni Muslims in particular, had no desire to be incorporated into an entity with a strong European and Christian orientation.

Naturally, this fact would inevitably generate a number of critical issues with respect to the legitimacy and function of the country. Would it be possible to create a national identity that could be embraced by all citizens of the new state irrespective of sectarian allegiances and cultural affinities? Furthermore, how would the political system account for the demographic balance of sharply divided confessional communities in the society? For example, while many Christians would presumably be happy to embrace an independent Lebanon closely allied with the West, the aspirations of many Arab Muslims were oriented towards the creation of a large Arab state incorporating Arabia, Iraq, Palestine and Syria, as well as the proposed Lebanese state. While the Christian elements wanted to secure an indefinite political predominance, the other sects clearly would prefer a system designed to take advantage of long-term demographic shifts that might favour them.[4]

A second problem was that the Arab world as a whole, and especially Syria, were opposed to the scheme. Arab opposition was based for the most part in broader Arab nationalist aspirations. Syrian opposition drew on pan-Arab issues, but also had a more specific and self-interested character. In effect, of course, the creation of *Le Grand Liban* would significantly reduce Syrian territory, especially coastal territory, and would rob it of its major Mediterranean ports.

It should be noted that there were some leaders, both in France and in the Maronite community, who foresaw these problems, and had serious reservations about the proposed territorial expansion as a result. However, those in favour of the plan exercised the decisive influence. It was implemented in 1920 and formally recognised by the League of Nations two years later.

The institutional foundations of the modern state

During the course of the mandate period, the French authorities did take significant steps to meet their mandatory obligations by fostering the development of indigenous political institutions. Indeed, the institutional foundations of the modern Lebanese state were established by the 1926 Constitution. Although it was amended several times, this document essentially remained in force until the late 1980s. For the most part, the institutions were modelled on the democratic system of the French Third Republic, with a Chamber of Deputies, a Council of Ministers headed by a Prime Minister, and a President elected by the Chamber of Deputies. However, the Constitution also specified that the French High Commissioner, and not the elected representatives, would exercise final authority.

Another significant feature of the 1926 Constitution was that it formally reflected the reality of confessional divisions in Lebanese society by establishing a distinction between criminal and civil law. While criminal matters were to be handled according to a secular juridical model based on the French system, civil matters, and particularly personal status and family laws, were governed by the respective religious codes of law and judicial practice. This mirrored a similar legal distinction which dated back to the *mutasarrifiyya*, and even, to a great extent, the Ottoman millet system.

On the subject of confessionalism, however, the Constitution was probably even more significant for what it did not specify than for what it did. In short, no formal system was elaborated to account for the interaction of the different confessional groups in the political sphere. Therefore it is of paramount importance to recognise the fact that, even at this early stage, the Lebanese political system was characterised by critically important informal rules governing the balance of power among the major confessional groups. Although there was no formal written requirement, in practice, the office of the Presidency was reserved for a Christian, just as the *mutasarri-fiyya* had always had a Christian governor. All of the sects were informally guaranteed some level of representation in the Chamber of Deputies, and so on. After the 1932 census, it became standard practice for fixed numbers of seats to be allocated in proportion to the relative sizes of the respective sects. For various reasons, the Lebanese state never conducted another census, and consequently the 1932 population figures continued to be used to determine confessional representation until the Constitution was reformed in 1990.[5]

It is important, at this point, to emphasise the crucial significance that these informal sectarian power arrangements would ultimately have on the shape of the modern state. While the French and the Christian groups, on the whole, were aiming to create a modern liberal democratic state along Western lines, realities in Lebanon effectively ensured that the state would never have a functional separation of the religious and political spheres. This was due not merely to the fact that many Muslims were opposed to the creation of a secular system with a Western orientation, but also to the fact that the Christians themselves, and their French sponsors, by extension, were unwilling to risk the loss of control that might result from the creation of a secular mass democracy.

By building in guarantees that major offices, a majority of seats in the Chamber, etc., would always go to Christians, the architects of the modern state were also ensuring that the citizens would never fully embrace a collective identity as simply "Lebanese", or participate in the political system as if sectarian divisions did not matter. On the contrary, they would always think of themselves as "Maronite-Lebanese", "Sunni-Lebanese", "Shiite-Lebanese", and so on. Furthermore, the representatives participating in the national institutions would effectively be representing not so much the "national" interest as the interests of their own sect within the national framework.

It is also important to consider the effect the emergence of national institutions had on the Lebanese political process. Traditionally, political influence in Lebanon has always been strongly associated with patron–client relationships. On one level, these relationships have always been the key to understanding how the elites within each of the various sects were able to secure their own position and mobilise the masses. On a second level, it also helps to explain the dominance of the leaders who were able to exercise influence across the sects, such as the small groups of notables who had governed the region in Ottoman times. The creation of a more modern state apparatus in the 1920s was significant largely because it created a new level of access to patronage for Lebanese elite elements, in the form of state revenue, jobs, access to national programmes and contracts, etc.

Those leaders who participated in the new state institutions, therefore, would be able to expand their influence at both levels: 1) at the sectarian level by distributing national patronage within their sects; and 2) at the cross-sectarian level by distributing national patronage to members of other sects. Needless to say, those leaders who opted out of the system, such as many of the Muslim leaders who opposed the creation of the Lebanese state, would be at a disadvantage in relation to those who chose to work within the new system. The importance and workings of the patron–client system in Lebanese politics is a point I will return to, and explore in greater detail, in the second section of this chapter.

Developments during the mandate period

For the most part, politics in mandate Lebanon were carried on in an orderly fashion, with no major disturbances. This probably owed more to the efficacy of French rule than to any overriding sense of unity among, or even within, the different sects. In fact, there were several currents of tension running through the political system during this period.

The most obvious of these originated in a reluctance among the Muslim communities, and the Sunni community especially, to embrace the idea of an independent and Westernised Lebanon. While they did not boycott the emerging national institutions completely, they also did not really endorse them. Ideologically, they remained committed to a Lebanon free from French rule and much more closely associated with the Arab world, as either part of an Arab state or some kind of federation. The fact that they clearly occupied an inferior tier in the political system gave them little incentive to cooperate more fully. Their second-class status was underlined by the fact that the French High Commissioner, Henri Ponsot, intervened in 1932 to prevent the election of a Muslim President when the Christian sects became deadlocked attempting to choose a leader from their own ranks.

As the latter point illustrates, there were also political tensions within the individual sects. The most notable example, which more or less paralysed the political system in 1932–33, was a serious rivalry between two powerful Maronite leaders, Bishara al Khoury and Emile Edde.[6]

Naturally, another significant source of tension was opposition to long-term French rule. This was not limited to the Muslim sects, but also emerged in Christian circles. While some scholars tend to see the Christians, and the Maronites particularly, as being submissive French clients, in fact, there were significant nationalist elements in the Christian sects pushing for greater self-determination and independent statehood. The French, for their part, seemed to aspire to a more open-ended controlling influence over the country, and were perceived by many Lebanese nationalists as high-handed and authoritarian. And the French authorities did suspend the Constitution on several occasions, and even went as far as unilaterally appointing some Presidents.

The end of the mandate

France's occupation by Germany in the Second World War naturally had a dramatic effect on the situation in Lebanon. The Vichy French government assumed power over Lebanon in 1940, but was unable to hold its position in the country against British and Free French troops in the spring of 1941. Following the withdrawal of Vichy forces, the Free French moved in, but acquiesced to Lebanese and international pressure, and declared the country independent on 26 November 1941. Britain, the United States, the Soviet Union, the Arab states and some other countries officially recognised this independence, and some even exchanged ambassadors with Lebanon. However, citing war necessity, the Free French continued to exercise decisive authority in the country.

During the remainder of the war, Lebanese leaders began making preparations for self-rule. These culminated in the 1943 National Pact, in which the leaders of the Maronite and Sunni sects agreed on a number of points that were to form the basis of the post-war power-sharing arrangements and settle the extremely important issue of Lebanon's West–East orientation. General elections were held in the summer of 1943, and a new President, Bishara al Khoury, was selected by the Chamber. On 8 November, the new Parliament amended the 1926 Constitution and abolished the mandate without first securing French consent. The French authorities responded by imprisoning most of the Lebanese leadership, leading to an open revolt across sectarian lines against the French presence in the country. International pressure forced the Free French authorities to concede and release the prisoners. Subsequently, it became clear that Lebanon would indeed be independent after the war, and the French withdrew the last of their forces at the end of 1946.[7]

The National Pact and creation of the modern state

As noted previously, the year 1943 constituted a crucial watershed in the genesis of Lebanese statehood due to a number of major developments. Almost certainly the most significant of these in the broader context of Lebanese history was the negotiation of the unwritten agreement that subsequently became known as "The National Pact". It marked the first occasion when the leaders of the two most powerful sects, Bishara al Khoury of the Maronites (also President at the time) and Riad Solh of the Sunni Muslims (the serving Prime Minister), were able to arrive at a mutually acceptable vision of Lebanon's nationhood and its standing in relation to the Christian West and the Arab/Muslim world.

Since the 1932 census, the Sunni Muslims had been officially recognised as numerically the second largest sect in the country. Prior to 1943, Sunni leaders had continually opposed the creation of an independent Lebanese state on ideological grounds. Essentially, they had always argued that Lebanon should be part of some kind of greater Arab/Muslim state. Obviously, the viability of the Lebanese national project would always be questionable, to say the least, without the active support of the Sunni community. Thus the Sunni leadership's decision to reverse their traditional position on this issue was a development of the highest importance.

To some extent, Solh's decision to negotiate with Khoury, and the Muslim sects' subsequent acceptance of the agreement, must be seen as a triumph of political pragmatism over ideology. In short, by 1943, it had become more or less clear that the emergence of a great pan-Arab state was extremely unlikely for the foreseeable future. On the other hand, the foundation of an independent Lebanese state had essentially become a *fait accompli*. Thus the leaders of the Muslim sects were left with a fairly stark choice: continue to hold out indefinitely for a new state that might never emerge, or accept somewhat inferior status in a state that seemed imminent.

Again, it should also be remembered that the national institutions represented a massive source of potential patronage, in the form of revenue, jobs, access to government programmes and contracts, etc., that could be used to win political influence both within and across sects. This patronage was a sort of double-edged sword. It could be used to secure the traditional patronage networks within the sects, or to undermine them. In order to prevent the latter, the traditional Muslim leaders simply had to gain access to the system.

Even given the Sunni community's new willingness to participate in the state for reasons such as these, compromise between the groups was absolutely essential in two particular areas: 1) Lebanon's relations with the West, on the one hand, and the Arab/Muslim world, on the other; and 2) the exact arrangements governing the disbursement of political power, and attendant patronage, within the national institutions.

With respect to the first area, both sides basically had to abandon their traditional preferences altogether. The Christians had generally aspired to ever-increasing ties with the West, while the Muslims had always pushed for integration in the Middle East. The two outlooks were irreconcilable, so the only compromise possible was for Lebanon to adopt a "neutral" stance in its culture and foreign relations. This did not amount to completely cutting off relations with the West or Lebanon's Arab neighbours. On the contrary, leaders in both sects recognised the advantages of maintaining good relations, as well as economic, cultural and spiritual links with the West and the East. In effect, they agreed to the principle that Lebanon would remain an independent state and not become too closely associated with either milieu.

As far as the second area was concerned, the Christians, and the Maronites especially, wanted to maintain their traditional predominance in the political system. However, it was obvious that they would have to concede some power to the Muslims, and the Sunni community in particular, if there was to be a functional state at all. This meant that a new set of mutually acceptable power-sharing arrangements had to be negotiated.

Although the distribution of major offices and seats in the Chamber had been arranged along sectarian lines throughout the mandate period, the traditional pre-rogatives of the major communities, as of 1943, were not strongly enough fixed to satisfy either the Maronites or the Sunnis. For example, prior to 1943, the Presidency had been reserved for a Christian, but not necessarily a Maronite, and the office of Prime Minister had no fixed sectarian designation. The National Pact provided stronger guarantees to the major sects by specifying that the President would always be a Maronite Christian, that the Prime Minister would always be a Sunni Muslim, and, as an additional concession to Muslim interests, that the Speaker of the House (i.e. the Chamber of Deputies) would always be a Shiite Muslim. The Council of Ministers was also divided along more fixed sectarian lines (six Christians to five Muslims).

It should also be remembered that, during the mandate period, the Maronites had always been able to count on the overriding authority of the French High Commissioner with respect to advancing their national agenda. The absence of such a compelling influence, while not an actual concession, meant that the Maronites' relative influence in the system would be declining to some extent from the previous norm. However, at the same time, in the absence of an external mediator like the High Commissioner, the President would be able to exercise an effective veto power over the whole of the political process. Thus, while the Maronites would not be able completely to control the national agenda, they did have the ability to prevent the other sects from passing legislation that would be seriously detrimental to their long-term interests. Therefore the Maronite leaders were reasonably happy with the new arrangements.

It is worth noting at this point that, like the sectarian power-sharing arrangements that had become standard practice during the mandate period, the National Pact was an unwritten, and in that sense fundamentally informal, arrangement. The Constitution was never modified specifically to incorporate the principles and arrangements established by the pact. This had both positive and negative implications for the new political order. On one hand, the informal nature of the agreement allowed for a great deal of compromise and accommodation among the sectarian elites. On the other hand, the lack of specific, written provisions in the context of the Constitution meant that there was no formal mechanism whereby the terms of the pact could be renegotiated and amended to account for changing circumstances.

In short, the political order established by the National Pact depended almost completely on the willingness and ability of the different sectarian elites to compromise with each other and settle any emerging disagreements among themselves. The pact itself did not envisage the need for more formal arrangements. Even if it had established such arrangements, a critical breakdown in the relationships among the major sectarian elites would cause the whole political order to collapse. Ultimately, it was such a failure of elite relations that led to the collapse of the system. Even with the benefit of hindsight, however, it is difficult to imagine how this problem could have been addressed without abandoning the confessional system entirely.

1.2 The functional state

The main features of the political order (1946–75)[8]

When considering the political order that emerged in Lebanon after independence in 1946, it is critically important to make a distinction between the country's ostensible and actual political processes. If one looks only at the ostensible processes, as defined by the revised 1926 Constitution, Lebanon would appear to conform to the essential characteristics of a Western-style liberal democratic state. It had a President, a Prime Minister and cabinet, a popularly elected chamber, and so on. Elections were held at regular intervals, and power changed hands in a relatively peaceful and orderly fashion in accordance with election results. There were a number of active political parties. There was an independent judiciary. And individual and collective political liberties were broadly respected. For example, the country had a free press, individuals were free to express their political views openly, right to assembly was upheld, etc. The one slightly remarkable difference from other liberal democratic frameworks was the distinction between different religious sects in certain areas of civil law.

However, even a cursory inspection of the country's actual political processes changes the whole picture. The most obvious characteristic that distinguished post-independence Lebanon from virtually all other ostensibly liberal democratic political frameworks was the ingrained confessionalism that existed at every level of political life. This was not so much a necessary consequence of the fact that Lebanese society was sharply divided along sectarian lines, as a result of the way that the sectarian leaders decided to adapt the political process to account for it. For example, there are other democratic countries (Belgium, Switzerland, Canada, etc.) with extremely significant religious, linguistic or ethnic cleavages. All of them have introduced either formal or informal measures to manage such tensions, but none has established anything comparable with the rigid and pervasive confessional system that developed in Lebanon after the 1943 National Pact.[9]

A second major difference was the critical importance of patronage in relation to all facets of Lebanese society. Again, the distinction is largely a matter of scale. Patron–client relationships continue to characterise, and influence the politics of, most liberal democratic states to a greater or lesser degree.[10] However, in most of these states, legal and practical frameworks have been established to monitor and restrict the role that such connections play in the political process. To cite a couple of examples: qualifications and examinations are used to assess the suitability of individuals applying for work in the state bureaucracy; government contracts are awarded on the basis of transparent bidding processes with clearly defined rules of competition; there are legal guidelines to establish the point at which there is a conflict of interest between a politician's public commitments and his personal or business dealings; and so on.

Lebanon, by contrast, never established truly effective mechanisms to regulate the political influence of patronage networks. On the contrary, it would be no exaggeration to say that a vibrant, omnipresent patron–client system continued to be the very essence of Lebanese politics. (And this remains the case, even to this day.) Since patron–client interactions take place largely outside the formal democratic framework, and structure loyalties that transcend election results and other expressions of the popular will, the liberal democratic character of Lebanese politics was muted to a considerable extent. In effect, post-independence Lebanon conformed more to the neo-patrimonial than to the liberal democratic mode of government.

I would stress here, however, that one should take care to avoid a reflexive conclusion that, because Lebanon did not have the liberal democratic government seemingly envisaged by the 1926 Constitution, it had a bad government. Up until the early 1970s, the system was broadly functional. If the government was not truly democratic according to the common Western understanding of the term, it was also not, as I will consider shortly, authoritarian, particularly arbitrary or oppressive. It enjoyed a fair degree of popular legitimacy. It is true that the sects remained divided and that the sectarian elites in particular were constantly engaged in competition over state patronage. But this actually meant, in practice, that every sect had a considerable stake in maintaining the existing system. In spite of continuing divisions, there was a growing sense of a common Lebanese identity. Indeed, many Western scholars came to view the Lebanese system as a potential imitative model for other societies deeply divided along ethnic and/or sectarian lines. Furthermore, as I will explain in due course, if one wishes to understand why the system failed, it is necessary to consider a number of different factors, some of the most significant of which were essentially external.

I will now proceed to consider in more detail how the new Lebanese state's fusion of liberal democratic and confessional/neo-patrimonial elements actually functioned up to 1975. First I consider how Lebanon's confessionalism and the crucial significance of patron–client relationships within the sects combined to become the dominant features of national politics. I then proceed to consider the nature of the "consociational democracy" that emerged, a political system that stands somewhere between the liberal democratic and authoritarian systems in the spectrum of governmental types. Finally, the susceptibility of the system to penetration by external factors is considered.

The confessional elites and the patron–client system

To a very great extent, Lebanon's confessionalism and neo-patrimonialism became so deeply ingrained because these two characteristics fed off each other. Neither element, in isolation, fully accounts for the extent to which both came to permeate the political process that developed after 1943.

No matter how liberal democratic the national institutions were designed to be, the deep ideological and political divisions among the sects made it imperative to establish some kind of balance of power. Only the pre-existing sectarian elites were in a position to establish and defend the national compromise. Therefore they could not be dispensed with. And, of course, their traditional power was deeply rooted in patron–client networks.

At this point, it is important to consider the composition of the sectarian elites and to look in more detail at their power bases. Within each sect, there were core groups of notables known as *zu'ama* (political bosses), and there were at least three distinct types.[11]

First, there was the semi-feudal variety, possessing large estates and traditional lordships. Their power rested on their position as landowner, their use of strong-arm men, and their ability to give protection and patronage. This type of *za'im* (singular form) was particularly prominent within the Druze and Shiite communities, and also the Sunni community of the rural Akkar region. Examples of this type of *za'im* included, among others, such prominent figures as Kamal Asad and Kamal Jumblatt.

The second type of *za'im* was the urban boss, found primarily in Sunni communities in Beirut, Tripoli and Sidon. Their power rested on the manipulation of the urban masses through patronage, ideological appeal and the use of strong-arm men. Examples of this type of *za'im* included Riad Solh and Rashid Karami, among others.

The third type of *za'im* was the "populist" variety, found in the predominantly Christian regions of Mount Lebanon. Their leadership was derived from the use of powers of protection and patronage and/or some kind of ideological appeal. This type included such noteworthy figures as Camille Chamoun and Pierre Gemayel.

It should be noted that some of the *zu'ama* from the first two categories were also attempting to develop more populist bases of support for themselves during the 1946–75 period, and these constitute a kind of hybrid group. Kamal Jumblatt was perhaps the most notable example.[12]

An important point that must be stressed with respect to all three types of *zu'ama* is that they were exclusive clubs, for the most part. It was very rarely possible for an individual from outside the establishment to become a *za'im* on the basis of personal political aspirations. For the most part, the *zu'ama* were family based, and power was transferred from the patriarch to a handpicked successor or successors within the family. Thus politics in Lebanon tends to be dominated by the same families from generation to generation. Occasionally, an outsider was able to develop an independent power base through capital accumulation or some kind of exceptional personal following, but this was rare. (Albeit, it has become considerably more common since the civil war.) Of course, even such new *za'im* generally aspired to join the system rather than change it. In short, they did not want to overturn the old dynasties or open up the political system more generally. They simply wanted to found their own dynasties.

Once these sectarian leaders became national leaders, it was almost inevitable that they would use their new positions to enhance their traditional neo-patrimonial bases of power. In fact, to a very great extent, negotiations about the disbursement of state patronage not only among the sects, but also among the individual *za'im* within the sects, became the fundamental preoccupation of the national government. There was intense negotiation among the sectarian leaders concerning the confessional and personal disbursement of virtually every conceivable source of patronage, not only high political offices and major state revenues, but even the most minor political appointments and contracts. One modern commentator has aptly referred to this as "splitting up the Lebanese pie".[13]

Naturally, the already existing confessional divisions were intensified by the fact that the leaders of the different sects were now in direct competition with each other, trying to gain access to the collective pool of influence laid open by the state institutions. Thus the relationship between confessionalism and neo-patrimonialism became a sort of dynamic vicious circle. The more sectarian competition increased, the more firmly neo-patrimonialism penetrated national politics, and *vice versa*. This naturally had detrimental consequences with respect to both national unity and the potential for evolving a more liberal democratic national government.

The nature and role of political parties in the context of the Lebanese system is a key example of how neo-patrimonialism has penetrated and subverted ostensibly liberal democratic institutions. While parties in liberal democratic systems are almost always based around ideology or a particular complex of issues, in Lebanon they tend to be built around a *za'im*. To cite just one of many possible examples, the Popular Socialist Party (PSP) was so completely dominated by Kamal Jumblatt that its focus was not socialist policy, but rather any policy that served to advance Jumblatt's interests. Some other prominent parties, such as the *Kata'eb* party, are more truly ideological, but have been associated for long periods with the interests of one particular family, the Gemayels in this case. Ideological parties that are not strongly tied into the *zu'ama* system tend to be very marginalised. For example, Lebanon has had a number of Communist parties, Arab nationalist and Arab socialist parties, and so on, but none of these has really had a major impact on the political system. Ultimately, this may be due to the fact that they are not really engaged in the sectarian and neo-patrimonial negotiations that have historically dominated the national political discourse.[14]

The consociational democracy

Although the post-independence Lebanese political system could certainly not be accurately described as a liberal democracy, it was also not an authoritarian system. Confessional divisions generally, and more specifically the unwritten but critically binding arrangements negotiated by the sectarian leaders, ensured that no single sect would be able to dominate the national agenda. Indeed, it was not generally possible even for a group of Christian sects acting in concert, or a group of Muslim sects acting in concert, to disrupt the carefully calculated balance of the confessional system. Furthermore, since the highest national offices were distributed as prerogatives to particular sects, this meant that the powers of the offices were also balanced. It would not, therefore, be possible for any President or Prime Minister to take personal control of the system through setting up a dictatorship.

Theoretically, the system might have evolved towards authoritarianism if the sectarian leaders participating in the national institutions had formed close alliances with one another and evolved into a tight, cross-confessional national elite. However, in practice, as noted above, the *zu'ama* tended to concentrate on using the state institutions to compete against each other for patronage. Their primary interest was to use such patronage to secure and enhance their own individual power bases, especially within their respective sects.

Another possible shift towards authoritarianism might have involved the military. After all, in many other Arab states during the same period, the military was becoming increasingly prominent in the political arena, usually with authoritarian consequences. And, as I explain later, the military did become more deeply involved in Lebanese politics, especially throughout the 1960s. However, the fundamental nature of the political system did not change. There are probably two main reasons for this. The first is that, like every other major national institution, the military was penetrated by confessional and neo-patrimonial allegiances. In short, the army was split up along sectarian lines just as carefully as the national institutions were. The commanding general was always a Maronite, a certain proportion of the officer corps was delegated to each of the sects, and so on. Additionally, the officers in the army often had client relationships with leading *zu'ama*. Consequently, the likelihood that the army as a whole would unite under the leadership of a single charismatic leader like Nasser, Asad, Qaddafi, etc., was not very great. The second reason for the limited influence of the army in politics is that the Lebanese army was never a particularly strong military force. To some extent, it was intentionally kept relatively weak precisely because the political elites were afraid that it would come to undermine them.

As a result, the Lebanese system remained fairly decentralised and the state remained relatively weak, particularly in comparison with the political systems and state structures that were being built up in most other Arab states during this period. The real power in Lebanese politics, and the authoritarian mechanisms that existed to a greater or lesser extent, were located not at the state level, but within the seventeen officially recognised religious sects.

Even when one considers the continuous grip exerted on Lebanese politics by the traditional sectarian elites, with the same tight groups of individuals and families tending to dominate sectarian and national politics for decades and generations, it would be a serious overexaggeration to suggest that the Lebanese state was completely undemocratic. Indeed, there were some significant functional aspects of democracy that were taken very seriously. For example, Presidents were restricted to a single six-year term. Elections were held at regular intervals. There were reasonably frequent changes of government, and transfers of power were generally peaceful and orderly. As I will demonstrate when looking at historical developments during this period, such as various Presidents' failed attempts to secure a second term, any attempt to contravene these norms was viewed as illegitimate and unacceptable at both the elite and mass levels.

In effect, the post-1943 Lebanese political system had virtually all of the essential characteristics of a distinctive form of government first identified by the political theorist Arend Lijphart in the 1960s: a consociational democracy.[15] This is defined as "government by elite cartel designed to turn a democracy with a fragmented political culture into a stable democracy". Although Lijphart conceded that a consociational system might be less democratic than a liberal democracy in a number of respects, he argued that it might be more democratic in other respects. For example, religious and ethnic minorities are often somewhat repressed in a mass democracy, whereas in a consociational system, every group is represented to a significant extent.

Lijphart outlined four necessary prerequisites or conditions for a consociational democratic framework to function successfully:

- First, there must be clear boundaries between subcultures, as limited contacts between mass groups tend to lessen the chance of hostility. Ideologies accepted by different groups within a society may be inconsistent without creating tension. The chance of greater tension arises only when the groups are in close contact.
- Second, it is absolutely vital for the elites of each subculture to work closely together, while at the same time maintaining the loyalty of their followers. A major threat to the system may occur if elites lose control over their followers.
- Third, there must be a multiple balance of power among subcultures. For instance, in a dual-culture society, the tendency is for the majority culture to attempt to dominate the other culture. However, in societies with several subcultures, none of which holds a clear majority, the likelihood is greater that the elite groups will be willing to cooperate with each other.
- Fourth, and finally, there must be a relatively low total load on the system. The stability of the system can be weighed in terms of its capacity to handle increased demands. Writing in 1968, Lijphart contended that the loads on the Lebanese system were not great and that this helped to explain its stability.

Susceptibility of the system to external pressures

A final major feature of the post-independence political order is that, in spite of the neutral foreign policy and cultural orientation adopted as part of the National Pact, the independent Lebanese state continued to be highly vulnerable to external pressures, especially currents emanating from the Arab world. Essentially, there were two particularly significant, and somewhat interrelated, sources of tension: 1) the ongoing Arab–Israeli conflict; and 2) the pan-Arab movement.

I will consider the specific effects that these two factors had on developments in Lebanon during the 1946–75 period in the next subsection. The point that needs to be stressed here is that, the National Pact notwithstanding, the Lebanese state had no practical mechanisms that enabled it to stave off the systemic instability that resulted from regional politics. The weakness of the state, the absence of a strong military, and, perhaps above all, the fragmented character of Lebanon's national identity laid the Lebanese political process open not only to active interference by external actors with transnational agendas, but also to periodic eruptions of internal ideological tension.

With respect to the Arab–Israeli conflict, Lebanon's geographical proximity made a neutral stance difficult to maintain. The national leaders were able to disarm internal tension to some extent by adopting a semi-detached pro-Arab stance. In short, the Lebanese government agreed with the other Arab nations in principle, supported resolutions in the Arab League, fostered Palestinian refugees, and provided mostly logistical and moral support during active military phases of the conflict. As a consequence, the pro-Palestinian (principally Muslim) elements in Lebanon were broadly satisfied with national policy for much of the period. However, there was periodic tension, especially during the 1967 and 1973 Arab–Israeli wars, when segments of the Lebanese masses felt that the government should be taking stronger military action in support of the Arab states. Furthermore, internal and external pressures on the Lebanese system increased dramatically after 1970, when the PLO established its political and military base in Lebanon, involving the country in the Arab–Israeli conflict to a much greater extent.

In theory, the National Pact resolved the whole issue of Lebanon's response to pan-Arab movements. The principle was that Lebanon should remain independent instead of becoming more and more closely affiliated with any external ideological or nationalist current, either Western or Arab. In practice, however, the popular currency of pan-Arabism, particularly when Nasser was at the height of his power, was so great that the Lebanese state had no functional defence from its influence. Thus the attempts of Nasser and other external pan-Arab agitators to undermine the existing order in Lebanon found no shortage of receptive elements within the country, again especially among the Muslim population. Ultimately, Lebanese governments responded to this pressure in two ways. The first was to seek external international support for the existing system. The second was to accommodate pan-Arabism to a limited extent. This mostly involved making purely rhetorical statements in support of Arab unity and brotherhood, but did sometimes require specific political concessions. As with the response to the Arab–Israeli conflict, Lebanese state efforts to maintain the system against pan-Arab tendencies were largely successful until the early 1970s, when the introduction of the PLO had disastrous consequences.

Dominant themes in the functional state context (1946–75)

Adherence to specified institutional norms

One of the major themes that characterised the Lebanese state context during the post-independence period was a strict adherence to most of the institutional norms set in place by the Constitution. In short, general elections and presidential elections were held at the regular intervals specified by the Constitution. Although some of the Presidents during this period made attempts to modify or circumvent the legal arrangements in order to expand their terms of office, these attempts were all unsuccessful. No President served for more than one six-year term during the period.

Changes of Prime Minister occurred even more frequently, largely because the Presidents were concerned with preventing any one Sunni figure from becoming too powerful. Thus Lebanon stands in sharp contrast to the other Arab states, where political leaders tended to stay in power for decades and to become increasingly authoritarian as their positions became more secure.

Fixed locus of elite politics

A second continuing theme throughout this period was that the *zu'ama* continued to be the locus of elite politics in Lebanon. As already noted, there were some challenges to their dominant position from ideological elements and also from the military, but these were blunted by the confessional and neo-patrimonial character of the political process.

Another point that needs to be stressed here is that the *zu'ama* of the different sects continued to cooperate with each other until the last few years of this period. Despite the fact that they continued to compete vigorously with each other for access to patronage, they frequently banded together to prevent any kind of major systemic change. For example, there were cross-sectarian alliances to prevent leaders such as Chamoun and Jumblatt from becoming too strong, to resist any moves to secularise the system, to prevent the military from gaining a stronger influence in the system, and to moderate the impact of popular agitation resulting from pan-Arab pressures. Interestingly, the *zu'ama* also worked together within the state context to prevent the Lebanese state itself from becoming too strong and therefore capable of impinging on their own regional power bases.

Economic prosperity[16]

Another continuing theme of the post-independence period was Lebanon's substantial economic prosperity, a feature that, once again, distinguished it from many other Arab states. Lebanon's relative wealth was built on its increasing status as a regional centre of banking and trade, a sort of bridge between West and East. While many other Arab economies were closed and socialist, Lebanon was open and capitalist, and benefited from the influx of external capital and investment. The country also became prominent as a cultural and tourist centre.

This prosperity had conflicting political implications. On one hand, it helped to reduce the overall loads on the consociational system, and gave many of Lebanon's citizens a stake in maintaining the *status quo*. On the other hand, it contributed to increasing urbanisation, and thereby helped to undermine the influence of the traditional rural *zu'ama*. By the 1970s, concentrations of urban poor, operating outside the spheres of influence of their traditional patrons, contributed to the radicalisation of Lebanese politics.

Presidential ascendancy

A final major theme that characterised the Lebanese political process during this period was the essential dominance of the Presidency within the state institutional framework. Readers who are somewhat familiar with contemporary Lebanese politics will be aware that the powers of the President, the Prime Minister and the Speaker of the House are now fairly evenly balanced, reflecting the post-civil war principle of sectarian parity. (This will be detailed in Chapter 3.) This was not the case prior to 1975. Although there was a functional sectarian balance of power, the President, and hence the Maronite sect, was in a position to exert a strong guiding influence with respect to state policy. While he did not have the power to push through a legislative agenda if other interests (from outside or inside the sect) united against him, he did have several tools he could use to block a competing agenda and encourage cooperation with his own.

The most powerful tool of the President was his power to block any legislation he considered undesirable with an absolute veto that could not be overridden by the other institutions. This encouraged the other leaders in the state context to cooperate with the President's political programme, because he would be able to retaliate against defiance by blocking all other legislative initiatives. Of course, such extreme measures were rarely necessary, as the President also had the power to appoint and dismiss Prime Ministers, and it was usually possible to find a cooperative Sunni partner. In any case, the Presidents during this period tended to replace Prime Ministers frequently, once every two or three years, in order to change the tone of government and prevent any Sunni politician from building up too strong a power base. The President also exercised a great deal of influence over cabinet appointments, and was commander-in-chief of the Lebanese military.

Not surprisingly, given the great influence associated with the post, several of Lebanon's Presidents attempted to find ways to extend their term in office, or to serve for more than one term. In each case, this was met with fierce resistance by virtually everyone in the country, sectarian affiliations notwithstanding. No one at the elite or mass level was willing to let any individual exercise such enormous power for more than a strictly limited term. If this constitutional safeguard had ever been successfully circumvented, the character of the whole political system might have shifted towards authoritarian dictatorship.

Major political developments (1946–75)

Khoury's Presidency (1946–52)[17]

The first President of the independent Lebanese state was Bishara al Khoury, the Maronite leader who had also served as President during the final years of French rule and helped to negotiate the National Pact. Essentially, his administration helped to reaffirm the cross-sectarian national compromise and establish the norms governing how the post-independence political process would actually function in practice.

One of the precedents that he established, but which he might not wish to be remembered for, was the rule that Presidents would be forced to respect the constitutional provision limiting them to a six-year term. In short, Khoury was reluctant to leave office in 1952, but was forced to step aside by a powerful cross-sectarian coalition of the other *zu'ama*. Needless to say, a great deal of pressure came from within the Maronite sect, because the other Maronite *zu'ama*, including Khoury's ultimate successor Camille Chamoun, wanted the chance to press their own candidacy for the office.

Chamoun's Presidency (1952–58)

The most significant development during Chamoun's administration was a considerable increase of systemic pressure as a result of the pan-Arab movement. This was a direct result of the 1956 Suez Crisis and the Egyptian leader Gamal abd al Nasser's dramatic increase in popularity across the Arab world. Nasser's calls for greater Arab unity and non-alignment *vis-a-vis* the Americans and the Soviets exerted a great appeal amongst Lebanon's Muslim masses. Ideologically, Nasser's pan-Arabism challenged the legitimacy of virtually all the existing Arab states, including Lebanon, and generated the first real threat to the post-independence political order of the country. This threat intensified following the formation of the United Arab Republic (UAR) by Egypt and Syria in February 1958.

Chamoun, who had already courted significant mass discontent by allying Lebanon with the West in support of the Eisenhower doctrine, chose to follow Khoury's example by demonstrating a reluctance to leave office as the end of his term approached. This provocation, combined with popular agitation in favour of joining the UAR, resulted in the outbreak of a brief civil war in spring 1958. This became more than a simple internal conflict, for two reasons: 1) the insurgents received vocal encouragement, and apparently some backing in the form of weapons shipments, from the UAR;[18] and 2) the United States, with the blessing of the Lebanese government, dispatched 15,000 marines to the country in order to help restore order.[19]

In fact, by the time the American troops arrived, the conflict had essentially been resolved. An internal coalition of *zu'ama* forced Chamoun to agree to leave office, and the new government under Fouad Chehab adopted a more conciliatory attitude towards pan-Arabism. Meanwhile, Nasser himself, perhaps troubled by the prospect of more significant Western intervention in the region, withdrew his support for the insurgents and toned down his rhetoric against the Lebanese regime. This enabled the Muslim *zu'ama* to reassert their control at the mass level.

Chehab's Presidency (1958–64)

The election of Chehab was something of a watershed in Lebanese politics, as it was the first time that someone from outside the *zu'ama* class was permitted to occupy the Presidency. He had been the leading general of the Lebanese military forces at the time of the 1958 uprising, and was popular with the troops and the masses. From the perspective of the Lebanese political establishment, his appointment was advantageous in two respects: 1) the very fact that he was an outsider would help to address mass discontent with a Maronite elite that many (perhaps Muslims especially) had come to see as self-serving and corrupt; and 2) he was perceived as a security specialist who would be able to restore stability and maintain the existing political order.

And indeed, the line of policy undertaken by Chehab was fundamentally oriented towards increasing state power at the expense of the sectarian elites and maintaining state security through a significant increase in internal intelligence-gathering and policing. The primary mechanism with respect to the latter was the Deuxieme Bureau, the internal security police, whose violations of previously unrestricted civil rights became increasingly resented throughout the next decade.

With respect to the economy and foreign policy, Chehab's agenda was somewhat populist. He introduced economic development programmes designed to improve conditions for Lebanon's poor, and successfully steered a narrow course between Muslim and Christian feelings on the pan-Arab issue. He played to Muslim sympathies by paying lip service to the achievements of Nasser and the pan-Arab movement, but allayed Christian concerns by strongly affirming Lebanon's sovereignty against foreign influences.

Unlike his two predecessors, Chehab stepped aside gracefully when his term expired. However, it should be noted that the next President was, to all intents and purposes, his handpicked successor, and that he continued to exert influence behind the scenes.[20]

Helou's Presidency (1964–70)

Like Chehab, Charles Helou came from outside the *zu'ama*, but unlike Chehab, he did not really have a personal power base. Effectively, he was a technocrat elected to continue the Chehabist lines of policy. This he was able to do successfully for the most part. Indeed, many scholars tend to classify the period from 1958–70 as "the Chehabist era" and view Helou's Presidency as an extension of Chehab's by proxy. By 1969, however, a combination of internal and external factors led to the end of the Chehabist era.

Internally, the *zu'ama* had come to resent the increasing power of the Lebanese state that had resulted from the Chehabist policies. This resentment was partly due to the close scrutiny of the security services in their affairs, but can also be attributed to more general concerns about the impact of populist policies on their own sectarian bases of support. In short, the administration was becoming a dangerous political rival.

At around the same time, developments concerning the activities and status of the PLO put the Lebanese system under considerable external pressure. It should be noted, at this point, that Lebanon had fostered significant numbers of Palestinian refugees since the 1948 Arab–Israeli war. As of the late 1960s, the refugee population of approximately 300,000 occupied a number of camps scattered throughout the country. For the most part, the Palestinians living in Lebanon were never permitted to take Lebanese citizenship or to become formally integrated into the system. This was largely because it was feared that giving them an official status would disrupt the delicate confessional balance and possibly lead to the radicalisation of Lebanese politics with respect to the Arab–Israeli conflict. The continuing presence of the Palestinians was fairly controversial in any case. While the Muslim sects tended to be very sympathetic to them, the Christians saw them as a threat.

In the late 1960s, PLO elements operating out of the refugee camps had begun using southern Lebanon as a base for anti-Israeli activity. Israeli reprisals forced the Lebanese government to initiate a military crackdown in the South. At this point, a combination of Egyptian diplomatic pressure and popular support for the PLO within the Lebanese Muslim sects forced the government to back down and conclude a document that became known as the 1969 Cairo Agreement. The agreement basically gave the PLO autonomous status over the Palestinian refugee camps and established the principle that they would have an unrestricted right to continue operations against Israel. Even the Muslim *zu'ama* had reservations about this arrangement. Needless to say, the Christians were more or less outraged at both the elite and mass levels. The major practical implication of the agreement was that the PLO continued their activities and the Israelis continued to strike back. Between 1968 and 1974, there were forty-four major Israeli attacks on Lebanon, causing the deaths of hundreds of people and considerable damage to Lebanon's infrastructure and economic stability.

Franjieh's Presidency (1970–76)

The 1970 Presidential election was one of the closest in Lebanese history. Sulayman Franjieh, the candidate representing the interests of the traditional *zu'ama*, defeated the Chehabist candidate, Elias Sarkis, by just one vote in the Chamber of Deputies. Despite Franjieh's lack of a clear mandate, the election effectively changed the course of Lebanese politics.[21] The Chehabist policies that had strengthened the state, placed a strong emphasis on internal security and promoted economic development in the poorer sectors of Lebanese society were abandoned, and in some cases deliberately reversed. Essentially, the Franjieh administration's policies were designed to reassert the supremacy of the *zu'ama* in both national and local contexts.

One of Franjieh's main initiatives was significantly to scale down the Deuxieme Bureau. The ostensible reason for this was concern that the organisation's intelligence-gathering activities, particularly with respect to the elite elements, violated civil liberties and constituted a threat to the democratic process. On a deeper level, it was a measure designed to restore the *zu'ama's* traditional freedom of action within their own spheres of influence. Additionally, the Bureau, along with the Lebanese army, constituted an important power base for the *zu'ama's* Chehabist rivals, so undermining it weakened the potential opposition to *zu'ama* dominance.

Another consequence of weakening the internal security establishment, which Franjieh may or may not have recognised at the time, was that it freed the *Kata'eb* party and other Christian elements to begin quietly creating their own illegal militias. This development was a response to Christian concerns about the future of the Lebanese state in the aftermath of the Cairo Agreement. In effect, the agreement had placed Palestinian elements outside the jurisdiction of the Lebanese security establishment, which meant that the Lebanese had no formal way to defend themselves against a potential Palestinian threat. The Palestinians now had an unrestricted legal right to build up their own military power. The fact that this was intended to allow them to conduct operations against Israel was not, in itself, a guarantee that the same forces would not be used at some point within Lebanon. For example, it was possible that the PLO might use its military strength to help set up a Muslim-dominated Lebanese state much more supportive to its cause. The new Christian militias were an unofficial safeguard against this contingency. Of course, the flaw in the Christian plan was that the decline of the Deuxieme Bureau did not just serve their interests; it also allowed disaffected Lebanese Muslim and Leftist elements to arm themselves.

In any case, the second major theme of the Franjieh administration was the abandonment of development-oriented economic policies designed to address the grievances of Lebanon's poor. As noted previously, the Lebanese economy was essentially prosperous during this period, but the wealth was not evenly distributed across society. Urbanisation had resulted in growing concentrations of poor unemployed and underemployed elements in Beirut. These people were largely cut off politically from the *zu'ama*, who had traditionally represented their interests when they had lived in rural areas, and were hence becoming more and more politically active on their own behalf. Increasingly, they tended to turn to the Lebanese Left in order to push for the kind of systemic change that would allow for more substantial economic reforms.

The urban masses' move towards the Left was intensified by the Franjieh government's perceived emphasis in the economic sphere. The suspension of the Chehabist economic programmes prompted many to view the new administration as, at best, indifferent to the plight of Lebanon's poor. To make matters worse, there was a widespread perception that the Franjieh regime was taking the long-standing nepotism and economic self-interest of the *zu'ama* class to new, and quite excessive, heights.

Lebanon had always had a number of Leftist parties, but up to this time, they had been politically marginal. This was partly because the *zu'ama* had effectively monopolised their popular constituencies through the successful use of patronage, and partly a result of the fact that the many Leftist parties tended to cancel each other out instead of presenting a unified front. Suddenly, the Left had a real popular base of support, and therefore aspired to become a truly significant player in the Lebanese political context for the first time. The Leftists were also becoming more politically unified at this time. Ironically, this change can be attributed largely to the efforts of one of the more influential *zu'ama*, the Druze leader, Kamal Jumblatt.

For reasons that had at least as much to do with his own political ambitions as with his Leftist sympathies, Jumblatt created the Lebanese National Movement (LNM), a sort of umbrella organisation for Leftist parties. The LNM's charter envisaged not just the creation of a socialist political order, but also the elimination of confessionalism within the Lebanese state context. In short, the organisation was calling for the abrogation of the National Pact. This represented a threat to the *zu'ama* of all the sects, because it challenged both their economic and their political predominance. It was also seen as a threat by most of the Christian masses, including the poor, because it threatened the traditional safeguards that prevented Muslims from taking control of the political agenda and involving Lebanon in the pan-Arab movement.

Increased PLO presence in Lebanon and the collapse of the Lebanese state

It is unclear how the Lebanese political establishment might have managed these new internal tensions under other circumstances. The fact is that these developments coincided with catastrophically intensified systemic pressure that resulted primarily from a major external event: the Jordanian expulsion of the PLO in the so-called "Black September" of 1970, and the subsequent relocation of its international head-quarters to Lebanon. The autonomy granted to the PLO in the context of the 1969 Cairo Agreement, combined with the fact that the PLO leadership was now present on the ground in Lebanon, meant that the Palestinians were able to establish a "state within a state" in the country. This, more than any other factor, led to the increasing polarisation of Lebanese politics, and particularly the breakdown in elite relations that ultimately made the civil war inevitable.

The main consequence of the new PLO status in Lebanon was that anti-Israeli activities based in Lebanon intensified dramatically. Israeli reprisals accordingly became more and more vigorous. This included military strikes on Lebanon's economic infrastructure. The prime objective of Israel's reprisal policy was not so much to attack the PLO directly as it was to put pressure on the Lebanese government to crack down on Palestinian activism. A similar policy had been successful with respect to Jordan and all the other Arab states that the PLO had used as a base for various operations.

The Lebanese elites recognised the detrimental effect that the PLO–Israeli conflict was having on the country, and they attempted to respond to it. On a number of occasions from 1970 to 1975, the government directed the Lebanese armed forces to take action to limit PLO cross-border operations. However, in each instance, the government was unable to sustain its security policy in the face of external condemnation from Egypt, Syria and other Leftist Arab states and, perhaps more importantly, internal condemnation from the Lebanese Muslim masses and movements such as the LNM.

With respect to Muslim mass attitudes, it should be recognised that these had always been quite sympathetic as far as the Palestinian issue was concerned. Of course, much the same might be said of mass attitudes in most of the Muslim states where the governments had ultimately decided that they could not continue to give the PLO free rein. A critical difference in Lebanon was that the PLO was able to forge an alliance with the LNM and other dissident elements, who were more than willing to mobilise the masses against the existing system and threaten the position of the existing Muslim elites.

A critical point that needs to be stressed here is that the Muslim *zu'ama* were confronted with an impossible dilemma. On one hand, they had a considerable stake in the existing system and wanted to preserve it against the danger that PLO activities were introducing. On the other hand, they had to placate their own constituencies or risk losing their traditional bases of support to populist elements such as the LNM. This meant that, whenever the Lebanese government attempted to take action to restrict the PLO, they would begin by supporting the action but ultimately would have to withdraw their support and join in the condemnation.

The Christian elites possibly sympathised with the problems of the Muslim *zu'ama*, but they were not themselves in much of a position to compromise. Popular opinion in their own constituencies was becoming increasingly anti-PLO with each new incident, and the Christian masses were infuriated that the government seemed to be completely unable to do anything about the situation.

As a result of the government's failures, the Christian communities, and the Maronites particularly, stepped up the development of their own militias, and prepared to take unilateral action against the PLO. The country split into two armed camps along Christian–Muslim lines. The government was paralysed by its own internal divisions, so there was no mediator who could help to resolve the internal conflict. Thus every minor dispute increased the already dangerously high level of tension until the system finally imploded in 1975.[22]

1.3 Understanding the collapse of the Lebanese state

I consider the specific events that led up to the outbreak of the civil war in some detail at the beginning of the next chapter. The purpose of this section is to provide an overview of the different schools of thought scholars have advanced to explain the failure of the Lebanese system, and to present my own analysis concerning the key causal factors.

The different schools of thought

While it is generally acknowledged that several factors contributed to the outbreak of the war, some authors would argue that certain ones were more crucial than others. Essentially, there are five schools of thought.

The first school of thought (including both Marxist and non-Marxist scholars) suggests that economic inequalities led to the breakdown of the traditional patron–client system. As explained in the previous section, the Chehabist governments attempted to offset problems created by the concentration of wealth around Beirut by assisting the poorer areas with development projects. These projects were met with great resistance by the traditional *zu'ama*, who feared that government aid would undercut their own control over the patronage system. Ultimately, the Franjieh government halted the development projects altogether.

The scholars in this school would argue that this somewhat shortsighted perspective led to *zu'ama's* undoing. Continuing poverty in the rural areas initiated a tendency toward urbanisation (in the form of migration to Beirut) that actually served to place much of the rural *zu'ama's* traditional client base beyond their influence. The urban *zu'ama* also suffered from the change in population distribution, as they were unable or unwilling to provide patronage for the great numbers of people entering their sphere of influence. As the government was also unable or unwilling to assist them, the new urban poor, facing extreme hardship, turned to an increasingly radical and aggressive Leftist movement. As Lebanon's poorer classes, under Leftist leadership, challenged the privileges of the rich, the Right resorted to coercive measures to disrupt the challenge, and a civil war ensued.

A second major school of thought, which includes some of the most prominent authorities of the Lebanese scene, including Kamal Salibi and Albert Hourani, does not accept the above as a sufficient explanation, arguing that it fails to account for the fact that Lebanon's population actually split primarily along sectarian, rather than class, lines. As an alternative explanation, they put forth the thesis that the Lebanese political system collapsed, above all else, because of a lack of political community. As noted previously, Lebanon had a divided political community – those, predominantly Muslim, who supported pan-Arabism; and those, predominantly Christian, who supported a pro-Western Lebanon. The National Pact was based, to a great extent, on a compromise between the major sects that ostensibly neutralised Lebanon's foreign policy orientation. Changes in the Arab world (namely the popularity of Arab nationalist and Arab socialist ideas) undermined public confidence in the workability of this compromise, and sectarian mistrust superseded class interest as a reason for conflict.

Like the first school, this school also places significant emphasis on the role of the Lebanese Left in the genesis of the civil war. However, it was not the Leftism of the Left that was the key component, but rather its pan-Arabism. As Arab socialism and Arab nationalism tended to be strongly linked, the Lebanese Left was perceived by many Christians (perhaps with some justice) as being too much in line with the Arab nationalist and pro-Palestinian agendas of pan-Arabism. Therefore, rather than seeing the Left primarily as a group opposed to the privileges of the wealthy, the Christian masses saw it as a disguise for a Muslim challenge to the basic Western nature of Lebanon and the traditional position of the Christian community. As the Leftists manifested increasingly aggressive tendencies and solidified their alliance with the Palestinians in Lebanon, the Christian masses flocked to, and encouraged, the Christian Right.

A third school of thought suggests that a major cause of the civil war involved increasingly ardent demands for the redistribution of political power by groups that perceived themselves as under-represented in the context of the existing decision-making process. In short, groups on the fringes of the Lebanese political system challenged proportional confessional representation on both demographic and ideological grounds.

Demographically, it was contended by many in the other sects that the Maronites were no longer numerically the largest group, and therefore had no legitimate claim to political dominance. The Shiites particularly began to lay claim to their share of political power. Ideologically, the Leftist movements were opposed to the *status quo*, calling for the deconfessionalisation of the political system and a change in Lebanon's foreign policy orientation in favour of support for pan-Arab issues, such as the Palestinian cause.

As already noted, many in Lebanon were opposed to such radical changes in the *status quo*. The *zu'ama* of all the sects naturally resisted deconfessionalisation, because it would strip them of their traditional prerogatives in the political system. The Christian masses were also strongly opposed, since it would eliminate the functional safeguards that prevented the Muslims from involving Lebanon in the pan-Arab movement. Hence demands for change were resisted and society became increasingly polarised, to such an extent that, when additional stresses arose to challenge the existing system, a major conflict ensued.

A fourth school emphasises the breakdown of elite–mass relations. In short, the elites were increasingly unable to control their followers. Their respective attempts to solve this problem led to a general breakdown in good relations between the elites themselves. In his 1986 study of Sunni patron–client relations, Michael Johnson argued that the Sunni *zu'ama* were unable to control their own "street", as their clients found alternative patrons including pan-Arab Leftist and Palestinian groups. In an attempt to retain the support of their clients, Sunni elites paid lip service to popular pan-Arab causes, particularly the armed Palestinian presence in Lebanon. This position, however, served to put them at odds with other elites, particularly within the Maronite sect, whose own community fervently opposed the Palestinian presence.[23] Tewfik Khalaf argued that the Maronite elite, like their Sunni counterparts, were prisoners of their own "street". Popular Maronite attitudes hardened as a result of the Palestinian presence in Lebanon and the increased demands of the Muslim communities.[24] As a consequence, it was difficult for Lebanon's elites to find common solutions to the problems facing the country. The increasingly poor intra-elite relations paralysed the government.

A fifth school, of which Iliya Harik and Georges Corm are leading advocates, argues that it was primarily the pressures originating from external factors, such as the Palestinian–Israeli conflict, which caused the civil war. The position of this school was summed up by Corm:[25]

> Lebanese society was not genetically flawed; ... [this is] not to say that Lebanon was a country without problems, but only that there was little time to adjust to and assimilate the tensions, imbalances and shortcomings which are also common to other societies before the regional conditions that destabilised the country appeared in 1967.

The Arab–Israeli dispute and the armed Palestinian presence, according to this school of thought, constituted a major external load on the Lebanese system that had the effect of greatly polarising Lebanese domestic politics. The regional loads on the Lebanese political system were commented upon by Walid Khalidi:[26]

> When a deeply divided society like Lebanon belongs to a regional system characterised by the level of turbulence prevailing in the Arab world, and when the Pan-doctrine is actively espoused within this system, the centrifugal tendencies within this member society are likely to be maximised.

A critical assessment

Having looked at all these approaches to understanding what happened, I would suggest that no single school presents a truly comprehensive and definitive account – and it is obviously not possible to develop a definitive account in this context. However, it may be useful to consider how elements of the different schools can be used together to explain the complex of forces that were working to undermine the Lebanese political order by the early 1970s. I would propose that it is necessary to pay particular attention to three factors or problems that reflected the extent to which the whole political system was fundamentally weak or even dysfunctional.

The weakness of the Lebanese state

The first systemic problem was the fact that the state structures were too weak to manage sectarian and class-based tensions. As mentioned above, the weakness of the state was primarily a result of the *zu'ama's* desire to protect their own dominance of the system. They did not want to allow the emergence of a strong state that could exert influence in their traditional spheres of influence, interfere in their activities or rival their ability to supply patronage to their constituents. Consequently, when the Chehabists introduced policies designed to strengthen state power, the *zu'ama* resisted them, and the Franjieh government either halted them altogether or even reversed them. This was a tragic mistake given the tensions that were besetting Lebanese society at this time. A strong state almost certainly would have been able to handle the situation better.

For example, I explained above how the Lebanese army was traditionally kept weak and how the Franjieh government undermined Lebanon's internal security establishment. A state with stronger coercive and internal security capabilities would have been in a better position to take action against the PLO and to resist internal and external pressures regarding the Palestinian issue. It also would have been able to prevent the illegal militias from coming into being. A state with a better developed economic capacity, or a more redistributive economic policy, would have been able to reduce tensions among the poor of Beirut, to give them a stake in the system rather than leave them feeling disenfranchised.

To understand the true significance of the fact that the Lebanese state was so weak, one only has to look at how the stronger Jordanian state was able to manage almost exactly the same problem in the late 1960s and early 1970s. Like Lebanon, Jordan had a population deeply divided over the PLO presence. Indeed, in that sense, the situation in Jordan was probably worse, because a much higher proportion of the population was actually Palestinian. Yet, when the Jordanian government decided that the PLO had to be expelled in 1970, they were able to carry through the policy in spite of internal opposition and protest from other Arab states. The key difference is that the Jordanian state and the Jordanian military were reasonably strong and stayed internally united during the crisis.

Demographic shifts and the power-sharing arrangements

The second systemic problem was that significant demographic shifts after 1943 had not been accounted for in the national power-sharing arrangements. The distribution of seats in the Chamber continued to be fixed according to the population figures for the 1932 census, ignoring the fact that the population balance shifted in favour of the Muslims in the three decades that followed. Furthermore, despite this change, the Maronite Presidency continued to be the single most significant and powerful of the national institutions. These facts had potentially very significant connotations with respect to the popular sense of national community. In short, many Muslims felt that they were second-class citizens in a state that would always have a predominantly Western and Christian orientation. The Shiites may have even felt that they were third-class citizens, since their population had increased very significantly and they had no increased representation to show for it, while the Sunni community at least had control of the office of Prime Minister.

If the Christians had been willing to renegotiate the power-sharing arrangements to give the Muslims effective parity, at least two significant positive consequences might have resulted. First, the Muslim masses might have felt a stronger sense of loyalty to the whole concept of a united Lebanese nation. They also, almost certainly, would have had a greater stake in maintaining the system, and accordingly might have been less likely to risk a major confrontation with the Christians over the PLO issue. Second, the Muslim *zu'ama* would have had more resources and a greater incentive to work consistently with the Christians to resist the pressure that the Palestinian presence was introducing into Lebanese society.

Another point that should be made here is that, even if the political will had existed to renegotiate the power-sharing arrangements, the system had no real mechanism or defined procedure to allow for such change. The Christian and Muslim elites would have had to come together informally in the same spirit that had culminated in the original National Pact. The polarisation of the elites over the PLO issue ensured that this spirit was absent at the critical time. If the power-sharing arrangements had been more formal, and if there had been a constitutional mechanism to provide for changing circumstances, it might have been possible to address Muslim grievances long before a critical breakdown in sectarian relations occurred.

External penetration of the Lebanese system

The third, and perhaps most significant, problem was the susceptibility of the Lebanese system to penetration by external actors.[27] Obviously, in the context of the early 1970s, the most notable and disruptive of these external elements was the PLO. However, the problems that Lebanon had encountered as a result of the pan-Arab movement in the late 1950s and early 1960s should be sufficient evidence to demonstrate that this was a continuing feature of the system and not a single extraordinary occurrence.

It should be recognised that Lebanon was not the only Arab country to have its internal sovereignty threatened, either as a result of the pan-Arab movement generally, or as a result of the specific pan-Arab issue that was the Arab–Israeli conflict. On the contrary, most Arab countries experienced significant internal tensions, and some states were actually overthrown in the 1950s as a result. However, by the 1970s, the pan-Arab movement had lost much of its initial impetus. The failure of the Egyptian/Syrian UAR and the catastrophic Arab defeat in the 1967 War had amply demonstrated the practical limits of Arab unity. Despite undiminished rhetorical support for pan-Arabism, the leaders of the Arab states were, almost without exception, beginning to adopt more pragmatic policies rooted in national self-interest. Virtually all of these states were strong enough by this point to manage internal tensions arising out of pan-Arab issues, and the fact that states such as Egypt, Syria and Jordan had taken measures to put a stop to PLO cross-border raids from their territories was a prime example of the new attitude.

However, the Lebanese state was not strong, and the country was weakened by a sectarian system that weakened the population's sense of national identity. Thus it was all too easy for external actors to penetrate the system and forge ideological, economic and/or military alliances with internal factions. Lebanon was also unlucky in geographical terms. If it had not happened to border on Israel, it would not have been such an ideal base for the PLO or such an easy target for Israeli reprisal attacks.

In any case, it was the PLO presence specifically that critically inflamed tensions between the Christian and Muslim sects. To begin with, it disrupted the traditionally neutral foreign policy orientation of the state, and therefore destroyed one of the key pillars of the National Pact. Furthermore, the PLO's cross-border raids and other anti-Israeli activities laid the country open to damaging Israeli reprisals and involved it directly in the Arab–Israeli conflict, something that Lebanese leaders of both Christian and Muslim sects had worked very hard to avoid for decades. And finally, although the PLO publicly claimed that it operated strictly within the bounds of its legal autonomous status and did not interfere in Lebanese internal politics, this simply was not true. In fact, the PLO, especially its Leftist elements, was very actively engaged in Lebanese politics and formed strong alliances with the Lebanese Left. The objective of this involvement, ultimately, was to topple the existing sectarian order and replace it with a secular socialist state that would be more amenable to Palestinian interests.

2

THE CIVIL WAR: 1975–90

When most people in the West think of Lebanon, they tend to think of the civil war. The fifteen-year conflict focused world attention on the country to an unprecedented degree, not least because it was an extension of the Arab–Israeli conflict and therefore had a significant international dimension. Ultimately, it involved not only regional powers such as Syria, Israel and Iran, but also such global actors as the United Nations and the United States. Its legacy has been a popular impression of Lebanon that includes violence and brutality, religious and nationalist fanaticism, hostage-taking and acts of local and international terrorism.

Not surprisingly, the war period has been the primary focus of a great proportion of Western scholarly literature about Lebanon. There have been numerous books and articles examining the causes of the war, looking at general or specific aspects of its genesis and development, and/or considering its implications.[1] One of my primary aims in this book is to correct this exclusive emphasis on the civil war by placing the conflict in the broader context of Lebanese history and proceeding to look at more contemporary developments. Consequently, it is not my purpose in this chapter to present a detailed and comprehensive history of the war. Rather, my aim is to provide a relatively brief analytical account that explains the transition from the pre-war political system to the post-war system.

The chapter is divided into two main sections. The first comprises a summary of major developments during the civil war; the second considers the lasting systemic implications that have figured very significantly in post-war Lebanese politics.

2.1 Major developments during the civil war period

The Lebanese civil war lasted for nearly fifteen years, but it was not a period of constant and intense conflict between a few sharply differentiated factions. On the contrary, it was a complex war with a constantly changing face. It ultimately involved a considerable number of domestic and international actors and was characterised by several fairly distinct phases. Periods of intense fighting were separated by transitional intervals in which new actors became involved, other actors built up their strength or became weaker, alliances shifted, and so on.

In the context of this account, the war can be divided into five more or less distinct phases. For the most part, I have distinguished the different periods on the basis of two elements: 1) the fact that key actors first became involved at a particular time; and/or 2) the phase identified can be characterised in terms of a major developmental theme.

Phase I: 1975–76 – the decline of the Lebanese state and Syrian intervention

The period from April 1975 to November 1976 was marked by intense battles and very heavy casualties. Of the estimated 100,000 people who were killed in the course of the whole fifteen-year conflict, approximately 40,000 died within these eighteen months.

Although there had been sporadic fighting between the Lebanese army and Leftist/ PLO elements, particularly from 1973 onwards, most observers date the actual outbreak of the civil war to a specific incident in April 1975, when twenty-seven Palestinians travelling on a bus in East Beirut were massacred by members of the major Christian militia, the *Kata'eb* (more commonly known in the West as the Phalange). The consensus is that the *Kata'eb* were trying to provoke an open conflict that would resolve the issue of Leftist and Palestinian activism in Lebanon once and for all. And, indeed, the Leftists and their allies within the PLO did respond by engaging the Christians in heavy fighting, particularly in and around Beirut.

Although the conflict spread periodically to other parts of the country, control of Beirut was seen by both sides as the major objective, and it was always the focal point of the most intense fighting. Not only was the city Lebanon's political capital and its major economic centre, it was also home to nearly two-thirds of the population. Furthermore, while the respective Christian and Muslim communities in the rural parts of the country had always been somewhat geographically separate, Beirut was more cosmopolitan and integrated, with the different sects interacting on a much more frequent basis.

In any case, Christian plans for victory were fairly heavily dependent on intervention by the Lebanese army. As they saw it, the Leftists and the PLO were the elements challenging the existing order, and they were the supporters of the state. Hence they calculated that they could count on the support of the army. As events actually developed, however, the army split along sectarian lines and became basically ineffectual. Once this occurred, the Lebanese state had no real coercive capacity. It was unable to bring the conflict under control, or to impose public order of any kind. The government became a helpless bystander as the country disintegrated into chaos. The feuding factions did not limit their activities to major battles against rival paramilitary elements, but also began to target civilians in a rash of massacres and revenge killings.[2]

Over the course of the next few months, Beirut became divided into a number of sectarian/ethnic enclaves. The Christian militias dominated the eastern half of the city, adjacent to the Christian heartland of the country, while the Leftist/PLO Muslim alliance dominated the western half, neighbouring predominantly Muslim territories. Those unfortunate Christian and Muslim pockets that happened to be located in the wrong parts of the city were subject to ethnic cleansing. Palestinian refugee camps located in the Christian sectors were effectively destroyed.

It is also important to note that the sectarian paramilitaries were able to extend their control over the whole country, with the Christian militias exercising decisive influence in Christian areas outside Beirut, and the Muslim paramilitaries controlling Muslim regions. The Lebanese government no longer had effective control over any part of the country.

By 1976, the balance of the conflict had shifted in favour of the Leftist/PLO alliance, largely because Yasser Arafat's Fatah organisation finally threw its weight behind the Leftist PLO factions that had previously joined with the Druze leader Walid Jumblatt's Lebanese National Movement (LNM). Arafat and Jumblatt now began to push for a total victory in the conflict that would allow Jumblatt to become the leader of Lebanon and establish a Leftist secular state with a heavily pro-Palestinian orientation. In other words, they wanted to end substantial Christian influence in Lebanese politics once and for all, and to dispense with Lebanon's traditionally neutral East–West orientation.

Nothing demonstrated this ambition more clearly than the Leftists' total rejection of proposed constitutional changes that would have given the Muslim sects parity with the Christians in a reconstituted Lebanese state. Initially, the Leftist/PLO alliance had claimed that it was only trying to redress the historic disenfranchisement of Lebanese Muslims by conservative Christian elements, but it became clear once they gained the ascendancy that their preferred solution involved an even more thorough disenfranchisement of Lebanese Christians. For them, the time for compromise was past. The conflict had become a zero-sum game.

These developments introduced a new element that was to have dramatic ramifications with respect to Lebanese politics for decades to follow. The potential implications of a Lebanon partly or wholly dominated by radical elements alarmed the Syrian leadership in Damascus to the extent that it felt compelled to intervene militarily in the country. The Syrian leader, Hafez al-Asad, felt that a Leftist victory would only serve to invite another major regional conflict between the Arab states on the one hand, and Israel and its Western patron, the United States, on the other. The consequences for the Lebanese Christians were yet another factor that would draw the major Western powers to get involved. Asad felt that the Arabs were not in a position to win such a conflict, and he was not prepared to risk it. The Syrians were also concerned that a potential cantonisation of Lebanon would set a precedent that might destabilise their own divided society.[3]

Consequently, when Arafat and Jumblatt ignored Asad's calls for a ceasefire and the acceptance of constitutional reform proposals, Damascus sent 30,000 troops into Lebanon with the formal approval of Lebanese President Franjieh. After a series of successful military operations, the Syrians prevented a Leftist/PLO victory and solidified the boundaries of the sectarian/ethnic enclaves. This brought an end to the first phase of intense fighting, but left many issues unresolved. Subsequently, the Arab League gave formal sanction to the Syrian military presence in Lebanon by creating an "Arab Deterrent Force", which consisted of the Syrian troops already in the country and small numbers of troops from other Arab countries that were sent in later. The Arab League also extracted promises from the PLO to respect Lebanese sovereignty, but this measure had no practical effect.

Phase II: 1976–82 – sectarian entrenchment and shifting alliances

Although the security situation prevented the election of a new Lebanese Parliament, the mandate of the 1972 Parliament was extended and a new President, Elias Sarkis, was elected in 1976. The Lebanese government, with substantial support from Syria, attempted to reassert state control over the country. However, the Christian and Muslim paramilitaries refused to disarm or allow for any reduction in their regional dominance. On the contrary, they devoted a great deal of effort during this phase to consolidating their positions and usurping the administrative and welfare functions that had previously been the exclusive province of either the state or the traditional *zu'ama*. The Christian militias, in particular, developed an extensive "state within the state", levying their own taxes, making military service compulsory, setting up illegal ports for imports and exports, establishing local public service and patronage networks, and even sending political representatives to foreign capitals.[4] Thus Syrian-backed government initiatives were almost wholly unsuccessful.

Within four months of the Syrian intervention, the LNM was dealt a critical blow with the assassination of its leader, Kamal Jumblatt. His importance to the Lebanese Left was demonstrated by the fact that the movement lost its functional coherence after his death. From this point on, the PLO became overwhelmingly dominant within the Muslim enclaves.

With the decline of the Left, the ideological focus of Muslim groups became more sectarian in nature. This tendency was particularly pronounced among the Shiites. The most prominent Shiite militia at this point was Amal (Hope), which was beginning to establish a power base that would become very significant in the 1980s.[5] It is worth noting that perhaps a great part of their strength was derived from an alliance with Syria, and to a lesser extent Iran, whose foreign policy since the 1979 revolution called for active support of Shiite Muslim communities throughout the region.[6]

During the same period, the Maronites were reorganising and asserting their dominance within the Christian enclaves. The *Kata'eb* under the leadership of Bashir Gemayel began to unify the various Christian militias into a new organisation, the Lebanese Forces. After a series of battles with rival Christian leaders, Gemayel succeeded in achieving nearly complete dominance over Christian areas, the main exception being the far North, which continued to be controlled by the Franjieh clan.[7]

The vital point to be stressed here is that neither the PLO nor the Christians were satisfied with the situation that had emerged from the first phase of the civil war. The

PLO wished to maintain its independence and, ultimately, to continue its anti-Israeli activities. To do this, it had to secure its position relative to the Syrians, on one hand, and the Christians, on the other. Syria's objective was to establish as much control as possible over the situation, but pressure from the other Arab states made it difficult for them to act decisively against the PLO leadership. Meanwhile, the Christians not only wanted to drive the PLO out of the country once and for all, but also wanted to force a Syrian withdrawal. Obviously, they were far too weak to accomplish these objectives alone in the long term. In the short term, they needed external insurance against Syrian interference while they were building up their forces. In order to satisfy these imperatives, they cultivated an increasingly strong alliance with Israel.

Obviously, Israel's key objective with respect to Lebanon was to end PLO activities in the country. Ideally, they wanted the PLO expelled or even fatally disrupted. In this sense, they were the natural allies of the Christians, who also wanted the PLO out of the country for good. Consequently, the Israeli government had given some aid and support to the Christians during the first phase of the war, and had taken considerable satisfaction from the Syrian–PLO conflict. During this phase, they began to work much more extensively with the Christians, developing contacts with the Christians in the South and providing clandestine military support to the Lebanese Forces.

After Menachim Begin and the Likud party came to power in Israel in 1977, Israeli opposition to the PLO became ever more strident. In 1978, Israel sent 25,000 troops into South Lebanon in an attempt to destroy the PLO. This operation was ultimately somewhat limited due to diplomatic pressure from the USA and Egypt, with whom the Israelis were, at the same time, negotiating the Camp David Accords. The result was that Israel withdrew its own forces to a so-called "security zone" that consisted of a narrow strip inside the Southern Lebanese border. They also helped to establish the South Lebanon Army (SLA), a militia consisting of their Lebanese clients. The SLA was led by a renegade Lebanese army general, Saad Haddad, and most of the senior officers were Christian, but many of the fighters were drawn from the Shiite villages straddling the Israeli border. The UN passed Resolution 425, which called for the withdrawal of Israeli forces from South Lebanon and established a multinational peacekeeping force (UN Interim Force in Lebanon, UNIFIL) to separate the PLO forces from the Israeli and SLA troops.[8]

Phase III: 1982–85 – the 1982 Israeli invasion and subsequent events

By the beginning of this phase, the major factions had built up their strength sufficiently that they were prepared for a full-scale resumption of the conflict. Violence had been steadily increasing throughout 1981 and early 1982, but the catalyst that fully reignited the war was another large-scale Israeli invasion in June 1982.

The conclusion of the Egyptian–Israeli peace treaty and the emergence of a more hawkish administration in Washington freed Israel's hand with respect to its Lebanon policy. Israel no longer had to worry about an Egyptian strike across its Southern border, or about substantial interference in its designs by the USA. Under these conditions, Begin's government felt the timing was ideal to settle the Arab–Israeli conflict by force. Their plan entailed invading Lebanon to eliminate the PLO and set up a friendly Lebanese government that would conclude a peace treaty with Israel. This would, in turn, isolate Syria, and thereby neutralise that country as an effective threat or, even better, force Damascus into separate peace negotiations.[9]

And so Israel launched a three-pronged offensive involving as many as 70,000 troops. The ostensible goal was to expand the "buffer zone" between the PLO and the Israeli border to around forty miles. In effect, however, the Israelis planned to destroy the PLO and drive Syria out of Lebanon.[10] Initially, the operation seemed to be a spectacular success. Between June and August of 1982, the Israelis and, to some extent, their Christian allies, were able completely to defeat the PLO and Syrian forces. By August, the PLO had agreed to leave Lebanon, and its evacuation to Tunisia was effectively carried out by the beginning of September.[11] The Syrian forces had been forced to retreat from Beirut and withdraw to the Biqa Valley. Thus the Israelis and the Christians had control of the capital and were on the verge of setting up a new national government under Lebanese Forces Leader, and now President-elect, Bashir Gemayel.

However, shortly thereafter, things started to go wrong from the Israeli perspective.[12] The first major blow was the assassination of Gemayel in September. With the death of their strongman leader, the Lebanese Forces was thrown into chaos as different Christian leaders tried to advance their interests. Ultimately, Bashir's Presidency was assumed by his brother Amin Gemayel. However, Amin was a much less forceful and influential figure who lacked his brother's power base within the Lebanese Forces. He was unable to bring the Christian militias under his government's control, and they proceeded to widen the internal conflict.

Partly, this took the form of massacres against their old enemies, the most infamous of which were those conducted against the Palestinian Sabra and Chatilla refugee camps. The Israelis, and particularly Defence Minister Ariel Sharon, were implicated in these atrocities, and this resulted in international pressure that forced them to withdraw their forces from Beirut. The Christian militias also challenged the Druze for control of their traditional heartland in the Shuf mountains. These incidents ensured that the new Lebanese government would be unable to assert its authority over the country.

Ironically, another major blow to the authority of the Gemayel government was dealt by the Israelis themselves. The so-called Lebanese–Israeli "withdrawal agreement" negotiated in 1983 amounted, in effect, to a humiliating unofficial peace treaty. It cost the Gemayel administration what little credibility it had left, not only among the Christians, but basically across all the sects. The most controversial feature of the agreement was the security arrangements, which effectively ceded the security of South Lebanon to Israel and the SLA, and gave Israel significant influence in all Lebanese security matters for an indefinite period.

Despite the fact that most Lebanese felt the withdrawal agreement represented a Lebanese capitulation to the Israelis, the Israeli government was actually not satisfied that it went far enough. They felt that Gemayel had been too uncompromising during the negotiations, and they were growing increasingly frustrated with his inability to secure the cooperation of even the Christian Lebanese elements. Largely as a sort of protest, they withdrew their forces from the Shuf. This was the beginning of a phased Israeli withdrawal that would see virtually their entire force redeployed to the security zone in the South by 1985. This process was probably encouraged to some extent by the fact that Gemayel and the Lebanese *zu'ama* held consultations in 1984, and it became clear that the Lebanese Parliament would not ratify the 1983 agreement despite the fact that the government had approved it. The Israeli occupation forces were suffering significant casualties, which put the Israeli government under pressure to show that something significant was being gained from their presence in Lebanon. The Gemayel government was either unable or unwilling to deliver. Gemayel, for his part, may have felt that the Israelis were not doing enough to support his position.

In any case, Syria considered the prospect of a continuing Israeli role in Lebanon a security threat of the first order, and the 1983 Lebanese–Israeli negotiations prompted them to start reinforcing their own presence. In addition, they began taking advantage of every possible opportunity to destabilise the country and encourage Lebanese opposition against the Gemayel government.

The withdrawal of the PLO had created something of a power vacuum in the Muslim sects. Syria moved quickly to back the newly emerging leaders. This included the leaders of the Druze, whose conflict with the Christian militias did so much to disrupt the country for the next couple of years. It also included Amal and, to some extent, influential new groups of Islamic militants such as Hizbollah, who received moral and tangible backing from a militant Iran. These essentially Shiite-controlled movements fought the government for control of West Beirut and other Muslim sectors of the country.

It should also be noted that, in the absence of any real authority, public order had completely broken down in many parts of the country. The resulting chaos was characterised by high levels of violence and the use of terror tactics. This included sectarian revenge killings targeted at civilian elements, attacks on foreigners, waves of kidnappings and hostage-taking, and so on.

The general levels of violence and chaos in the country persuaded the international community to redeploy the multinational force that had originally been sent in to assist with the PLO withdrawal. Their main aim was to help the Gemayel government to restore order and assert state authority in the country. This included military action in support of Lebanese government troops. The American elements particularly were drawn into the Christian–Druze battles over the Shuf. American naval bombardments against Druze elements were probably intended primarily to help the Lebanese army assert some kind of control on the ground, but the Muslim sects naturally interpreted them somewhat differently – as US participation on the Christian side of a Christian–Muslim war. They no longer perceived the Westerners as peacekeepers, but as allies of the enemy.

Shortly thereafter, in October 1983, Muslim elements began launching bomb attacks against US and French compounds. A total of 241 US servicemen and fifty-eight French paratroopers died in these attacks. Subsequently, it became increasingly clear that the major Western nations would ultimately withdraw from the country. It was only a matter of time. Finally, in February 1984, after the Lebanese army imploded once again due to internal sectarian tensions, the multinational force had no official indigenous power to support, and the Western powers used this as a pretext to pull out their forces.

This left the respective sectarian militias with effective control of the country. It is interesting to note that, shortly after the withdrawal of the multinational force, President Gemayel travelled to Damascus to meet with Asad. This amounted to implicit recognition that Syria was now the predominant actor in Lebanon, due not only to its continuing armed presence, but also to its influence on many of the key militias and other disruptive elements.

Phase IV: 1985–88 – militia rule[13]

Basically, from this point up until 1988, the Lebanese government continued to administer the country in name only. The whole period was marked by unprecedented levels of chaos and public disorder, and whatever true government there was emanated from the militias that had secured enclaves in different parts of the country. Of course, the Syrian government continued to exert great influence in the Muslim areas through its close ties with the leaders of the Druze and Shiite Amal militias, as well as Hizbollah. To some extent, however, it was in Syria's interest at the time for the situation to remain somewhat unstable. Furthermore, the Christian enclaves controlled by the Lebanese Forces continued to be largely independent of Syria, and still hoped to force a Syrian withdrawal at some point.

This phase of the civil war essentially represented the peak of sectarian cantonisation in Lebanon. The Christian enclaves were overwhelmingly Christian and dominated by the Maronites, and the Muslim enclaves were overwhelmingly Muslim and dominated either by the Shiite militias or by Syria. Vast numbers of people were displaced during this period as the borders of the sectarian enclaves once again became more strongly fixed. For example, when the Druze militias finally defeated the Christian elements in the Shuf region, hundreds of thousands of Christians were forced to leave and seek refuge in the Christian enclaves to the Northeast.[14]

It is important to note that it was also during this period that the wars of succession in the Muslim enclaves were finally resolved. As noted previously, the departure of the previously dominant PLO had left a power vacuum in these areas. Increasingly, the Leftists and other elements were suppressed by the Shiite militias, Amal and Hizbollah. Amal had existed since the mid-1970s, and had become the dominant Shiite militia by this time, with considerable assistance from its Syrian patron as well as from Iran. Hizbollah[15] was founded after the Israeli invasion, and drew its ideology from Ayatollah Khomeini's Iranian revolution. The movement also received a considerable amount of direct material support, in the form of funds, arms and training, from Iran. As a consequence, Iranian ambitions in both the region and towards the West (especially the USA) were carried out by their client, Hizbollah. As the movement developed, Syria also became involved as an influential sponsor, never displacing the Iranians entirely, but becoming increasingly powerful as Syrian dominance of Lebanon increased. The PLO made some effort to reassert its authority during the mid-1980s, particularly in the Palestinian refugee camps, but the Shiite militias, with the aid of Syria and Iran, were able effectively to shut them out.

This phase also saw the greatest extremes of terrorist violence, kidnappings and hostage-takings, spectacular hijackings and general lawlessness throughout Lebanon. Much of this activity had a distinctly anti-Western orientation, and was organised by Muslim extremist groups including Hizbollah and Islamic Jihad. Although both Iran and Syria had considerable influence over these groups, they did not really discourage this sort of activity. In fact, the Biqa valley, which was undeniably under direct Syrian control at the time, became a notorious centre for international terrorist activities and training.

This can probably be seen as part of Iran's and Syria's overall regional and international strategy. On one hand, there was a sincere desire in both Tehran and Damascus to eliminate Western interests in Lebanon and elsewhere in the region. On the other hand, the two countries were also able to use their potential ability to rein in terrorism as a bargaining chip in ongoing relations with the West. It should be remembered that the USA was making serious attempts to undermine both the Iranian and Syrian regimes during the 1980s, and this was part of their retaliation.[16] Naturally, the effect on Lebanon's international reputation was devastating. If the earlier violence of the civil war had created the impression that Lebanon was an unstable and dangerous place, developments during this period elevated it to the status of an international pariah.

As noted previously, by 1985, Israel had withdrawn virtually its whole military force to the security zone in the South. Although the departure of the PLO from Lebanon had removed the ostensible reason for their presence in the country, it was clear that the Israelis planned a long-term occupation. The increasing Syrian dominance of Lebanon obviously posed a threat. More importantly, Hizbollah emerged as a new, and possibly even more radical and dangerous, enemy. Continuing violence in the South was thus another feature of this phase of the civil war.

Phase V: 1988–90 – "dual government" and the end of the civil war

Although the Lebanese government under Amin Gemayel had been almost irrelevant since early 1984, a crisis with respect to the choice of the next President actually ushered in the decisive phase of the civil war. In short, when the Chamber of Deputies convened at the end of Gemayel's designated term in 1988, they were unable to reach agreement on a replacement. Ultimately, Gemayel was forced to fall back on a contentious legal provision allowing him to transfer executive power to an interim Council of Ministers.

For this Council, he selected three Christians and three Muslims from the reconstituted Lebanese army. In a shocking break from the National Pact and decades of Lebanese tradition, the interim Prime Minister was a Maronite, Michel Aoun, the chief general of the army. The Muslims were incensed, and the Muslim nominees to the new Council refused to serve. This left only Aoun and two other Christians in the new government. The serving Prime Minister from the previous government, Salim Hoss, refused to recognise the new government and, with Syrian support, established a rival Lebanese government in Muslim West Beirut.

Aoun was not deterred by Muslim and Syrian opposition to his rule, or indeed by opposition from the Christian militias. He intended to use his military power base to extend the control of his government over the whole country. He began by challenging the Lebanese Forces militia for control of the Christian enclaves. He was only partially successful with respect to this objective, and the essentially inconclusive struggle was halted by a ceasefire arranged through Catholic religious authorities. This did not mark the end of Aoun's military activism, however. Before long, he initiated a series of measures designed to undermine all the militias and also Syrian influence in the country. The result was a serious escalation of the military conflict on the same scale as the initial phase of the civil war and the period of the 1982 Israeli invasion. This culminated in a six-month "war of liberation against Syria". For this undertaking, Aoun and the Lebanese army formed an uneasy alliance with the Lebanese Forces, and even had some support from Iraq. Needless to say, the Syrians were able to count on the support of the Muslim paramilitaries.

These developments greatly concerned the international community, and the end of the Cold War had created an atmosphere in which the USA and the Arab League (particularly the Saudis) were both willing and able to step in and try to moderate the conflict. This resulted in peace negotiations involving sectarian delegations of Lebanese parliamentarians at the Saudi town of Ta'if in the Autumn of 1989. The result was a document known as the "Ta'if Accord", which called for constitutional reforms establishing Christian–Muslim parity in government, and attempted to set out terms for the disarmament of the militias and the withdrawal of all foreign forces from the country.

Aoun's government rejected the proposed settlement on two grounds: 1) that it recommended an excessive reduction in the powers of the Maronite Presidency; and 2) that it was far too underdeveloped concerning when and how the Syrian withdrawal from Lebanon would take place. Despite the fact that Aoun's alliance with the Lebanese Forces had collapsed in the meantime due to his rivalry with its leader, Samir Geagea, he continued to resist the implementation of the Ta'if Accord and put up a military resistance to the Syrian presence for roughly another year. By this point, geo-political realities had seriously shifted against him. In order to secure Syrian cooperation in the anti-Iraqi "Gulf War Coalition", the USA and its other Arab allies turned a blind eye to Syrian air strikes against Aoun's forces. He was militarily defeated, and fled to exile in France.[17]

With Aoun's departure, the last real obstacle to the implementation of the Ta'if Accord was removed. The USA and the Arab League backed the plan, and due to interests that I consider in more detail in Chapter 3, Syria and its Lebanese allies also supported the accord. Geagea, the last remaining Christian leader with substantial military resources, acquiesced to it in exchange for what he anticipated would be a significant role in the new Lebanese government.

2.2 Critical systemic implications of the civil war

The loss of state authority

One of the most obvious long-term implications of the civil war was the effective loss of authority by the Lebanese state. As explained above, this dates back to the initial collapse of the Lebanese army in the first phase of the war. From this point on, even when the military was reconstituted to some extent during several subsequent phases, the state institutions never really regained the dominance of the system that they had enjoyed from 1943 to 1975.

There are three fundamental points that one needs to bear in mind here: 1) the fact that the Lebanese state was relatively weak to begin with; 2) the continuing inability of the sectarian elites to resolve their differences; and 3) the essential reliance of the state on external supporters from 1976 to the present day.

The weakness of the state prior to 1975 and its implications as a causal factor with respect to the war have been commented on in some detail above. The point that is stressed here, and in subsequent chapters, is that this feature of the pre-1975 system has been carried over into the post-war system. The Lebanese state is still relatively weak with respect to both internal and external politics. The army is still weak, and although the regime has been criticised for repression and human rights abuses, the strength of its internal security mechanisms is still questionable. Of course, this weakness has an added dimension. In the pre-1975 set-up, the *zu'ama* and their desire to continue controlling the system acted as the main check on the power of the state. This factor holds to some extent in the post-1990 system, especially with respect to Hizbollah. However, for most of the post-1990 period, the most significant obstacle to a stronger Lebanese state was posed by Syria's desire to keep the Lebanese government weak.

The inability of the sectarian elites to resolve their differences was another major problem for the Lebanese state throughout the war period. The Ta'if Accord was meant to resolve the central dispute by giving the Christians and Muslims parity in the post-war order. Again, as explained later, developments did not quite go according to plan. The Maronites were marginalised for the most part in post-Ta'if Lebanon, and sectarian deadlock became a regular feature of the new "troika system", the tripartite executive in which the Maronite President, the Sunni Prime Minister, and the Shiite Speaker of the House all have roughly equal powers.

Finally, perhaps the most significant lasting implication of the war with respect to Lebanese state power was the fact that, ever since the Syrian intervention in 1976, the different Lebanese governments have been largely reliant on external sponsors. The Franjieh government depended on Syria. The Gemayel government ran the spectrum from relying on Israel, to relying on the multinational force, and finally turning back to Syria for support. Hoss's half of the "dual government" was dependent on Syrian support, and even Aoun had some external backing. Indeed, ultimately, Aoun's government failed because he was unable to maintain enough external support to protect him from Syria. The point to stress here is that this situation did not end with the war, but has become a lasting feature of Lebanese politics. In fact, as I demonstrate throughout the rest of this book, Syria, rather than the Lebanese state, has been the dominant player in Lebanon for much of the post-civil war period.

Change within the Lebanese elites

Another lasting implication of the war was the effect it had on the composition of the sectarian elites. It was argued in Chapter 1 that the traditional *zu'ama* class was basically exclusive and familial in nature. The war forced the elites to become more open to new elements, with two lasting consequences. The first is that the new elite elements created during the war have persisted in the post-war system. The second is that, to some extent, the system remains more open than previously to the introduction of new blood.

The elite introduced by the war was essentially made up of militia leaders, the Lebanese "warlords". This class includes men such as Michel Aoun, Nabih Birri and Samir Geagea. In some cases, the militias themselves came to be significant parties in the political establishment. This is particularly true of Amal and Hizbollah, the Shiite ideological parties which have persisted and which continue to be very influential in the post-war political system. These parties have effectively replaced the traditional Shiite *zu'ama* altogether. The Lebanese Forces also continues to be significant as a political complex, although it remained outside the system for most of the post-war order until Syria withdrew from the country in 2005.

New *zu'ama* have also emerged in the post-war context with greater frequency than the pre-war elite system allowed. These additions fall into two groups. The first group is made up of political figures who owe their position and influence largely to Syrian political imperatives. This includes many of the Maronites who have participated in the post-war governments, including most notably President Hrawi. Arguably, it also includes President Lahoud, although he was also able to draw considerable popular support and backing from the army. The second group consists of individuals who have been able to "buy" their way into the system due to their personal financial resources. The most significant example of this class was the post-war Prime Minister Rafiq Hariri[18.]

Penetration by external actors

As I have detailed before, a high level of susceptibility to external penetration has been a fundamental characteristic of the Lebanese system from the very beginning. Prior to the 1970s, the Lebanese state was able to use a combination of international backing and moderate rhetoric to stave off major instances of external interference in Lebanese affairs. The PLO managed to circumvent Lebanese state efforts in the early 1970s, and the sectarian tension this produced was probably the single most significant cause of the war. Although the PLO was expelled in the course of the conflict, an even more severe level of external penetration survived into the post-war period. This penetration emanated, and continues to emanate, from at least three different sources.

The first source was the continuation of the Israeli presence in the Southern "security zone" until the spring of 2000. This resulted in constant tension and a very high level of potential instability for a decade after the end of the war. The intermittent South Lebanon conflict has had an impact on post-war Lebanese politics that is somewhat difficult to quantify without looking at a number of different factors. I consider all of these to at least some extent in the following chapters.

The second source of penetration includes Iran and Islamic movements with other national and international bases. The manifestation of this influence is particularly obvious in the case of Hizbollah, but also has less overt components. It should suffice to say that Lebanon is still regarded in some quarters in the West, and the USA especially, as a major breeding ground for international terrorism, a perception that has become particularly damaging in the aftermath of September 11. As I discuss in later chapters, Iran's influence in Lebanon, via its client Hizbollah, increased considerably after 2005, the year Syria withdrew its military forces out of Lebanon.

The final and most significant source of external penetration is Syria. In short, for most of the post-civil war period (1990–2005), Syria came to dominate Lebanese politics to the extent that it exercised virtual hegemony over most aspects of Lebanese domestic and foreign policy. Even after the Syrian military withdrew from Lebanon in 2005, Syrian influence in the country has remained significant. The examination of Syria's influential role in Lebanon and its implications is the major theme of the remaining chapters of this study.

Lebanon becomes a pariah state

Another legacy of the civil war was considerable long-term damage to Lebanon's image and international standing. Before the war, Lebanon was viewed by many in the international community as an island of stability and relative democracy in a region dominated by ideologically radical and repressive authoritarian regimes. It was a bridge between West and East, an important centre of trade, banking and tourism. It was also regarded as a model of ethnic and religious tolerance, a society where a great number of different sects and groups with deep ideological and religious divisions managed to live together harmoniously.

Obviously, the war dramatically altered this perception. Lebanon became strongly associated with religious bigotry and fanaticism, violence and lawlessness, brutal massacres, terrorism, kidnappings and hostage-taking, and so on. In short, Lebanon came to be seen as the reverse of the previous popular perception. Particularly in the West, the country came to be regarded as dangerous. It was not safe to travel there, to do business there, or to have any dealings with the country. It was a hot-bed of terrorism and radical Islamic ideology.

Needless to say, this change posed a serious problem for the post-war governments as they tried to attract international aid and support for their attempts to reconstruct the country and restore its traditional role as a centre of international trade and finance. It would have been hard enough to rehabilitate the country's image if there had been a complete halt of violence and terrorist activity. The fact is that all of the country's attempts to regain its international standing have been seriously undermined by the ongoing conflict between Hizbollah and Israel, among other things. This is another point that I will revisit several times in the following chapters.

Economic devastation

Another long-term problem posed by the war was the effect it had on the Lebanese economy.[19] The country's physical infrastructure was devastated. Vast numbers of people were rendered homeless and displaced. Many of the vital middle-class elements fled the country and took their capital and their skills with them. The currency collapsed and the country began to run up huge debts. Furthermore, and perhaps most significantly, the country lost its traditional role as the regional centre of international trade and finance. In the course of the fifteen-year conflict, other centres emerged to replace it, and one must now question whether it will ever be possible, in the new competitive environment, for Lebanon to recover its traditional economic base. I look at the economic consequences of the war, and the post-war governments' attempts to address them in some detail, in Chapter 4.

3

THE POST-WAR POLITICAL SYSTEM

The defeat of General Aoun and his mainly Christian supporters in October 1990 removed the last real obstacle to the implementation of the Ta'if Accord and marked the end of the civil war. Although the vast majority of the Lebanese people continued to be opposed to crucial aspects of the Ta'if arrangements, the accord became the fundamental blueprint for the post-war political system. The manner and circumstances of its implementation established the basic priorities and constraints that have defined the political process ever since, and that will almost certainly continue to do so for the foreseeable future.

This chapter is divided into two parts. Part I examines the main features of the post-war political system until 2005, the year that the so-called "cedar revolution" forced the Syrian military to quit the country. Part II examines the implications of Syria's unexpected military withdrawal for the post-war political system.

Part I is divided into three main sections.

- In the first section, my aim is to place the contemporary political process in historical context: 1) by examining how it synthesises core elements of the pre-war system with the Ta'if arrangements; and 2) by considering whether or not the new system actually corrects, or compensates sufficiently for, the major systemic weaknesses of the pre-war era. I will argue that, for various reasons, Syrian hegemony in the Lebanese context being the most important factor, the post-Ta'if system fails effectively to remedy any of these weaknesses.
- My purpose in the second section is to examine in greater detail the two essential characteristics that have defined the 1990–2005 post-war political system: 1) the overwhelming dominance of Syria in Lebanese affairs; and 2) parity among the major confessional groups within the restructured national institutions. First, I look at Syria's interests in Lebanon and consider the domestic and international factors that have enabled Damascus to penetrate and control the Lebanese political

process so thoroughly; second, I proceed to examine the post-Ta'if shape of the national institutions and explain how the parity system works in practice.

- Finally, in the third section, I present a brief analytical account of major political developments from 1990 to 2004. These include the initial post-war governments; the accession of Rafiq Hariri as Prime Minister in October 1992; developments from 1992 to Hariri's resignation in December 1998; the election of Emile Lahoud to the Presidency and Salim Hoss's government of 1998–2000; and events since the return of Hariri to government from October 2000 until October 2004, including increased international pressure on Syria to withdrawal from Lebanon.

Part II is also divided into three main sections.

- The first section discusses the cedar revolution, which led to the withdrawal of Syrian troops.
- The second section identifies the limitations of the cedar revolution.
- The third section provides a brief account of the major developments following the revolution.

PART I: THE LEBANESE POLITICAL SYSTEM FROM 1990 TO 2005

3.1 Continuity and change in the post-war context

Analysis of the Ta'if Accord and its implementation[1]

If one wishes to really understand the historical significance of the Ta'if Accord and the changes that it introduced into the Lebanese political context, one must begin by considering whether or not, or to what extent, the accord actually addressed the most significant systemic weaknesses that led to the outbreak of the civil war. After all, the accord's overriding aim was not only to bring an end to the conflict, but also to reform the political system so that it would be stronger and more stable in the long term.

Systemic weaknesses in the Lebanese political context and the provisions of the Ta'if Accord

To briefly reiterate, the pre-war political order had become dysfunctional in three important respects: 1) the Lebanese state was too weak to manage tensions generated by internal and external circumstances; 2) already deep sectarian divisions were exacerbated by the fact that significant demographic changes were not accounted for within the power-sharing arrangements defined by the 1943 National Pact; and 3) sectarian tensions were critically inflamed due to the penetration of the Lebanese system by foreign elements, especially the PLO, which disrupted the traditional neutrality of Lebanese foreign policy and forced the country to become engaged in the Arab–Israeli conflict.

The Ta'if Accord was certainly not designed to address the first of these systemic weaknesses. Although it established the preconditions for a reassertion of central authority, no substantial changes were envisaged with respect to the power or role of the state in the political system or the economy. The political system would continue to conform to the basic model of a consociational democracy arranged along confessional lines. The political process would continue to be dominated by extensive patronage networks operating within each of the respective sectarian communities, with the formal state institutions essentially serving as a forum for the sectarian political elites to settle disputes and negotiate arrangements for the distribution of patronage among the communities. Consequently, for the system to remain functional, the four necessary preconditions of a consociational democracy (clear communal boundaries, elite cooperation, balance of power, and a relatively low total load on the system) would need to be maintained.

By contrast, the accord gave considerable attention to the second weakness, the fact that many viewed the 1943 power-sharing arrangements as illegitimate in light of subsequent demographic changes, particularly a significant increase in the relative size of the Muslim communities. Indeed, the framers of the accord viewed this as the major problem that needed to be addressed in the post-war context, a priority that is quite defensible, given the need for elite cooperation and a communal balance of power within a consociational framework. Consequently, the prime aim of the accord, in addition to ending the war and setting the stage for the reassertion of central state authority, was to address this issue by establishing parity among the major confessional groups as the fundamental principle underlying the post-war power-sharing arrangements. This parity was to be achieved mainly through constitutional changes that would reshape the national institutions, giving Christians and Muslims an equal number of seats in the Chamber of Deputies and redefining the powers of the three highest offices (the Maronite President, the Sunni Prime Minister and the Shiite Speaker of the House) to guarantee that no sect would be able to dominate the political process.

The accord also attempted to deal with the third problem, as it contained a number of provisions designed to lessen, and ultimately end, the destabilising penetration of the Lebanese system by foreign elements. This entailed, first and foremost, disentangling Lebanon from the Palestinian–Israeli conflict by establishing that Lebanon would no longer serve as a base for Palestinian or pro-Palestinian aggression against Israel, and by calling for the withdrawal of Israeli forces from Lebanon. Additionally, the document called for the normalisation of relations with Syria and established a timetable for the redeployment of Syrian forces as a prelude to their eventual withdrawal. More specifically, the accord stipulated that Syrian forces should be redeployed to the Biqa Valley within two years of its implementation. Significantly, this delay was ostensibly explained as a function of the special status granted to Syria as a guarantor of the accord. In short, because the Lebanese authorities continued to occupy a somewhat tenuous position, the Syrian forces, which remained the most formidable power on the ground in much of the country, were empowered to assist the Lebanese authorities with the implementation of the accord, especially of those provisions relating to the disarmament of the militias and to the reassertion of central authority.

With respect to this arrangement, it might be argued that the Ta'if Accord was self-defeating. Rather than guaranteeing that the Lebanese state would be able to reassert autonomous control of the country, it actually placed the Syrians in a strong position to establish the overwhelming predominance of their own interests in the Lebanese context. The majority of the Lebanese people certainly had serious reservations on this point, and it had unequivocally been Aoun's main reason for opposing the accord so strenuously.

On the other hand, it is probably worth noting that, with respect to the whole issue of external (and particularly Syrian) entanglement in Lebanese affairs, the practical obstacles to what the Lebanese people might have regarded *en masse* as a satisfactory resolution were overwhelming at this point in time. First and foremost, the nature of the external penetration did not allow for a clear-cut solution to the problem. Subtle factors, such as the establishment of the foreign-sponsored Hizbollah and Amal movements as effectively leading *zu'ama* of the Shiite community, guaranteed that freeing the Lebanese system from potentially destabilising outside influences would be much more complicated than simply evicting foreign military forces from the country. Furthermore, it was by no means clear that the Lebanese state forces alone would be able to disarm the militias or maintain a stable environment. Finally, and perhaps rather critically, the fact that the Syrian forces were the dominant military power on the ground in Lebanon automatically made any peace settlement that Syria would oppose virtually unworkable from the start.

As will be seen, Syria's continuing foreign policy agenda towards Israel meant that Damascus had compelling reasons for maintaining a powerful, if not overwhelming, influence in Lebanese affairs. This consideration surely would not have escaped the predominantly US and Saudi architects of the Ta'if Accord. In the absence of any means for compelling an immediate Syrian withdrawal, short of yet another costly and dangerous military intervention, the framers possibly hoped, realistically or otherwise, that circumstances would change over the course of the following years to allow for a better resolution of the issue. In any case, as the accord clearly posed no immediate threat to its position in Lebanon, Syria became one of its most enthusiastic supporters.[2]

Implementation of the Ta'if Accord

As noted at the end of Chapter 2, the Ta'if Accord was ratified by the Lebanese Parliament on November 5 1989, but its implementation was delayed until the rival government of Michel Aoun was defeated in the summer of 1990. The implementation process ultimately began only in August and September of 1990, when the Parliament approved the recommended institutional changes and amended the Constitution to officially put the new sectarian power-sharing arrangements in place.

It became clear almost from the earliest stages of the process that, rather than merely assisting the Lebanese government, Syria would play the dominant role with regard to interpreting and enforcing the accord's provisions. Indeed, there is over-whelming evidence to suggest that Syria exercised a decisive influence with respect to the composition of the "government of national reconciliation" that was formed in December 1990 to preside over the disarmament of the militias and the reassertion of state authority. To the exasperation of much of the public, the then Prime Minister, Salim Hoss, the President, Elias Hrawi, and other leading Lebanese figures openly made trips back and forth to Damascus to discuss the formation of the government, and, in a strikingly open display of contempt for the formal procedures, the new Prime Minister, Omar Karami, was actually announced as Hoss's successor in the Syrian press two days prior to his nomination in the Lebanese Parliament.[3]

The militia disarmament process that followed was largely successful and allowed for the restoration of central authority to most of the country by the spring of 1991. However, in a move that greatly upset many, particularly within the Maronite community, the decision was taken that some militias, most notably Hizbollah, would not be required to disarm as the Ta'if Accord specified. The official reason given was that Hizbollah had the right to continue its attempts to liberate territory illegally occupied by the Israelis, but this explanation clearly made very little sense in relation to the interests of the Lebanese state or the people as a whole.

Even if one assumes that there was a compelling need to take forcible action against Israel at this time, which is not at all clear, given an already war-devastated Lebanon's other critical priorities, it is still difficult to understand why it was deemed necessary to involve paramilitary irregular troops rather than employing the recon-stituted state forces. As events developed, and as any informed observer of the Lebanese scene surely would have anticipated, continuing Hizbollah operations against the Israelis merely served to give Israel a pretext to maintain its occupied "security zone" in South Lebanon indefinitely and to launch reprisal attacks against whatever Lebanese targets it could justify in terms of its leaders' prevailing objectives at any given time. In short, the main result of the decision not to disarm Hizbollah was to establish that a high level of potential instability and conflict would continue to be a long-term feature of the Lebanese context. Needless to say, this was not at all helpful with respect to the country's attempts to reconstruct itself and rehabilitate its image on the international stage.

The situation did, however, give the Syrians a bargaining chip in their ongoing dispute with Israel, as it enabled them successfully to represent themselves, to the Israelis and the international community as a whole, as the only force capable of reining in Hizbollah and securing the Lebanese–Israeli border. It is by no means incidental that the possibility of a major resurgence in the border conflict also supplied Damascus with an effective pretext for continuing its own indefinite occupation of Lebanon. And indeed, given these considerations, it is hardly surprising that Hizbollah's continuing armed status can almost certainly be traced, in the first instance, not to the Lebanese government or even to Lebanese–Syrian deliberations on the issue, but rather to an agreement negotiated by Syria and Iran in April 1991.[4]

Furthermore, Syria's influence over the Ta'if implementation process was not limited to "assisting" with security issues. The accord also called for a normalisation of relations between Lebanon and Syria, a process that was meant to entail equal negotiations between the two countries on a whole range of bilateral issues. As it happened, the most prominent result of these provisions was "The Treaty of Brotherhood, Cooperation and Coordination" signed in Damascus on 22 May 1991 by the Lebanese and Syrian heads of state. This document stipulated that the two states agreed to work for the highest possible level of coordination in all matters of political, economic, security and cultural policy, and to establish a joint institutional framework to that end. The chief institution was a "Supreme Council" chaired by the heads of state and empowered to make "mandatory and enforceable" decisions in virtually all policy areas. Additional coordination committees were established for specific areas, including a Foreign Affairs Committee and a Defence and Security Affairs Committee, to cite only the most significant examples.[5]

It should be clear from Lebanese popular opposition, and from intense protests by international observers such as France and Israel, that the agreement did not represent, and was never intended to establish, anything remotely resembling a true bilateral partnership between the two states. There was very little question in anyone's mind that what "coordination" really meant was that Lebanese policy in all areas would correspond to Syrian preferences in virtually every respect. The institutions created by the treaty simply gave Syria a technically legal and very effective means to exercise decisive influence over all policy decisions.[6] The Israeli Foreign Minister at the time, Moshe Arens, summed up what many felt when he referred to the treaty as the "*Anschluss*", harking back to Nazi Germany's annexation of Austria in 1938.[7]

As if all of these developments did not sufficiently undermine the intent and spirit of the Ta'if Accord, when they did not contradict the letter of it outright, they ultimately had a very heavy impact even on the agreement's core provisions relating to sectarian parity. The leaders of the Muslim sects, and most of the minor sects, tended to acquiesce to Syrian dominance, perhaps grudgingly in many cases and in the hope that it would afford them enough influence to moderate the damage Syria might do to Lebanese national interests. However, the most influential leaders of the Maronite elite continued to call vociferously for Syria to withdraw its forces from Lebanon. Although the Christian militias did cooperate with the disarmament process, the Maronite leadership consistently (but unsuccessfully) attempted throughout the early 1990s to resist, or at least delay, the implementation of the Ta'if Accord's other provisions. They established Syrian troop withdrawal as a precondition for their support.

Although it is undoubtedly true, as some observers have commented, that the Maronite community was really opposed to the new sectarian arrangements, and the Ta'if Accord as a whole, because of what it regarded as an excessive reduction in the traditional powers of the Presidency (i.e. the basis of the community's traditional veto power in the pre-war system), I would argue that it is not clear that this objection would have been critical in other circumstances. Very serious Maronite concerns about the accord's legitimation of Syria's role in Lebanon were at least as significant, and probably even more so, in terms of explaining their continuing opposition to the Ta'if arrangements throughout the implementation period.

In any case, the 1992 parliamentary elections became an important watershed in the development of the post-war Lebanese political system, for all the wrong reasons.

Damascus needed to secure a pliant Chamber of Deputies that would not openly challenge its dominant influence in Lebanon or attempt to force the implementation of the Ta'if provision requiring the redeployment of the Syrian forces to the Biqa Valley later that year. Indeed, the timing of the elections was essentially dictated by Syria's desire to forestall an open debate about this particular point.

For various reasons, there was a broad consensus across the sectarian elites that it might be preferable to postpone the elections until there was a more conducive atmosphere among the Lebanese masses. Nevertheless, the government, at Syria's urging, insisted on pressing ahead according to schedule. The Maronite leadership expected (correctly, as some observers would later point out) that Syria would use its influence to gerrymander, intimidate the public and tamper with votes. In protest, and as a last desperate attempt to strip any remaining veneer of legitimacy from the post-Ta'if political process, they staged a successful Maronite boycott of the elections.

However, although there was a fair amount of international protest, the Syrians, for their part, seemed perfectly happy with the results. The boycott simply gave them an opportunity to completely bypass the legitimate Maronite elite and, eventually, to install their own favoured Maronite clients in the Maronite seats of the Chamber. The formal political process was effectively closed to the more popular Maronite leadership, and the Syrians relied on figures such as Hrawi and Emile Lahoud, who owed most of their influence to Syrian largesse.[8]

Needless to say, the redeployment of Syrian forces was subsequently postponed indefinitely. Any substantial resistance to Syrian imperatives by popular Maronite leaders was silenced by force. For example, in the early 1990s, Samir Geagea, the leader of the Lebanese Forces, agreed to support the Ta'if Accord and participate in Karami's national reconciliation government, apparently on the understanding that the Syrians would deal with him as the most important leader of the Maronite community. But, when he later attempted to assert what Syria considered to be an unacceptable degree of independent initiative, he was arrested, convicted of the sort of crimes that could just as legitimately have been attributed to many other leading figures in the government, and locked up in prison. The whole affair was a sore point for most Maronites.

The legacy of the Ta'if implementation process, therefore, is not the functional sectarian parity that the framers of the accord had hoped for, but rather the almost complete marginalisation of one of the three most important sectarian communities. Moreover, even those leaders of the other communities that continued to enjoy substantial access to the political process had very little real influence, given the overwhelming dominance that Syria exercised both informally and through the parallel system of institutions set up under the auspices of the Treaty of Brotherhood.[9]

Conclusion

To summarise, the pre-war political order in Lebanon was characterised by three major systemic weaknesses, each of which contributed to the genesis of the civil war: 1) a state that lacked the power to effectively manage internal and external tensions; 2) the fact that subsequent demographic shifts called the legitimacy of the 1943 power-sharing arrangements into question, generating tension among the different sects; and 3) the penetration of the system by external elements (especially the PLO and other Palestinian groups) that critically exacerbated sectarian tensions through disrupting Lebanon's traditional neutral foreign policy and involving the country in the Arab–Israeli dispute.

The Ta'if Accord envisaged no major changes to the power or role of the state in the Lebanese system, and thus failed to address the first weakness. By contrast, a real (and potentially viable) effort was made to neutralise the destabilising effect of demographic changes by redefining the allocation of power within the central institutions on the basis of Christian/Muslim parity. However, although the accord also attempted to deal with the third problem, external penetration of the system, its own provisions actually allowed Syria to hijack the implementation process and penetrate the system to an unprecedented degree. Indeed, the new circumstances were such that the existence of Lebanon as an independent political entity for much of the post-war period could be legitimately questioned. If this fact alone did not completely strip the new parity system of any real meaning, the long-term marginalisation of the Maronite community, due to its continuing opposition to Syrian hegemony, ensured that the continuing ostensible function of the balanced institutions would not reflect genuine parity among the sectarian elites.

Thus it is difficult to escape the conclusion that the Ta'if Accord, as it was ultimately implemented, did not definitively address any of the systemic weaknesses and tensions that led up to the civil war. It did bring an end to the war, but in terms of the architects' own stated goals and their claims concerning the agreement's historic significance, it was a catastrophic failure that could have deprived the Lebanese people of their sovereignty for many generations to come.

3.2 The essential characteristics of the 1990–2005 post-war political system

Syrian hegemony in the Lebanese context

Having examined the origins and early development of Syrian predominance in post-war Lebanon through their manipulation of the Ta'if implementation process, it is now useful briefly to consider: 1) the underlying Syrian interests that made control of the country a crucial imperative for Damascus, as these developed over time; and 2) the international and domestic factors and interests that facilitated Syrian hegemony by neutralising most of the potential sources of effective opposition to it.

Syria, South Lebanon and the Arab–Israeli conflict

Simply put, the fundamental reasons for Syria's refusal to withdraw its forces from Lebanon were grounded initially in Syria's long-term objectives *vis-à-vis* the Arab–Israeli conflict. These objectives also explain its interest in exerting almost complete control over the country, especially in the areas of defence and security policy. Subsequently, other factors, particularly Syrian economic interests and internal politics, also became increasingly important.

The recovery of the Israeli-occupied Golan Heights, irrespective of any over-arching peace settlement, has been a major pillar of Syrian foreign policy since the end of the 1967 Arab–Israeli War. However, short of either threatening a direct military conflict over the issue or offering the Israelis a unilateral peace settlement, both of which Damascus was unable or unwilling to countenance throughout the 1980s and early 1990s, Syria had very little that it could use to influence the Israelis in negotiations.[10] As I indicated briefly above, the ongoing conflict between Hizbollah and Israel along the South Lebanese border presented the Syrians with a new bargaining chip. They were able convincingly to assert to the Israelis that only they were able to rein in Hizbollah effectively and resolve the conflict. It was generally understood that the return of the Golan Heights would be their asking price for this favour. Consequently, most observers and involved parties came to see the resolution of the South Lebanon conflict, and the broader issue of Lebanese relations with Israel, as inextricably intertwined with the resolution of Syria's territorial claims.

The sweeping geo-political changes of the early 1990s had a strong impact on regional politics, and affected Syrian policy accordingly. The decline and eventual dissolution of the Soviet Union, their long-time superpower patron, left them in a weaker position strategically, but their support for the anti-Iraqi alliance in the Kuwait War of 1991 improved their relations with Washington somewhat. It also defused much of the tension that had characterised their relations with other key Arab states such as Egypt and Saudi Arabia throughout the previous decade. The Israeli–Palestinian Oslo Accords and the Israeli–Jordanian peace settlement in 1993 apparently paved the way for Syria to negotiate its own peace agreement with Israel. Although the practical obstacles to a settlement were more difficult than those that had figured in the Israeli–Jordanian negotiations, many observers hoped that an agreement could be concluded quickly. Yitzakh Rabin's Israeli government and the Clinton administration in Washington anticipated that the "final status" negotiations of the Oslo process would be difficult, and they wanted to neutralise Syria as soon as possible to secure the peace process for the long term.[11]

With respect to Lebanon, these developments simply made the continuation of the South Lebanon conflict an even more urgent priority from the Syrian perspective, as Damascus clearly intended to use the issue as a lever to extract concessions from the Israelis. It should be remembered that, even as late as 1992, no one would have been particularly optimistic about the prospect of serious peace negotiations between Syria and Israel. The Syrian government under Hafez al-Asad had long been adamant in its ideological refusal to negotiate a separate peace until the grievances of the Palestinians had been addressed. The Oslo Accords took the world by surprise and apparently removed this obstacle. If an Israeli–Syrian peace deal had been successfully negotiated shortly thereafter, an Israeli–Lebanese agreement would almost certainly have followed, and the South Lebanon conflict would have ended much more quickly than anyone would have expected the previous year.

As events developed throughout the 1990s, the initial Israeli–Syrian negotiations were inconclusive, and the Oslo process developed into a long and frustrating war of wills between the Israelis and the Palestinians. Leaders in the region and in

Washington became preoccupied with the stalled and increasingly tense Israeli–Palestinian process, and the Israeli–Syrian negotiations became a background priority. They were pursued only sporadically, and never bore substantial fruit. Consequently, the South Lebanon conflict continued unabated as Asad's government waited for a confluence of circumstances that would allow Syria to use the issue to its advantage.

In the meantime, due largely to internal political considerations, the Israeli governments of the mid-1990s became increasingly obsessed with security and launched occasional reprisal attacks against Lebanon to demonstrate to the Israeli people that they were willing and able to take action to protect the Northern Israeli border. The reprisals included two large-scale military operations, one in 1993 and another in 1996. The 1996 attack, which was dubbed "The Grapes of Wrath", was intertwined with Shimon Peres's unsuccessful attempt to win that year's Israeli elections by demonstrating his competence in the security domain. It was, however, successful in the sense that it inflicted substantial damage on the South Lebanon infrastructure, led to a significant number of civilian Lebanese casualties, and seriously undermined the Lebanese government's vital economic reconstruction programme.

The "Peace with Security" platform of Peres's successor, Binyamin Netanyahu, did not allow for any substantive change in the Lebanese situation during the next few years. However, the election of Ehud Barak did inaugurate some significant developments that raised hopes both in Lebanon and in the international context, and that complicated matters from the Syrian perspective. Barak was elected with a mandate to push ahead vigorously with the peace process, and part of his platform included withdrawing Israeli forces from South Lebanon and attempting to negotiate a definitive peace settlement with Syria.

And indeed, Israeli forces did withdraw from their security zone in South Lebanon in May 2000, in a move that many Lebanese and international observers hoped would mark the final end of Israeli–Lebanese border disputes.[12] Unfortunately, it was not in the interest of either Syria or Hizbollah to let the matter rest at that, and the relatively minor issue of Israel's continued retention of the Shiba Farms was seized on as a pretext for Hizbollah to retain its arms and its belligerent stance against Israel. The continuing potential for a conflict over this issue was, in turn, used to justify the continued presence of Syrian troops in Lebanon. The Israeli–Syrian negotiations were once again inconclusive despite real pressure from Washington. The complete collapse of the Oslo process and a renewal of the Palestinian *intifada* ensured that additional negotiations would have to be postponed until the crisis in Israeli–Palestinian relations could be resolved.

The death of Hafez al-Asad in 2000 and the accession of his son Bashar al-Asad to the leadership in Damascus further complicated matters, because it was not clear that Bashar would be able to exert the same kind of dominance within the Syrian context as his father had. There was little question that Hafez was in a strong enough position *vis-à-vis* the Syrian political elite to make the difficult decisions that a settlement with Israel might require and push through with their implementation. Bashar, it was feared, could face stiffer opposition.[13]

Syria's role in Lebanon and the international community

It must be understood that these continuing developments in relation to the Arab–Israeli conflict and the delicate balance of regional security constituted the main reason that the international community stood by for over a decade and took no real action to pressure Syria about its ongoing penetration of the Lebanese system. Although there were occasional protests from various countries, including France, Israel and the USA, about developments in Lebanon, no significant action was taken to back these up. As time passed, even the protests became fewer and farther between. International human rights watchdogs such as Amnesty International tried to call attention to increasing human rights abuses perpetrated, ostensibly, by the Lebanese government against opponents of the system. However, even in a period during which the human rights issue became the focus of considerable international attention, most of the world chose to ignore the situation.

For a while it seemed that, as long as the Israeli–Syrian dispute remained unresolved, the international community would be loath to damage the prospects of an eventual settlement by engaging in any policies that might alienate Damascus. The absence of an active border conflict between the two countries lessened the urgency of the issue, especially considering the more active conflict between the Israelis and the Palestinians, and the more intractable nature of the issues that stood (and still stand) between those two parties. Everyone, with the possible exception of the Lebanese masses, appeared content to wait for a settlement of the Israeli–Syrian dispute before placing substantial pressure on Syria about its effective hegemony in Lebanon.[14]

Ironically, events in the context of the post-9/11 "war on terrorism" resulted in a considerable amount of negative world attention towards Lebanon. The country continued to be seen as a hot-bed of international terrorism, and the major Western powers urged the Lebanese government to do something about Hizbollah and Islamic radicalism within the Lebanese context. It should be clear, by this point, that the Lebanese government, in and of itself, was not really in a position to do very much about the situation. Syria, for its part, took a very ambiguous line, openly condemning terrorism in principle, but also taking every possible opportunity to highlight the grievances of the Islamic world. Above all, Damascus continued to point to the absolute lack of progress in the Israeli–Palestinian dispute as a justification for the sort of hard-line rhetoric Hizbollah espoused.

Until the late summer of 2004, the major Western powers, meanwhile, showed little indication that they were prepared to depart from their policy of treading very carefully where Damascus was concerned.[15] Thus it seemed likely that the Lebanese leadership would continue to be a largely helpless scapegoat as far as the terrorism issue was concerned.[16] However, in the early autumn of 2004, the international community departed from this policy and for the first time took significant diplomatic measures to show their displeasure at Syria's continuing dominance of Lebanon's political system. The UN Security Council passed resolution 1550, which effectively called for Syria to withdraw from Lebanon or to face international sanctions. As I demonstrate below, these developments set the stage for the events of 2005 that ultimately led to Syria's departure from Lebanon.

Other Syrian interests and domestic factors in the Lebanese context

As time passed, Syria's interests in Lebanon, quite independently of its desire for leverage in the Arab–Israeli dispute, increased steadily. One might certainly make a case that these interests alone became sufficiently important for Syria to be very reluctant to cede any of its influence in Lebanese affairs, even if the dispute with Israel were to be resolved to their satisfaction with immediate effect.

To begin with, it must be recognised that the Lebanese and Syrian economies became increasingly intertwined over the course of the 1990s. For example, in the autumn of 1994, the Syrian and Lebanese leaders signed a Labour Accord that essentially served to legitimise the penetration of the Lebanese labour market by Syrian workers. Estimates of the number of Syrian workers in Lebanon at the time varied from 500,000 to around 1 million, contributing something like a billion dollars to the Syrian economy. Naturally, Lebanese workers strongly resented the Syrian presence, and a number of mass demonstrations and strikes were held over the years in protest about this and the penetration of other Syrian economic and business interests. The continued occupation by Syrian military forces was probably the most effective lever Syria had to prevent such protests from escalating into a more damaging form of opposition.

In addition to this sort of macro-economic tie, it should also be noted that the individual members of the Syrian political elite developed extensive personal business interests in Lebanon throughout this period, which they no doubt wished to protect. Indeed, it would probably be no exaggeration to say that continuing economic and political control of Lebanon had become a vital component of internal Syrian politics, as access to the country represented a vast source of patronage, which the leadership could use to placate powerful individuals who might oppose them.

Obviously, effective control of the Lebanese context also enabled the Syrian leaders to co-opt many of the Lebanese leaders who participated fully in the post-Ta'if institutions. The disbursement of patronage has always been at the heart of the Lebanese political process, and up to 2004 the Syrians had the final say concerning which concessions and opportunities would be granted to which individual leaders and sectarian communities. This undoubtedly critically handicapped the ability of the Lebanese leaders to express even rhetorical opposition to Syrian dominance within the context of the Parliament and other national institutions.[17]

The post-Ta'if character of state institutions

Overview

As noted, the role of the Lebanese state in the 1990–2005 political system had not changed substantially in comparison with the pre-war period. Lebanese politics continued to be dominated by extensive patronage networks operating within each of the respective sectarian communities, with the formal state institutions essentially serving as a forum for the sectarian political elites to settle disputes and negotiate arrangements for the distribution of patronage among the communities. Although the constitutional changes implemented as a result of the Ta'if Accord theoretically increased the powers of the Chamber of Deputies to a considerable extent, in practice, the executive institutions continued to predominate, actually to an even greater extent than in the pre-war system.[18]

Ostensibly (apart from the extra-legal *de facto* control of all state institutions by Damascus and the marginalisation of the Maronite Christian community that followed from this) the major distinguishing characteristic of the post-war set-up was parity among the sectarian communities. The Christian and Muslim communities were allocated equal numbers of seats in the Chamber, and the three major executive offices, President, Prime Minister and Speaker of the House, were balanced to prevent any one of the major sects from exerting a dominant influence in national politics.

The Chamber of Deputies

On 16 July 1992, the Lebanese Parliament passed a new electoral law increasing the size of the Chamber of Deputies from its pre-war size of 108 seats to 128 seats. In accordance with the Ta'if provisions for sectarian parity, there was an equal balance of Christian and Muslim seats. The Maronite Christians continued to have the single largest allocation of any sectarian group, while the Sunni and Shiite confessions were given the same number of seats as each other, giving them more seats collectively than the Maronites. However, the allocation of seats to the other Christian sects balanced this, and other significant groups, such as the Druze, were also allocated a fixed number of seats.

The members of the Chamber were to be elected for four-year terms. The first post-war election, as noted previously, was held in 1992, and subsequent elections were held in 1996 and 2000. Obviously, the Chamber is Lebanon's supreme legislative body, but it has traditionally been a very weak component of the Lebanese institutional set-up, essentially serving as a rubber stamp for decisions taken by the executive. The Ta'if Accord was supposed to give the Chamber more power, but, in practice, it became probably weaker than it had ever been. This was partly a result of the fact that the Speaker of the House, the traditional prerogative office of the Shiite sect, was elevated to the extent that it was now a part of the executive for all intents and purposes. Many of the formal measures designed to give the Chamber more power were simply taken over by the Speaker. Another factor that reduced the significance of the Chamber was the absence of any real opposition to the executive within it. In order to understand the reason for this, one must appreciate the workings of political alliances and power blocs within the Chamber.

As explained in Chapter 1, developed political parties with ideological or policy-based agendas have never really been a significant feature of the Lebanese political process. Although certain ideological parties, especially Hizbollah, played a significant role in the post-war political process, it should be understood that these are sectarian parties that operate in the same manner as traditional *zu'ama*. In short, the Lebanese system continued to be dominated by more or less formal alliances headed by prominent individuals, particularly the leading sectarian figures. Most significantly, each member of the "troika" (the Maronite President, the Sunni Prime Minister and the Shiite Speaker of the House) commanded massive influence within the Chamber. For example, many members of the Chamber secured their election by participating in electoral lists headed by the prominent leaders. Furthermore, as the executive had overwhelming control over access to political and economic patronage (including cabinet appointments, committee chairs and memberships, etc.) cooperation with one or more members of the executive was an essential prerequisite for gaining any significant influence within the system.

Additionally, many of the members would also have strong ties to the executive through the sectarian patronage networks that ran parallel to the formal political system. Even supposed opposition elements, such as the largely Shiite Hizbollah, for example, could not really function outside the sectarian networks, and thus must deal extensively with the Shiite Speaker of the House.

As a result of all these factors, what opposition there was to executive decisions tended not so much to originate among the members of the Chamber itself, but rather to reflect divisions among the members of the troika. There were some independent individuals and small blocs of independent members within the Chamber, and these tended to include some of the Maronite community's more significant post-Ta'if leaders, but these elements had little influence as a general rule.[19]

The cabinet

Although technically the cabinet is the executive branch of the Lebanese parliamentary system, in practice, even in the pre-war system, it always occupied a secondary tier underneath the real executive consisting of the major sectarian leaders. This demotion was even more pronounced in the post-Ta'if context, with the troika exerting overwhelming predominance. The size of the cabinet was variable but, in accordance with the parity system, always equally balanced between Christians and Muslims in the post-war set-up. It should be noted that, unlike many parliamentary systems, the Lebanese cabinet was open to individuals who were not members of the Chamber.

To a great extent, the composition of the cabinet was supposed to be decided through negotiations among the members of the troika. Of course, in practice, Syria exercised the decisive influence with respect to the disbursement of all cabinet portfolios throughout this period. In any case, the cabinet, like the Chamber, tended to reflect divisions within the troika, and the individual leaders tended to defer to their patron in the executive with respect to all significant decisions. Having said this, there have been some individual cabinet ministers, particularly Michel Murr, the long-time Interior Minister, who were able to exert considerable personal influence independently of the troika. However, these ministers owed their influence almost exclusively to the Syrians and represented Syrian interests, or at the very least were deferential to them.

The troika system

As noted, the core of the post–Ta'if institutional arrangements was the fact that the powers of the three most important confessionally allocated political offices would be balanced to prevent any one sect from dominating the political process. The result, in practice, was the emergence of a tripartite executive, or what is commonly referred to as the troika system, consisting of the Maronite President, the Sunni Prime Minister and the Shiite Speaker of the House.

The President sits for a single, non-renewable, six-year term, although, very controversially, this actually did not hold in the case of Elias Hrawi, who occupied the office from 1989 to 1998, essentially because Syria was not comfortable with any other candidate for the office during that time. As well, and for similar reasons, President Emile Lahoud's term was extended in the autumn of 2004, despite Lebanese and international opposition. The Prime Minister may hold office for as long as he/she can maintain their government, and there are no limitations on the number of times any given individual can be selected to form a government. The Speaker of the House is elected every four years by the Chamber of Deputies, and this post is renewable with no limit on the number of terms an individual may be elected to serve.

One important functional characteristic of the troika system is what some observers have referred to as a "confusion of powers". In essence, the Ta'if provisions did not provide a clear delineation of the powers of each office, but left them rather ambiguous. The key point is that each of the three offices is capable of exercising an effective veto power over the political system by interfering with the passage of legislation through the chamber or obstructing its formal acceptance into law. This meant that in the post-war Lebanese political system, no law could be passed if any one of the major sectarian communities had serious objections to it, and thus no one sect, or even an alliance of Muslim groups or an alliance of Christian groups, could effectively take control of Lebanon's destiny.[20]

In terms of everyday decision-making, the primary characteristic of the post-war political process is constant bargaining among the three members of the troika. Apart from the strict functions of designing, passing and enforcing legislation, the primary object of these negotiations is to resolve how patronage will be distributed to particular individuals or groups, or across the sectarian communities as a whole. This patronage can take the form of political, financial or cultural influence, and may be a feature of the system (such as a political office, a civil service appointment, etc.) or the result of legislation (an award of funds, the administration of a particular state project or body that is to be created, etc.). The troika also controls how much patronage is distributed to each troika member. Surprisingly, this is not considered a conflict of interest. The lines between state patronage and personal patronage within the Lebanese system are very blurred indeed. Perhaps to an even greater extent than traditional *zu'ama* competition, negotiations among troika members can be characterised as "splitting up the Lebanese pie".

Another feature of the troika system, as it has functioned in practice, is periodic deadlock among the troika members when they cannot reach an agreement on a particular issue or complex of issues. Within the pre-war system, the President was clearly in a dominant role, and was able to resolve disputes by dismissing the Prime Minister, calling for new elections and so on. In the post-Ta'if context, however, there is no formal dominant arbiter to resolve intractable disputes. Theoretically, the possibility of deadlock should be moderated by the fact that none of the troika members is that secure in office. The President only has one term, and must accomplish his agenda, if any, in the course of it. The Prime Minister can lose the confidence of the government and be dismissed from office if he is seen to be excessively obstructing the system. And the Speaker can also be removed if the need arises. In reality, however, there have been frequent and often quite bitter instances of deadlock among the troika members. These have not been resolved by any internal systemic mechanisms, but rather, in every case, by Syrian intervention as the dominant arbiter by its own design on all disputed points.

On the one hand, this might lead one to question whether or not the troika system would actually be a particularly functional form of government without the presence of a strong external actor such as Syria to resolve disputes. On the other hand, it should be recognised that Syria has played a fairly significant part in the genesis of the disputes. It is by no means clear that the disputes would have been as frequent, or as intractable, as they have been: 1) if the parties did not know that Syria would resolve disputes when they could not reach internal agreement; and 2) if Syria was not actually working hard behind the scenes to play off the troika members against each other, to prevent any one from gaining too much influence and possibly attempting to assert a popular, authentically Lebanese, political agenda.

Obviously, all of the individuals who have participated in the troika during this period owed a considerable amount of their influence to Syria. Indeed, one did not become a member of the troika without Syrian approval, and this was not extended to anyone about whom the Syrians had real reservations. Some of the troika members, such as President Hrawi, Speaker Nabih Birri and Prime Minister Omar Karami, owed virtually all their influence to Syria. Others, like Prime Minister Hariri and President Lahoud, had more of a domestic power base independently of Syrian support. However, even these individuals were constrained by very strong and intricate ties to the Syrian establishment.[21]

Extra-institutional elements in the post-war system

No account of the 1990–2005 post-war Lebanese system would be complete without considering the important role that certain elements operating outside of the formal institutional context played in the political life of the society. Obviously, Syria played an incalculable role outside the institutional context, and I have examined that fact in some detail throughout this chapter. Another crucial extra-institutional element was the leadership of the still otherwise marginalised Maronite community.

The pre-eminent figure within the Maronite community in the post-war context was the Maronite Patriarch, Boutros Sfeir. Although ostensibly a religious figure, he was the most prominent individual to articulate openly the concerns of the Maronite community, both within Lebanon and through his visits to many countries throughout the world, including the USA, Canada, Australia and major European countries. The Maronite masses came to see him as the authentic political leader of the sect, and, to some extent, the post-war establishment was forced to recognise the significance of his influence.

The Maronite community in Lebanon also continued to have strong ties to prominent individuals from the pre-war and civil war periods then living in exile. These included such figures as Michel Aoun. Other exiled leaders, for instance the former President Amin Gemayel, returned to the country and made plans to re-enter the political fold as representatives of the Maronite community. As we will see, these individuals were to play a prominent role in the political process following Syria's withdrawal in 2005.

In the meantime, the Maronite elite living in Lebanon felt that they had little choice but to come to terms with the reality that a reduction in Syrian hegemony over Lebanon was an unlikely prospect unless international and regional circumstances changed dramatically. The end result of this was that a more pragmatic attitude emerged among some former Maronite *zu'ama* and others who had gained influence through the militias during the civil war period. These elements came to recognise that they could ultimately be supplanted in the community by those who cooperated with Syria. The longer the order continued, the harder it became for them to maintain their influence against the predations of Maronite Syrian clients. They were now, ironically, in much the same position as the pre-1943 Muslim leaders who had boycotted the then new national institutions but ultimately had had to accede to them or risk becoming politically irrelevant.

To some extent, it was also in Syria's interest to find ways to accommodate Maronite leaders who wished to abandon the boycott. Provided that these leaders were prepared to accept effective Syrian hegemony, this would allow Damascus to secure its long-term influence against Maronite opposition much more rapidly and thoroughly than they had been able to do through cultivating their own Maronite clients. As long as the more traditional and legitimate leaders were outside the system, they could continue to stay above the fray and criticise the whole prevailing order. Once they had been brought inside the system and became engaged in the neo-patrimonial wheeling and dealing that Syria now dominated, it would be much harder for them to take the moral high ground, even if they were inclined to do so.

3.3 Major political developments in the post-war period

Having examined the Ta'if Accord and the results of its implementation in some detail, and having commented extensively on the essential features of the post-war political system, I now present a brief analytical account of the major political developments that have taken place in the Lebanese context since the war. Particular attention is paid to: 1) the different governments that have been put in place; 2) the agendas that these governments have attempted to pursue; and 3) the problems and underlying factors that have affected them most significantly.

The first two post-war governments: 1990–92

As indicated above, the first government of the post-war period was the "government of national reconciliation" formed by Omar Karami in December 1990. The main stated purpose of the government was to disarm the militias, to reassert state power in the country and to implement the other major provisions of the Ta'if Accord. In fact, however, Syria exercised a decisive influence over the composition of the government, and its real purpose can, perhaps, best be described as ensuring that the Ta'if Accord would be implemented in such a way as to secure the long-term dominance of the Lebanese system by Syria.

The government's approach to achieving this purpose was not particularly subtle, and largely as a result of this, it was deeply unpopular with much of the Lebanese public almost from the beginning. To make matters worse, in the course of presiding over such controversial policies as the selective disarmament of the militias and the negotiation of the Treaty of Brotherhood, the Karami government failed to establish any kind of effective or coherent economic policy, and never made any serious attempt to begin the badly needed reconstruction of the country's infrastructure. This neglect inaugurated an economic crisis that became steadily worse throughout 1991 and the first half of 1992. A series of mass demonstrations and general strikes protesting against the economic situation were held in the spring of 1992, and, after consultation with Damascus, Karami took the decision to resign on May 6 of that year.

One might have assumed that the next government would be formed with the prime objective of resolving the economic crisis. However, this was not the case. The new government formed under Rashid Solh, a moderate and conciliatory figure who had been Lebanon's Prime Minister at the time the civil war broke out in 1975, differed very little from the Karami government in its composition or its line of policy.

Its essential purpose was to ensure that the Lebanese parliamentary elections scheduled for the summer of 1992 would take place on time. Although there was a broad consensus among the sectarian leaders that it would be better to delay the elections until a more conducive atmosphere could be created among the public, the Syrians badly wanted the elections to go ahead on schedule because they needed to install a pliant Lebanese Parliament that would not challenge their role in the country or try to enforce the Ta'if provision that called for the redeployment of Syrian forces to the Biqa valley later in the year. Although it was no more popular than the Karami government had been, the Solh government successfully managed to push ahead with the elections as Syria had hoped.[22]

The 1992 parliamentary elections and the accession of Hariri

Lebanon's previous parliamentary elections had taken place in 1972, three years before the outbreak of the civil war. The 1992 elections, therefore, from the standpoint of the Lebanese people, should have been a welcome event that inaugurated a new era and introduced some new personalities, new chemistry and new energy into the political system. Instead, as I noted when looking in detail at the implementation of the Ta'if Accord, the lasting legacy of the elections was to add further legitimacy to Syria's hegemony in Lebanon and almost completely to shut the authentic leaders of the Maronite community out of the formal political process for an indefinite period of time.

The one positive development, from the perspective of the Lebanese masses, was that Syria acquiesced in the selection of Rafiq Hariri as the country's new Prime Minister from October 1992. This was viewed as a very significant development because Hariri was a genuinely popular figure. He had been tipped as a potential Prime Minister in the past and the Syrians had rejected him, essentially because they regarded him as having an independent power base strong enough for him to possibly create problems for them as they pursued their own objectives in Lebanon. The fact that they were now prepared to let him take office raised hopes, both in Lebanon and in the international community, that the new government would be able to establish an agenda independent of Syrian interests.

It is very important to understand the nature of the Syrians' calculations at this point in time. The Karami government and the 1992 elections had essentially enabled them to secure their long-term position in the country, and the primary threats to their continued influence were now: 1) mass Lebanese discontent due both to the state of the economy and to Syria's apparently total control of every facet of the political system; and 2) protests within the international community about the extent of Syrian influence in the country. The only real way to alleviate these pressures was to allow the creation of a government that: 1) seemed more independent (even if it would still be tightly controlled behind the scenes); and 2) was geared towards stabilising the economy and initiating the badly needed reconstruction of the country's war-devastated infrastructure.

Although Syria had become increasingly involved, and hence increasingly interested, in the Lebanese economy throughout the post-war period, its compelling interest in the early 1990s was related to controlling Lebanese foreign and security policy in order to facilitate its own overall policy *vis-à-vis* Israel. It is probably fair to say that none of the Syrian political establishment had any great desire to become deeply engaged in the dauntingly massive task of Lebanese economic reconstruction, albeit they probably had no objection to profiting personally from it, if that could be arranged. Consequently, Syria was almost certainly reasonably happy to let the new government exercise some real independence in the sphere of economic decision-making, as long as it was firmly understood and accepted that no independent agenda would be permitted outside those carefully defined and monitored margins.

Such an arrangement had two other great advantages for Syria. First, it did generate a very real sense, both inside and outside Lebanon, that the Lebanese people were finally being permitted to exercise some control over their own destiny. Economic affairs have always been of particular importance to the Lebanese people, as their traditional prosperity was deeply rooted in trade and banking. Consequently, the apparent concession of some independence in the economic sphere was perceived as no small matter by much of the population, and it went further towards blunting their opposition to the Syrian-dominated system as a whole than a similar concession might have done in many other societies. Second, ceding apparent control of the economy and the reconstruction process allowed Damascus effectively to distance itself from further economic problems and problems with the reconstruction process. Public discontent about these issues would henceforward fall primarily on the Lebanese government rather than being directed at Syria.

Hariri was practically the perfect candidate for the job in light of these considerations. He was a prominent, self-made Sunni billionaire who had cultivated close relations with the Saudi royal family and gone on to make his fortune, mostly in the construction industry. In the years prior to the election, he had contributed extensively to the development of the state's economic reconstruction plans, and he was widely perceived, both at the mass level and by many economic commentators, as the one man who could stabilise the economic situation and attempt to tackle the massive task of managing the economic reconstruction process.

Furthermore, he was from outside both the traditional Muslim *zu'ama* class and the paramilitary elites that had grown up during the civil war period. Therefore he was not as obviously tainted by association with Syria as these elements were. At the same time, however, he was a pragmatist about the Syrian domination of the Lebanese system. Although it is true that he had a considerable personal power base, in terms of his wealth, his popularity and his international connections he also had personal and business ties with members of the Syrian establishment. Moreover, he was primarily interested in the economy and the reconstruction programme, and was happy enough to concentrate on these issues and let Syria continue to exercise overall control.[23]

In a speech to the Lebanese Parliament shortly after taking office, he spoke very candidly about the relationship between the two countries, asserting: "There are no parties with any reservations about the full and complete coordination between Lebanon and Syria. When they stop, we stop. When they step backwards, we step backwards. There is no argument over this."[24]

The first Hariri period: 1992–98

From 1992 to 1998, the performance of the economy and the progress of the economic reconstruction programme became the central focus of the Lebanese political discourse, to the almost total exclusion of any other issues. Obviously, this was exactly according to Syria's plans. There were no significant protests or debates within the national institutions about Syria's influence in Lebanon. The substantial exclusion of the Maronites from the political process was accepted as a *fait accompli*. No attempt was made to negotiate an end to the South Lebanon conflict, or to put a stop to Hizbollah activities against Israel, even though this would have been beneficial for the economic recovery process. In short, there was no challenge to Syria or Syrian objectives within the bounds of the formal Lebanese political process.

The economy and the progress of the economic reconstruction programme throughout this period are the primary focus of Chapter 4 so I will not detail them here. However, it is worth noting that two primarily political factors significantly affected the final outcome of the Hariri government's efforts: 1) the continuation of the South Lebanon conflict; and 2) constant conflicts within the troika about the disbursement of the massive patronage associated with the reconstruction process. Needless to say, Syria played no small role in both of these areas.

Although much of Lebanon's physical infrastructure was successfully restored and modernised, financial problems and increasing deadlock in the troika compelled Hariri to abandon many of the more ambitious aspects of his master recovery plan. One consequence of the reconstruction process was the accumulation of a huge national debt. This and other macro-economic factors contributed to an economic crisis in 1997 and 1998. Although Hariri did not bear sole responsibility for these problems, he was the one who took most of the blame.

Furthermore, encouraged by Syria, Hariri's nemesis in the troika, Speaker Nabih Birri, began to raise questions and accusations concerning corruption and conflicts of interest in relation to Hariri and many of his allies. Many of these criticisms were perhaps justified from an objective standpoint, and the massive corruption of the government certainly had become a source of significant public discontent by this time. However, if they are viewed strictly within the context of the post-war Lebanese system, they must be recognised as basically malicious. The whole system was shot through with conflicts of interest, and Birri and his associates were no less guilty of offences than those they were accusing.

In any case, the combination of economic problems and personal attacks, along with the election of Emile Lahoud to the Presidency on an anti-corruption platform, persuaded Hariri that his long-term political interests might be better served outside government, and he resigned as Prime Minister in December of 1998. Although he had previously resigned, or used the threat of resignation, on a number of occasions to persuade the Syrians and the other troika members to grant him concessions in pushing forward the recovery process, this resignation was accepted. He was useful to Syria only as long as he could moderate Lebanese mass dissent by keeping the economy in decent shape. With the economy in recession, public finances dogged by chronic debt, and tensions among the public rising accordingly, he clearly was no longer meeting Syria's needs at this point. Hariri retained his seat in Parliament, however, and soon began using his massive influence and patronage to start building a stronger base of support for the parliamentary elections of 2000.

The Lahoud Presidency and the Hoss government: 1998–2000

With Hariri's departure, Salim Hoss was selected as the new Prime Minister, and the new President, Emile Lahoud, became the predominant personality in the troika. Interestingly, like Hariri, Lahoud was a genuinely popular figure across all the major sects. He was the General who had led the reconstituted Lebanese state forces in the post-war era, and who was credited with successfully rebuilding the military along non-sectarian lines. Although not a member of the traditional Maronite establishment, he did enjoy considerable popularity (at least initially) in the Maronite community, a fact that distinguished him significantly from his predecessor, Hrawi. Lahoud's other great selling point was that he was widely seen as being honest and incorruptible.

Of course, the all-important point from Syria's perspective was that he was also firmly pro-Syrian.

Hoss was also greatly respected as an honest and principled politician, in addition to being an experienced and capable former Prime Minister. As was the case with Lahoud, the perception of incorruptibility was a key element, for the visible focus of government from late 1998 up to the elections of summer 2000 was to be cleaning up corruption and inaugurating a much-needed fundamental reform of the civil service.

Ultimately, this was probably more of a distraction from economic hardship than a policy agenda that anyone was really thoroughly committed to. The anti-corruption drive was applied very selectively. The main targets were out-of-favour Hariri associates and individuals who had been the worst offenders in the mismanagement of public funds and state projects. A great number of individuals who might otherwise have been indicted were left alone because they continued to enjoy Syrian approval. The civil service reform consisted of little more than replacing Hariri appointees with new appointees more friendly to Lahoud, Hoss or Birri.

While Lahoud maintained his popularity and Birri's position was largely unaffected, Hoss increasingly became the focus of public discontent with the new government. Essentially, he was held responsible for the failure of the government to pursue stronger anti-corruption and civil service reform programmes, and was also associated with the continuing poor performance of the economy. This left him in a rather weak position in the approach to the 2000 parliamentary elections.

The return of Hariri and increased international pressure on Syria: 2000–04

The main outcome of the 2000 elections was a clear victory by Hariri, which can be explained in large part by his extensive use of patronage and the impressive organisational network he set up to prepare for the elections after his departure from the government in 1998. His personal electoral list swept much of the country, and as the Sunni leader with the largest bloc of supporters in the Chamber, he was the clear choice to form the next government.

Despite his impressive victory, Hariri's influence in the executive was not what it was during most of his first period as Prime Minister. This was partly because the other two members of the troika were significantly stronger. Lahoud, who had extensive support within the military and security apparatus, and was strongly backed by Syria, was a considerably more influential President than Hrawi, and Birri continued to be more closely tied to the Syrian establishment than Hariri. It was also a consequence of increased tension between Hariri and the Syrians. In fact, the relationship between the two turned acrimonious, and was increasingly played out in public. Syria and the other two members of the troika clearly worked to undermine the Hariri administration to the point that, at times, the troika was at an impasse and the government stopped functioning.

Hariri's diminished influence was also due to the fact that he did not emerge from the 2000 elections with the same kind of new, large and exciting economic programme as that with which he had begun in 1992. He had continuously asserted his intention to push ahead with the economic reconstruction from the point where his original programme left off, but his poor relations with the Syrians and other members of the troika, and continuing financial problems, imposed severe limits on what he could actually do. His economic expertise and influence did retain some of their old force, however, and the economic situation did improve somewhat after he returned to office.

The period from 2000 to 2004 had also seen some important changes with respect to the Lebanese political discourse as a whole, although this had generally not been widely reflected in the state institutions, and certainly not within the confines of the troika system. The withdrawal of the Israeli forces from South Lebanon in the spring of 2000 led many Lebanese, including some prominent public figures, to start calling publicly for Syria to withdraw its forces as well.[25] The death of Hafez al-Asad, also in 2000, led many Lebanese to entertain further hopes for a positive change of some kind in Lebanese–Syrian relations. Bashar al-Asad represented himself on the international stage as one of a new generation of Arab leaders with a more liberal orientation than the leaders of the past.

To the increasing frustration of the Lebanese masses, however, neither of these developments really resulted in any change in Syrian policy. The Syrians simply seized on the Shiba Farms dispute and the continuing fluidity of Israeli–Palestinian tensions to justify their enduring support for Hizbollah and their ongoing military presence in Lebanon. There had been no concrete manifestation of Bashar al-Asad's supposed liberal orientation.

By late 2003, Syria was facing, for the first time since the civil war ended in 1990, significant international pressure to withdraw from Lebanon. The pressure was emanating largely from the Bush Administration, which, in the context of post-9/11 and the "war on terror", pursued an aggressive foreign policy against its perceived enemies in the Middle East, including Syria. The Bush Administration had determined that Damascus was undermining US interests in the Middle East, including in Iraq, in the Palestinian territories, and in Lebanon, through its support of Hizbollah and other radical groups. As a result, Washington was determined to contain Syrian influence in the Middle East region, and took a number of steps in this direction.

In December of 1993, President Bush signed into law a congressional bill called the Syrian Accountability and Lebanese Sovereignty Restoration Act. Of particular relevance in this context, it called for Syria to withdraw its troops from Lebanon or face punitive sanctions and diplomatic isolation. Nine months later, on 2 September 2004, the United States, in cooperation with France, co-sponsored UN Security Council Resolution 1559, which called for the end of Syrian occupation of Lebanon, as well as for the disbanding and disarmament of all Lebanese and non-Lebanese militias, a move largely directed at Hizbollah. Further, Resolution 1559 made explicit reference to calling for free and fair presidential elections in Lebanon, a clear response to concerns that Syria was trying to amend the Lebanese constitution to allow for the extension of the term of President Lahoud, a close ally of Damascus.

Syrian dominance of the Lebanese political system was further reflected in the autumn of 2004, when Syria pushed for the Lebanese constitution to be amended in order to allow President Lahoud to run for a second term. Against wide-scale Lebanese opposition, as well as unusually strong reaction to the move from the international community, the Syrians secured a second term for Lahoud. This ultimately led to a situation where Hariri, who strongly opposed the move, resigned the prime ministership. Syrian ally and former Prime Minister Omar Karami was asked to head the next government; he faced a number of particularly daunting challenges. He had to deal with a weak economy, a population and political opposition angry at recent political developments and Syria's continuing role in the country, an international community now openly opposed to Syria's presence in Lebanon, and the generally negative international attention Lebanon had received since 9/11.

PART II: POLITICAL DEVELOPMENTS IN LEBANON SINCE 2005

The purpose of this part of the chapter is to describe political events in Lebanon since 2005, a period that could have transformed the political system as it had developed under Syrian tutelage.

Part II is divided into three sections: the first discusses the cedar revolution, which led to the withdrawal of Syrian troops; the second identifies the limitations of the cedar revolution; and the third provides a brief account of the major developments following the revolution.

3.4 The cedar revolution – the end of a Syrian-dominated Lebanon?[26]

In the early months of 2005, two interrelated events created the equivalent of a political tsunami in Lebanon, shaking the very foundations of the arrangements that had dominated the political system since the end of the civil war in 1990.

The first event occurred on 14 February, when the former Prime Minister Rafiq Hariri was assassinated by means of a remote-controlled truck bomb as he travelled by motorcade through the streets of Beirut.[27] As noted, Hariri was an influential Lebanese politician and leader of the Sunni community, the father of Lebanon's reconstruction, and the only politician with sufficient power to provide a counter-weight to Syrian influence. Syria was widely blamed for the assassination. Hundreds of thousands of people took to the streets of Beirut in the weeks that followed the assassination to protest against Syria's continued domination of the Lebanese political system and to demand an immediate withdrawal of Syrian troops.

The second event occurred by the end of March, when Syria succumbed to both Lebanese and international pressure (including from Saudi Arabia) and withdrew its military from Lebanon, ending a thirty-year presence. As discussed elsewhere, the military was a key pillar of Syria's control over the Lebanese political and security systems, so its withdrawal raised considerable hopes in Lebanon, the West and elsewhere that Syrian control over Lebanon was indeed over.

The mass protests (or uprising) that ultimately led to the Syrian military withdrawal were popularly referred to as the "cedar revolution" or, sometimes, the Independence *Intifada*. It was expected that the cedar revolution would not only free the country from Syrian control, but also: 1) introduce political reform and democratic change; 2) realign Lebanese foreign policy toward the West; and 3) bring about the disarmament of Hizbollah and other radical Islamist groups.

While the political system opened up in the few years that have passed since the cedar revolution, few of the changes expected actually materialised. Indeed, political figures previously excluded from the Lebanese political scene, such as Michel Aoun and Samir Geagea, could now participate more robustly than during the 1990–2005 period. In the end, however, this did not lead to true political reform.

Rather, the post-2005 political system was noted for the intense and often acrimonious rivalry between two roughly equal yet ideologically opposed Lebanese political movements, which fell largely along sectarian lines. The intense political stand-offs between the two movements, the so-called "March 14 Alliance" (which was Sunni-dominated) and "March 8 Alliance" (which was Shiite-dominated), created serious political instability and made the country vulnerable to significant external penetration.

As we shall see, the post-2005 political system suffered from the same three systemic weaknesses that had existed in both the pre-civil war (before 1975) and post-civil war (1990–2005) periods. First, the Lebanese state remained far too weak to manage tensions generated by internal and external circumstances. Moreover, it was too ineffective even to prevent the continuing decline of the security situation (a number of pro-Western, i.e. anti-Syrian, members of Parliament and journalists were killed). Second, sectarian tensions, particularly between the Sunni and Shiite communities, reached levels not seen in decades and became, perhaps, the defining feature of the post-2005 system. The militant Shiite group Hizbollah came to the fore of Lebanese politics and was able to dictate to a considerable extent the country's political and security agenda. And third, despite Syria's military withdrawal from the country, for all intents and purposes Lebanon remained a heavily penetrated state, susceptible to the interests of foreign powers and, by extension, to regional and international tensions. Syria retained much of its influence and Iran, through Hizbollah, significantly extended its reach into Lebanon, ensuring that Lebanon became part of its strategic manoeuvring *vis-à-vis* Israel, the USA and conservative Arab states.

In short, despite the early expectations and hopes raised by the cedar revolution, the Lebanese political system since 2005 was barely functional, and at times even came close to imploding.

3.5 The limits of the cedar revolution

The cedar revolution was hugely popular with Lebanon's Christians, but also received significant support from the Sunni and Druze communities. Hundreds of thousands of people marched and demonstrated in the weeks following the assassination of Hariri, calling for an end to Syrian rule. The demonstration on 14 March was particularly significant, and saw as many as one million people turn out, nearly a third of the entire Lebanese population. While each of these three communities differed in their vision of Lebanon, they were united in their desire to see the occupation end.

With respect to the three communities, as explained in Part I of this chapter, the Maronite Christians had been effectively marginalised in the post-civil-war Syrian-dominated order, with many of their most popular political leaders living in exile or languishing in prison for having opposed Syrian rule. The Sunni community was still reeling from the assassination of their main political leader, Rafiq Hariri, which they blamed squarely on Syria. Further, they had long resented Syria's bolstering of the rival Shiite community at their expense. The Druze, under the leadership of Walid Jumblatt, strongly resented the high-handed manner of Syrian rule in Lebanon, and even before the events of early 2005 had joined the Christian opposition against Syria and its Lebanese allies.

The cedar revolution gave rise to the March 14 Alliance (named for the day of the massive anti-Syrian demonstration), which included a group of anti-Syrian politicians, among them the most influential political leaders from the Sunni, Maronite and Druze communities. The alliance was led by Saad Hariri, the son and heir of Rafiq Hariri, and Walid Jumblatt, and included a number of Maronite political figures who had returned from exile or had been released from prison, such as Michel Aoun, Samir Geagea and Amin Gemayel.

With respect to the March 14 programme, it included, above all, freeing Lebanon from Syrian control and beginning a process of negotiating the normalisation of relations between the two countries on the basis of respect for each other's sovereignty. The programme also called for: 1) the re-establishment of Lebanese state control over the whole of Lebanon, which included disarming Hizbollah and other groups; 2) establishing a tribunal to investigate the death of Rafiq Hariri; and 3) working with the international community to establish the basis of a strong Lebanese economy.

The March 14 Alliance was victorious in the two parliamentary elections that were held in Lebanon after the Syrian withdrawal. From 2005 to 2009, the Lebanese government was headed by Prime Minister Fouad Siniora, a close ally of the Hariri family and long-time cabinet minister under Rafiq Hariri. The 2010 election resulted in the formation of a government headed by Saad Hariri.

Despite success in winning parliamentary elections, the effectiveness of the March 14-led Lebanese governments was very limited. The Lebanese opposition, and their external patrons, Syria and Iran, effectively blocked their platforms. This included most prominently the failure to disarm Hizbollah and the inability to progress on the investigation of the assassination of Rafiq Hariri.

At least four major reasons account for the general ineffectiveness of the March 14 movement and, by extension, of the two governments that it led, including: 1) inherent political and ideological differences among alliance members; 2) the strength of the opposition led by Hizbollah; 3) the continuing interference of Syria, the main sponsor of the opposition; and 4) the lack of sustained support from the international community.

Internal problems with the March 14 Alliance

With respect to this first point, the March 14 Alliance was simply a fluid, loosely organised and diverse group of politicians and political parties from the Sunni, Christian and Druze communities. They had come together because of their common goal to remove Syria from Lebanon, which, in the aftermath of Hariri's death, seemed possible, given the public mood within their respective communities. Their ability to move beyond this, however, depended very much on the dynamics of the various actors involved in the group and their political goals. The populist Christian leader Michel Aoun, for instance, had well-known political ambitions to become the president of Lebanon. When it became clear that he did not have the support of the other leaders, he simply withdrew his Free Patriotic Movement from the alliance, rather strategically just prior to the 2005 parliamentary elections. This was to be the first serious blow to the alliance. Indeed, even though March 14 won the 2005 elections (seventy-two seats to the opposition's fifty-three), it cost them the majority of the Christian vote, which was split between Aoun and the alliance. Had they retained Aoun's allegiance, March 14 would have had approximately double the number of seats in Parliament held by the Shiite-led opposition, in all likelihood creating the sort of margin of victory that just might have allowed substantial reforms to take place, and for the momentum of the revolution to continue.

As noted, Aoun's ambitions to be president created one of the most surprising turns of events in post-2005 Lebanese politics. Not only did he withdraw from the March 14 Alliance, but he then also proceeded to join the Syrian- and Iranian-backed opposition. This move should be seen as little more than a self-centred, opportunistic political attempt to gain the support of the opposition in order to secure the Presidency, a position he had coveted since at least 1988. The move also gave many of his Christian supporters pause. Aoun's popularity was based on populist politics and his unflinching criticism, since 1990, of the Syrian occupation of Lebanon. The outcome of Aoun's political realignment not only weakened March 14 and the proponents of the cedar revolution, but also divided and, ultimately, weakened Lebanon's Christian community. March 14 was now very much dominated by the Sunni community led by the Hariri family and their Future Movement. The Shiite community and Hizbollah, on the other hand, dominated the Lebanese opposition. Lebanon's once-dominant Christians became junior partners in both.

The Lebanese opposition: the March 8 Alliance

A significant, if not outright fatal, weakness of the cedar revolution was that it did not appeal to all the major sectarian communities in Lebanon. Noticeably missing from the mass anti-Syrian protests was Lebanon's influential Shiite community, arguably the largest sectarian community in the country. In fact, rather than unite the country, the cedar revolution reaffirmed the country's polarisation along sectarian lines, with the Sunni, Christian and Druze communities supporting it, while the vast majority of the Shiite community were either opposed or deeply suspicious. The leadership of the Shiite community, the Amal and Hizbollah parties, remained Syria's staunch allies and key pillars of continuing Syrian influence in Lebanon. However, Amal lost much of its political power to Hizbollah, which positioned itself as the community's dominant leader.[28]

For every mass demonstration led by the anti-Syrian forces, the pro-Syrian opposition matched it in kind. In the weeks following Hariri's death, both groups mobilised hundreds of thousands of their supporters. The opposition, officially referred to as the March 8 Alliance, named after the day on which it orchestrated a massive pro-Syrian rally, was led by Hizbollah and, to a lesser extent, by Amal.

With respect to its political platform, March 8 was adamant about maintaining close ties to Syria and Iran, and ensuring that Hizbollah be allowed to maintain its arms in order to continue its "war of resistance" against Israel. Besides actual weapons, this included an entire infrastructural network amounting to the equivalent of a "state within a state" in Hizbollah-controlled parts of Lebanon. These points were non-negotiable for the Shiite-dominated March 8 Alliance. Moreover, the alliance set out to ensure that the Lebanese government adopt the language of resistance, thus institutionalising and legitimising their notion of permanent conflict with Israel.

March 8's influence in Lebanon has been significant. It exploits a number of formal and informal tools to ensure that its views are heard and that its interests (and those of its patrons) are protected.

With respect to the formal governing institutions, as mentioned in Part I, one of the three most senior positions, the Speaker of the House, is reserved for a member of the Shiite community. Since 1992, Nabih Birri of Amal, a strong Syrian client, has held the position, giving him important control over government decisions. With regards to Parliament, since 2005 the opposition has held as many as fifty-seven seats, as opposed to the seventy-two held by the March 14 majority. This encompasses every seat allocated to Lebanon's Shiite community. Since traditionally all major sectarian communities need to be represented in government, the opposition rightfully demanded a number of cabinet seats. In fact, a major point of contention since 2005 has been the opposition's demand that it be allocated one-third of all available cabinet seats. The controversy that ensued stems from the fact that, if this were granted, the opposition would gain an effective veto over any major government decision. The implications are obvious: 1) Syria would once again be at the helm of the country, this time without it being physically present; and 2) Hizbollah would not only maintain its arms, but would actually play a decisive role in any security decisions. In effect, the March 14 programme would be dead.

With respect to the informal mechanisms, I will emphasise three.

- The March 8 Alliance, through Amal and Hizbollah, exerts considerable influence outside the formal bodies of government outlined above. Their strategic alliance with both Syria and Iran is rather intricate. At its most basic level, it enables the continuing flow of Iranian arms and money to Hizbollah via Syria. In return, Syria and Iran use their Lebanese clients to protect and further their interests in Lebanon. The patron–client relationship is, of course, far more complex than this. For instance, Iran and Hizbollah share a similar ideological view of the world, and work closely together strategically by sharing intelligence, by actively supporting Hamas, and by challenging Western and Israeli interests.

• March 8 has greatly used to its advantage its ability to mobilise tens of thousands of its followers against the government. This extends not only to demonstrations and strikes, but also to indefinite occupations of government buildings and even of pro-opposition neighbourhoods. This heavy-handed approach has been used since 2005 for extensive periods, and has caused a heightened level of tension with Lebanon's other sectarian communities.

• As a last resort of persuasion, it should be obvious to all that the opposition is also well armed. Since 1990, Hizbollah has gone on to develop an extensive security apparatus purportedly for use in its conflict with Israel. In fact, the Lebanese army is now considerably weaker than Hizbollah. As a consequence, neither the state nor any of the other sectarian groups (who were disarmed after the civil war) are in a position to resist Hizbollah should it decide to flex its military muscle to settle political scores, a point I return to below.

The role of Syria

One of the main themes of this book is the overwhelming influence of Syria on the contemporary Lebanese political process between 1990 and 2005, to the point that one could justifiably call into question Lebanon's sovereignty during that period.

The events that followed Rafiq Hariri's assassination, in particular the enormous pressure by both Lebanese groups and the international community for an end to the occupation, shook Syria without question. Even international actors such as Saudi Arabia, who had long acquiesced to Syrian control of Lebanon, told Damascus it was time to go. When Syria did finally withdraw its troops in April of 2005, it was clearly on the defensive.

However, initial hopes in some quarters that Syria would cease to play an important role in Lebanon were soon to be dashed, as they clearly underestimated the level of control and influence that Syria would maintain in the country after its withdrawal.

First, the Syrians would retain control over two of the three key executive positions. Indeed, both President Lahoud and Speaker of Parliament Nabih Birri were key Syrian clients, and although Lahoud's extended term would end by 2008, Birri could hold on to the Speaker's Chair indefinitely (he has held it since 1992). Further, with its key allies in the March 8 movement in the cabinet, Syria's influence now effectively extended to all three executive branches.

Second, Syria's intricate network of control of the security and intelligence services, its influence with key personnel in the Lebanese army, as well as with Palestinian groups and various Islamist groups, gave it a range of coercive tools to: 1) ensure that its interests in Lebanon were protected; 2) demonstrate its unhappiness with the

Beirut government; and 3) deal with politicians or other leading figures that strongly criticised it. From 2005 onward, the security situation in the country declined to such an extent that numerous anti-Syrian politicians were assassinated, including four MPs from the March 14 movement, as well as high-level journalists who openly criticised the Syrian regime. There was also a general flow of arms from Syria to militant groups in the Palestinian camps, adding to further tensions with Lebanese authorities. Syria's penetration of the security services was such that, at the very least, even if it was no longer calling the political shots, it was in a position to cause considerable instability in Lebanon should political developments become hostile to key Syrian interests. In other words, Syria would hold the key to the normalisation of the security situation in Lebanon.

In short, the overall basis of the Syrian–Lebanese relationship was renegotiated. Although very much a dynamic process, Syria has succeeded in reasserting its influence over the Lebanese political process. Its confidence was regained as a result of several additional factors, including the realisation that: 1) the regional and international political climate was moving in its favour; and 2) external actors, including the West and conservative Arab states, and key internal players (none other than Walid Jumblatt), were losing confidence in the March 14 movement. All of this gave Syria more latitude in Lebanon. In fact, by 2010, many of the leading anti-Syrian politicians had paid visits to the Syrian capital, an acknowledgement of Syria's continued influence in Lebanon. This included Walid Jumblatt, who withdrew from the March 14 Alliance, in part in recognition that the winds of political power were changing once again in Lebanon. It also ironically included the current Prime Minister, Saad Hariri, son and heir to the assassinated former Prime Minister Rafiq Hariri.

The role of other external actors

External actors have always had influence in Lebanon through key Lebanese clients.

Iran's influence in Lebanese affairs has existed since the early 1980s, when it created Hizbollah among the ranks of the Lebanese Shiite community to fight Western interests and help spread the Iranian revolution. As Hizbollah developed into an effective force – it was credited with forcing Israel out of South Lebanon in 2000 – its importance to Iran increased significantly. Iran has provided both material and financial support to Hizbollah over the years. Between 1990 and 2005, the Iranian–Hizbollah relationship was filtered and controlled to a considerable extent through Syria, but following 2005, the situation changed somewhat. Indeed, although the Iranian–Syrian–Hizbollah alliance remained strong, Iran was now in a strong position to bypass Syria to some extent on issues related to Hizbollah, should the need arise. Hizbollah has come to figure greatly in Iranian strategic thinking, particularly as an important front against Israel, should Israel and Iran go to war over issues such as Iranian nuclear power. Thus the continuing armament of Hizbollah and the possibility of opening up a conflict with Israel along the Lebanese border figure as key elements in Iranian strategic calculations.

Western and Conservative Arab influence in Lebanon runs through the various leaders of the March 14 Alliance, particularly the Sunni community. It was a combination of US, French and Saudi Arabian pressure in support of March 14 that forced Syria's hand in April 2005. Western and Arab diplomatic support has been important to the March 14-led Lebanese governments, and financial aid from them was key to the continuing stability of the Lebanese economy. However, fear over the extension of Iranian influence in Lebanon has created a complicated dynamic. On one hand, it has heightened conservative Arab support for the Western-backed Lebanese government; but on the other hand, it has also created a dynamic where countries such as Saudi Arabia, and even Western countries such as France, would consider Syrian concerns in Lebanon, if this meant that Syria would distance itself from its Iranian/Hizbollah axis.

3.6 Political developments 2005–10

The purpose of this section is to detail the major political events that have occurred from 2005 to 2010. In particular, I focus on: 1) the National Dialogue process; 2) the Hizbollah–Israel war of 2006; 3) the political crises of 2006–08; and 4) the 2009 parliamentary elections.

The National Dialogue process[29]

Within a year of Prime Minister Fouad Siniora taking office, Lebanese political leaders launched the National Dialogue process. This involved a series of talks among the main sectarian communities and their leaders to discuss the fate of the nation, and to come to some consensus on the main issues facing Lebanon. It was the first time that such talks had been held since the end of the civil war, and proved to be a promising, even if short-lived, attempt to move the political climate in a positive direction.

A number of rather divisive issues were on the table, including the normalisation of relations with Syria, the disarming of Hizbollah, and political reform. Perhaps not surprisingly, the talks did not progress well at all, as the various sides differed substantially on these issues. Hizbollah's arms, for instance, always divisive since the conclusion of the civil war in 1990, and even more so after Israel's withdrawal in 2000, became the polarising issue for Lebanon in the years that followed 2005.

For a substantial number of people in Lebanon, including the leaders of the March 14 movement, there was no legitimate justification for Hizbollah to maintain its arms. As they saw it, this served only to keep Lebanon entangled in the conflictual regional dynamics of Israel–Iran–Syria and embroiled in the wider Iranian–Western rivalries. Moreover, it created enormous tensions with the other sectarian communities, who had grown weary and deeply suspicious of Hizbollah's motives and actions, which only served to weaken further the political, economic and security fabric of Lebanon. Finally, those who strongly favoured the disarmament of Hizbollah pointed to the fact that both the Ta'if Accord and UN Resolution 1559 called for all militias in Lebanon, including Hizbollah, to disarm.

To Hizbollah, however, discussing its arms was a non-starter, as it considered itself a resistance movement. According to its narrative, its arms, and the various supporting infrastructural networks, were necessary to protect Lebanon from Israel. It would point to its success in forcing Israel from Lebanon in 2000. At the very least, and within the context of the National Dialogue, Hizbollah pushed for changing the focus of the discussion to a national defence strategy, in which it would, of course, figure prominently, retaining its arms.

While the strongly opposing views on this and other issues meant that progress would be slow, the National Dialogue process was soon overtaken by events on the ground, which triggered a political crisis lasting until the end of 2008, for much of the Siniora term. The National Dialogue process was suspended and was resumed only after the political crisis passed.

The Hizbollah–Israel War of 2006[30]

Just over a year after the cedar revolution raised substantial hopes about the country's future, Hizbollah and Israel fought a devastating thirty-three-day war, largely in South Lebanon. The war was a stark reminder of the risks associated with having a militia with its own dynamics – agenda, international links, etc. – operating as an autonomous entity outside of state control. As had happened all too frequently since the late 1960s, Lebanon was again used as the base for a devastating conflict over which it had little control, and which was largely tied to regional dynamics.

There has been much debate regarding the reasons for the war: 1) who started it; 2) the motives of Hizbollah; 3) the nature of the involvement of its external patrons Iran and Syria; and 4) the agenda of Israel. Suffice to say, Hizbollah was roundly criticised by its Lebanese opponents for either starting the war (possibly in consultation with Iran and Syria), or behaving in such a manner (the kidnapping of Israeli soldiers) that it overplayed its hand and triggered Israel to react to the extent that it did. Although there was widespread sympathy for the victims of the fighting (who were largely from the Shiite community), the conflict exacerbated considerably the sectarian divide within Lebanon at both the political elite and mass levels.

The war killed nearly 1500 Lebanese civilians, displaced approximately a million from their homes, and caused hundreds of millions of dollars' worth of damage to the country's civilian infrastructure (including the airport). The cost to the Lebanese economy, and in particular to its critical summer tourism season, was in the tens of billions. UN Security Council Resolution 1701, approved by both the Lebanese and Israeli authorities, brought the conflict to an end. The Resolution called for the immediate cessation of hostilities; the withdrawal of Israel from Lebanon; the expansion of the UN interim force and the deployment of Lebanese troops to the border; and, most significantly in this context, for the disarmament of Hizbollah.

Aware of the widespread criticism of its role in starting the conflict, Hizbollah took a number of steps to ensure a political victory from the war. First, it declared a military victory, pointing to the fact that Israel had been incapable of stopping rockets launched onto its territory, and that it had needed to rely on the UN for settlement of the conflict. Hizbollah would also reiterate its long-standing narrative that it had once again protected Lebanon from Israel (as it claims it has since the 1980s), making it the only Arab military force capable of challenging Israel.

Second, the Hizbollah leadership distributed hundreds of millions of dollars (received from Iran) to its Shiite clients to rebuild their homes and infrastructure, in a bid to retain their loyalty.

Third, Hizbollah used the war to bolster its political position, and to that effect made a number of demands on the Siniora government. Critically, this included the demand that the opposition be awarded a third of all cabinet seats, which, as noted above, would give them the much-coveted veto over government decisions, including ultimately the terms under which Hizbollah would be disarmed.

In short, Hizbollah would proceed to use the various tools at its disposal to push its agenda and demands on the government over the next two years, precipitating a calculated political crisis aimed at bringing the government down or, at the very least, severely undermining its ability to govern effectively for the remainder of its term. The crisis ultimately required the intervention of the international community, including the respective external patrons of each of the Lebanese parties.

The 2006–08 political crisis and the Doha Agreement[31]

The political crisis instigated by Hizbollah and its allies in the March 8 opposition began in November of 2006, when Shiite cabinet ministers resigned, thereby denying the government the full legitimacy associated with having representation from all of the major communities. It ended in May 2008 with the signing of the Doha Agreement, which set out the terms for the governing of Lebanon until the 2009 parliamentary elections.

Following the resignation of the Shiite cabinet ministers, Hizbollah and its allies initiated a series of protests and sit-ins aimed at forcing the Lebanese government to acquiesce to opposition demands that a new unity government be formed, ensuring the opposition got one-third of all cabinet seats and thus the prized veto over government decisions. Failing that, the opposition hoped to bring down the government and precipitate new elections.

The Siniora government rejected the opposition's demands. This led to a nearly two-year stand-off, and raised enormous tensions between the respective communities. This was especially true within the Shiite and Sunni communities, as many of the Hizbollah protests and sit-ins occurred in the Sunni neighbourhoods of West Beirut. To the Sunnis, this was not only a clear form of intimidation, but also a sign that the opposition was trying to bring down a Sunni-led government.

The political stand-off was elevated to a near civil war in May of 2008, when two controversial decisions by the government led Hizbollah to turn its guns against its Lebanese political foes, particularly the government, by taking over West Beirut, the airport and other parts of the country controlled by pro-government forces. For many commentators, this amounted to a *coup d'état*.[32] This latest crisis began when the Siniora government dismissed the head of security at the country's airport because of revelations that Hizbollah had installed surveillance cameras in a particularly sensitive area, which purportedly gave it the capability to monitor the comings and goings of high-level visitors to the country. Further, the government took the daring step of closing down Hizbollah's telecommunications network, used to conduct intelligence operations independently of government. These two decisions led Hizbollah's leadership to accuse the government of declaring war. In response, Hizbollah flexed its military muscle against its own countrymen for the first time since the civil war. The Lebanese army stayed neutral in the conflict, but clashes between Hizbollah (and its allies) and Sunni and Druze groups led to what can be described as the worst sectarian violence since the end of the civil war. Hundreds of people were killed before Hizbollah pulled back its fighters after a week of hostilities, thus allowing the Lebanese army to enter the neighbourhoods it had occupied.

Arab and international diplomatic efforts succeeded in bringing the crisis to a conclusion with the signing of the Doha Agreement on 21 May 2008. In short, the Agreement was a major victory for Hizbollah and its allies and patrons, as it gave them the long-desired veto in a national unity government, thus allowing them to block any decisions on the question of disarmament, the international tribunal on Hariri, etc. In return, the opposition agreed to allow Parliament to move forward to elect the next President of Lebanon. This critical position had been vacant since September of 2007. Although the opposition favoured Michel Aoun, in the end all sides agreed that a neutral candidate (but still acceptable to Syria), such as General Michel Suleiman, would be better. Finally, no significant mention was made of disarming Hizbollah, but only that no groups should use their weapons for political advantage. In other words, the Agreement cemented Hizbollah's stranglehold over the government.

Although the Doha agreement ended the political crisis and allowed the Siniora government to remain functional until the June 2009 elections, it created long-term tensions between the Sunni and Shiite communities. Indeed, it increased the appeal of Sunni extremist Islamist groups who are critical of a political solution to the question of disarmament, thus setting the stage for a possible future military conflict that would oppose the two Muslim factions.

June 2009 elections and the March 14-led Saad Hariri government[33]

In June of 2009, the second parliamentary elections since Syria's withdrawal were held in Lebanon. The elections could be viewed as a moral victory for the March 14 Alliance, as it won seventy-one seats to the opposition's fifty-seven, and was therefore in a position to form the next government. However, the results were similar to the 2005 elections, and within the context of the Lebanese political system, this meant the need for a unity government and the probability of opposition demands for veto power.

The results were, in fact, rather predictable. March 14 under Hariri's leadership has a monopoly on the Sunni community, while March 8 under Hizbollah's leadership has a monopoly on the Shiite community. As long as the Christian community remains divided, splitting their votes between the two blocs, Lebanon's political system will remain fractured between two relatively equal blocs, but ones divided along sectarian lines, aligned to different global players, and subscribing to different visions of Lebanon. The result will be a fractured system for many years to come.

After five months of intense negotiations, a unity government under Saad Hariri was formed. March 14 secured fifteen cabinet seats, the opposition ten, with five remaining to be appointed by the President. However, in a sign of continuing shift of the balance of power, one of March 14's principal leaders, Walid Jumblatt, withdrew from the group. Whether or not Hariri can be successful at stabilising Lebanon remains to be seen. His job, in any case, will be a difficult one.

4

POST-WAR RECONSTRUCTION AND THE ECONOMY

The economic reconstruction process, and the state of the economy more generally, were the issues that dominated the Lebanese political discourse, almost to the exclusion of all others, at least until 2004. Other issues, however pressing they may have been, were not dealt with. These were, for instance, the effective marginalisation of the Maronite community from the political process, the South Lebanon conflict, Hizbollah's activities against Israel, and so on. But, most importantly, there was no challenge to Syria or Syrian objectives within the bounds of the formal Lebanese political process.

The reason for this, as already noted, was that Syria exercised virtually total control of this process. Even before the Treaty of Brotherhood and the establishment of the various coordination committees gave Syrian hegemony a legal veneer, Damascus made all the major decisions concerning the composition of the Lebanese government and the policy agenda it would pursue. However, by the conclusion of the 1992 parliamentary elections, a situation had emerged whereby it was in Syria's interest to allow the new Lebanese government to exercise more independence in the economic sphere.

Essentially, Syria was under considerable pressure, due to: 1) mass unrest in Lebanon, resulting from the fact that the first two post-war governments had neglected the growing economic crisis in order to concentrate on Syrian-dictated priorities; and 2) protest in the international community about Damascus's manipulation of the 1992 elections to secure a pliant Lebanese Parliament that would not challenge its continuing military presence in the country. In order to relieve this pressure, Syria acquiesced in the selection of the relatively popular and influential Rafiq Hariri as Lebanese Prime Minister and afforded his government substantial, albeit closely monitored, autonomy in the sphere of economic decision-making.

As economic interests have always been at the heart of Lebanese politics, this decision placated the Lebanese masses to some extent. It also raised hopes in the international community that the Lebanese government would ultimately be allowed more autonomy in areas outside the economic sphere. Finally, it had the further advantage for Syria that, if the economic situation failed to improve, the Lebanese government, rather than Damascus, would be blamed. In that sense, the restricted autonomy policy would, ironically, help to further secure Syria's continuing role in Lebanon.

The purpose of this chapter is to examine, and to present a critical evaluation of, the economic policies pursued by successive Lebanese governments since autumn 1992.[1] The primary focus will be on "Horizon 2000", the major reconstruction programme that was the centrepiece of Rafiq Hariri's attempts during the 1990s to restore the economy and re-establish Lebanon as the major regional centre of finance and trade. The chapter is divided into three main sections. The first looks at the economic crisis that confronted Hariri when he took office in 1992 and explains his plans for resolving the country's economic woes. Particular attention is given to the nature and aims of the Horizon 2000 programme. The second section presents a brief summary and assessment concerning the progress of the reconstruction programme from 1993 up until the end of Hariri's first tenure as Prime Minister in December 1998. The major obstacles and problems the Hariri government encountered with the programme's implementation are examined, followed by a consideration of the extent to which the programme achieved its stated objectives. Finally, the third section briefly considers the economic policies of subsequent Lebanese governments, including: 1) Prime Minister Salim Hoss (1998–2000); 2) Prime Minister Rafiq Hariri (2000–04); and 3) the post-2005 governments of Prime Ministers Fouad Siniora and Saad Hariri.

4.1 The state of the post-war Lebanese economy and Hariri's reconstruction plan

The state of the Lebanese economy in 1992

The civil war had a devastating effect on Lebanon's economy, and the problems this entailed were only exacerbated by the fact that the first two post-war governments almost completely neglected the economic welfare of the country. When one considers the sheer scale of physical and social disruption in the country, not to mention the consequences of the continuing South Lebanon conflict and the severe limits imposed on the government's autonomy by Damascus, one must allow that the task facing Hariri when he initially took office would have been an extremely formidable challenge for anyone, no matter how well intentioned or competent. It is important to state this because, in subsequent years, as Hariri's programmes faltered, he became the target of increasingly harsh personal criticism for failing to resolve Lebanon's economic woes.

To demonstrate just what Hariri was up against, I would cite the following figures from 1992. According to the United Nations, around 20 per cent of the population had been displaced; about 55 per cent suffered from severe overcrowding; 21 per cent did not have private access to the water supply; and 48 per cent were housed illegally.

Furthermore: the monthly minimum wage had decreased steadily; real per capita GNP had fallen to approximately one-third of the 1975 level; and approximately 35 per cent of the labour force was unemployed. During the course of 1992, the value of the Lebanese pound fell from L£879 to US$1 to L£1500, then L£2100, and then L£3000 in just a few months. This violent devaluation was coupled with runaway inflation.[2]

Damage to Lebanon's physical infrastructure was estimated to run into billions of dollars: the telecommunications sector was devastated; electricity was rationed to about six hours a day; there were no functioning sewage treatment facilities in the entire country; 80 per cent of water samples collected from springs, wells and reservoirs were polluted; the system for solid waste collection was destroyed; most schools, hospitals and vocational and technical training colleges were damaged; and nearly a quarter of all housing was at least partially damaged.[3]

Finally, and perhaps above all, it should be pointed out that Lebanon emerged from the civil war as a pariah state with very little to offer the international business community and potential investors. During the fifteen-year conflict, its traditional economic role as a key centre for commerce and banking had been largely usurped by a number of regional competitors. Furthermore, for various reasons ranging from scattered acts of terrorism and hostage-taking to the possibility of a major recurrence of violence, Lebanon had come to be perceived as a bad business risk. Therefore one of the greatest challenges facing the country at the end of 1992 was to convince the world that: 1) Lebanon still had an important economic role to play; and 2) it was stable enough to play that role.

Hariri's economic reconstruction plan[4]

Upon assuming office, Hariri formed a "government of economic salvation" and set about trying to restore some macro-economic stability to the country. This entailed efforts to stabilise the Lebanese pound, bring inflation under control and balance the public budget. However, the true centrepiece of Hariri's economic policy was the massive Horizon 2000 programme, the cost of which was initially estimated at $11.7 billion. The stated aim of the plan was for the government to restore confidence in the Lebanese state and the future of the country generally, and to provide the private sector with an environment conducive to investment. Its real, and somewhat more ambitious, goal was to restore Lebanon's traditional status as a key regional centre of finance and commerce.[5]

Pursuant to this, the government was to provide a comprehensive, state-of-the-art physical infrastructure including electricity, telecommunications, clean water, public transport, port and airport facilities, etc. Second, the government was charged with providing an acceptable social infrastructure including, most significantly, adequate housing and resettlement, public health and education. And third, the government was expected to provide aid to the agriculture, industry and tourism sectors.[6]

Funding for the project was to originate from three sources. The first and most significant portion of financing was supposed to come from government budget surpluses, which the planners believed would materialise beginning in 1996. The surpluses were expected to amount to $8.7 billion or 47 per cent of gross financing requirements. The second major source of financing was to originate from foreign currency borrowing. This was supposed to contribute $4.9 billion or 34 per cent of the programme, and none of the money was expected to be allocated to non-recovery expenditures such as government debt. Finally, funding was also expected to come from foreign grants, which were to account for 6 per cent of financing, and from repayments under a credit support programme, which were to contribute 4 per cent.[7]

Even the most dedicated adherents of the Horizon 2000 programme recognised that the ultimate success or failure of the plan depended on financing. Furthermore, it was generally recognised that the fate of the Lebanese economic recovery as a whole depended on the private sector. Indeed, the primary goal of Horizon 2000 was to facilitate and stimulate private-sector activity. It is worth noting, at this point, that the authors of the Horizon 2000 plan included a cautionary note about both of these conditions.[8]

> The Horizon 2000 plan is indicative in that although it gives a well-defined public recovery programme, it allows the private sector activities to evolve at will. The plan cannot be considered as static. It has been established as a starting point in the quest for progress.

In other words, the authors of the plan were acknowledging that the ultimate costs of the plan, and even its contents, might be subject to change. Furthermore, they wanted to stress that, in any event, the success of the reconstruction would be dependent upon the performance of the private sector. Therefore it would ultimately be out of the government's hands, perhaps to a very great extent.

As part of the government's overall policy for encouraging the private sector, it provided for the creation of a number of large, privately funded and administered property development plans. By far the most significant and controversial of these was the plan for the reconstruction and development of the Beirut Central District, which was to be spearheaded by Solidere, a company effectively created for this purpose and in which Hariri himself exercised a controlling interest.[9]

This point raises one of the key criticisms directed at the recovery plan by its opponents, namely the possibility that, as one of the key architects of the plan, Hariri's primary interests were to: 1) make a massive personal financial profit from some of its many reconstruction and development contracts and projects; and 2) use the allocation of other contracts and projects as a source of personal patronage. To at least some extent, this criticism must be viewed as valid. However, it is important to bear a couple of points in mind.

First, although Hariri and his leading allies were closely associated with the development of the Horizon 2000 plan, it was not a radical departure in most respects from previous reconstruction plans developed by earlier Lebanese governments and privately commissioned consultants. Some aspects of the plan dated back to as early as 1978.[10]

Second, conflicts of interest and the use of state institutions and policies to enhance personal patronage are endemic characteristics of Lebanese politics. Thus what most

Westerners would probably consider to be abuses of political office are often ignored in the Lebanese context unless they are taken to severe extremes. It is unclear that Hariri was taking advantage of his position to a greater extent than his critics might have done had their situations been reversed.

In fact, it is quite possible that a significant amount of the resentment expressed by Hariri's political opponents was a response not to the Horizon programme as such, but rather to the institutional arrangements he planned to use to implement it. This involved removing the implementation process, the awarding of contracts, etc., from the conventional state sector, inasmuch as it was possible to do so, and transferring control to an institution known as the Council for Development and Reconstruction (CDR).[11]

Like many aspects of Hariri's reconstruction plan, the CDR dated back to the late 1970s. It had been created by the wartime government of President Elias Sarkis and Prime Minister Salim Hoss. From the very beginning, its intent was to facilitate and accelerate economic recovery plans by circumventing both political disputes in the national institutions and the inefficiency of Lebanon's bureaucracy. However, exactly because it bypassed existing institutions, it was always somewhat controversial. During the course of the 1980s, there were several attempts to abolish it in the Lebanese Parliament. Naturally, the controversy only intensified when Hariri increased the importance of the CDR's role and ensured his own control of the institution by installing close allies in its top positions.

And, of course, it could be argued that this institutional arrangement was designed by Hariri primarily to guarantee his control of Horizon 2000 and to keep the patronage associated with it out of rival hands. However, the ostensible purpose of Hariri's use of the CDR was also undeniably valid: to protect the implementation process from two significant systemic problems.

The first of these was the Lebanese system's ubiquitous inter- and intra-sectarian competition over potential sources of patronage. In short, Hariri contended that the implementation of the plan would be slowed and perhaps even fatally undermined by protracted debates and the interference of *zu'ama* who wished to gain access to the plan's contracts and projects as sources of patronage for themselves. In addition to introducing delays and other problems, such interference might have an incalculably negative impact on programme finances, since it would disrupt the competitive bidding process for individual projects and subject the state to effective political extortion.

The second problem was the widely acknowledged inability of Lebanon's notoriously corrupt and inefficient public-sector bureaucracy to manage the reconstruction process. Thus Hariri pointed to the need to have a central institution that would be able to support the government ministries as they attempted to implement the individual recovery projects in their respective sectors.

The inadequacies of the post-war Lebanese public sector are closely related to a final major criticism of the Horizon 2000 plan. Since a major proportion of the infrastructure reconstruction and development projects were ultimately to be administered by the public sector, the long-term value of the plan would be dubious in the absence of major public-sector reforms.

To a certain extent, the public-sector problem was a natural consequence of Lebanon's fusion of confessionalism with a neo-patrimonial system. In this sense, the public sector had been somewhat dysfunctional even before the civil war. In short, government jobs were always viewed as a key source of patronage. The competitive nature of the Lebanese political process, with all of the different sectarian *zu'ama* constantly looking to increase their influence, ensured that patronage-based rather than merit-based appointments were made at every level from the top public-sector jobs to the very lowest. The fact that sectarian balance had to be achieved also increased the overall number of appointments and served to introduce a new check on the emergence of a merit-based system. Overstaffing was common. With reference to this problem, one commentator described Lebanon's Central Bank as a "favourite dumping ground" for numerous patronage appointments. The sheer size of the public sector alone made it a major drain on state revenue.[12]

The civil war, however, made the system's inherent problems much worse. For one thing, the state's ability to collect revenue fell off sharply and it ran up huge deficits trying to maintain basic services and to pay its vast numbers of employees. To make matters worse, many of the better qualified and more capable civil servants left the country to escape the war, resulting in a severe shortage of skilled staff. The war also introduced absenteeism and corruption on an unprecedented scale. A great number of people stayed on the state payroll despite turning up at work rarely or never. Bribery became a virtually institutionalised feature with respect to just about every sort of interaction between the public and state ministries. Moreover, these new conditions naturally did not reverse themselves once the civil war ended, but continued to a greater or lesser degree. Returning the public sector to pre-war levels of professionalism and competence therefore represented a major challenge for post-war governments.[13]

The Hariri government recognised this as an imperative. In the course of an early speech setting out the different aspects of his economic recovery plan, Hariri emphasised the need for bureaucratic reform, and fired a warning shot across the bow of entrenched civil servants who owed their positions and job security to the confessional patron–client network:[14]

> The implementation of administrative reform requires the lifting of immunity for a certain period of time on all civil servants and public sector employees, and the adoption of a policy of reward and sanction to get rid of corrupt employees, and reward honest ones.

4.2 Progress of the reconstruction programme (1993–98)

Obstacles and problems in the implementation process

With respect to its efforts to implement the recovery process from 1993–98, Hariri's government encountered a considerable range of significant problems. Some of these were primarily economic in nature, but others emanated from the political sphere.

The first point that must be considered relates to public finances. As noted above, almost half the funding for Horizon 2000 was expected to come from projected budget surpluses. Furthermore, the other major source of financing, foreign aid and borrowing, was not supposed to contribute to the debt situation. Even in the early 1990s, some critics considered these assumptions highly questionable. In retrospect, they can be seen as dramatically over-optimistic.

The budget surpluses never materialised and government borrowing exceeded all expectations, to the extent that it contributed massively to the national debt. As early as 1995, the debt situation was so bad that a confidential World Bank report placed Lebanon on its shortlist of states that were at a high risk of bankruptcy. Moreover, the problem continued to escalate throughout Hariri's tenure as Prime Minister. By 2000, the debt had reached about $25 billion. This is equivalent to approximately 150 per cent of GDP, with debt servicing costs that account for 50 per cent of Lebanon's annual budget.[15]

A second problem was linked to the failings of Lebanon's public sector. As noted, it was widely feared that the notorious corruption and inefficiency of the Lebanese bureaucracy would both endanger the implementation of the Horizon programme and undermine its achievements. Hariri sought to evade at least part of the problem by assigning primary responsibility for the implementation to the CDR, a semi-autonomous body outside the traditional public sector. In practice, however, the ministries assumed a siege mentality and attempted zealously to defend their spheres of influence against CDR interference. Although Hariri was able to use his influence to push through CDR initiatives in many cases, this competition had detrimental consequences for the implementation process. Furthermore, as events developed, Hariri was unable to bring about any kind of substantive public-sector reform. This meant, among other things, that major public concerns, such as the nationalised electricity company, Electricité du Liban (EDL), continued to tie up public finances by operating at massive losses.[16]

The CDR was also supposed to help immunise the implementation process against the rampant competition over patronage that is such a fundamental characteristic of the Lebanese political process. In fact, however, since the CDR was almost entirely dependent on Hariri's influence, it was only as free from sectarian wrangling over patronage as Hariri was himself. And, of course, due to his position as Prime Minister and the very nature of the troika system as a focal point of cross-sectarian dispute, it was not particularly well protected at all.

The third major problem therefore was that the implementation process was subjected to a considerable level of political infighting between Hariri and other key governmental figures, especially the Speaker, Nabih Birri. Such disputes ruined any chance of putting the plan into effect with the greatest possible efficiency and speed. Birri and the President, Elias Hrawi, both had the constitutional power to hold up legislation, including the state budget and approval of the individual Horizon 2000 projects. They frequently used their prerogatives to extract concessions from Hariri. He also had to make deals with influential cabinet ministers such as the Interior Minister, Michel Murr.

Negotiated settlements over major projects and the patronage associated with them created significant delays and ensured that government contracts were all too frequently awarded as patronage rather than on the basis of: 1) a given company's proven capacity to undertake the work contracted; and/or 2) the most competitive bid. This contributed to cost over-runs and significantly hampered the implementation of many parts of the Horizon programme.

To cite just a few of many possible examples of this sort of thing, Birri's leadership of a quasi-state organisation known as the "Council of the South" allowed him to exercise great influence over many of the infrastructure projects in that part of the country. He also secured the award of one-third of a contract for building a major coastal road to a company owned by his wife. Another third of the contract was awarded to a company owned by Hariri's brother, and the final third to a company associated with Syrian Vice-President Abdel Halim Khaddam. This sparked a controversy in Parliament, where opposition figures claimed that the companies' charges were excessively high and that the contract had never been proffered for a competitive bid. The companies agreed to cut their prices by 20 per cent, but observers noted that they would still make a massive profit. Another prime example of political interference in the recovery process concerned a project to restore the Jeita Caves, a famous Lebanese tourist attraction. The Tourism Minister, Nicolas Fattouh, allegedly used his influence to secure the contract for a friend's company, which apparently lacked the technical and geological expertise to do the work properly.[17]

These examples also serve to lead into the consideration of a fourth, and closely related, problem which became increasingly serious throughout the 1993–98 period: the tension introduced into the political system by the perceived corruption surrounding the reconstruction and development process. As I have noted several times, a certain amount of conflict of interest must be taken for granted within the Lebanese political context. However, it can become an issue if leading figures are seen to be taking the normal process of "splitting up the Lebanese pie" to excessive lengths. Naturally, with a project as big and pervasive as Horizon 2000, there was always a danger that one or more of the leading politicians would be targeted for going too far.

The controversial 1996 media law provides an excellent example of the lack of subtlety that created problems in this area. The law limited the number of private television stations in the country to four, and the number of private radio stations to eight. Of the four television licences issued, one was awarded to Future Television, owned by Hariri; one to the National Broadcasting Network, owned by Birri; and a third to Murr Television, owned by the brother of the Interior Minister, Michel Murr. Hariri and Birri also owned companies that were awarded private radio licences.[18]

As Chapter 3 explains, Hariri was the prime target of frustration with this sort of thing, and increasingly came under direct attack for perceived corruption. To some extent, this was inevitable, since Horizon 2000 was widely seen as Hariri's personal programme, and since questions about his intentions had been raised by critics even before the implementation process began. However, it is ironic, to say the least, that one of Hariri's chief accusers, particularly after 1996, was Birri, a man just as deeply implicated as Hariri himself in some of the more clear-cut examples of corruption.

Hariri had never responded well to criticism of his motives, and his irritation about what he considered to be unwarranted personal attacks was partly responsible for several threatened resignations throughout the 1990s. His relations with Birri, never cordial at the best of times, became increasingly strained, and the corruption issue contributed greatly to the troika deadlock that frequently paralysed the political process and the recovery programme for the last few years of his tenure.

It should be recognised that Syrian penetration of the Lebanese system contributed to the political interference and perceived corruption problems, perhaps to a very great extent. In essence, it was in Syria's interest to limit Hariri's power, and keep him dependent, by playing him off against other leading members of the Lebanese political establishment. A strong Lebanese economy might be in Syria's interest, but a strong Hariri would be a potential threat. Therefore it was imperative for the Syrian leadership to make sure that Hariri would not be afforded too much personal control of the reconstruction process. Furthermore, if the troika were to become deadlocked, it would only serve to remind Hariri that he needed the support of Damascus if he wanted to get anything done.

There is considerable evidence to suggest that Damascus took advantage of many of the issues raised by the recovery process to encourage internal disputes. Unlike Hariri, both Birri and Hrawi owed their positions largely to Syrian sponsorship. Cabinet ministers such as Murr also had strong Syrian connections. Thus, in addition to their natural desire to gain access to the patronage the recovery projects represented, they also had to concern themselves with Syrian interests. If this meant that they had to concede some battles when Hariri had Damascus on his side, it also meant that they frequently had the power to force concessions from Hariri, as Damascus would often reward their loyalty by helping them to gain additional status and patronage. Syria's aim, after all, was to maintain a fairly even balance of power so that no Lebanese politician would be too strong. Damascus supported (encouraged) Birri's use of the corruption issue as a weapon against Hariri essentially because it served this interest. Birri, for his part, would certainly have been aware that an opponent with similar sanction from the Syrian leadership would be able to use the same weapon against him.

Naturally, Syria was the mediator whenever the troika became deadlocked or there was a major dispute within the Council of Ministers. This made Damascus a kind of super-patron. Accordingly, leading Syrian figures were generally able to negotiate their own personal access to recovery projects and other forms of Lebanese patronage when it suited them. Thus Syria did not just contribute indirectly to the political interference problem; Syrian leaders were directly involved as well.

A final major problem faced by the Hariri government as it attempted to implement the recovery programme was Syria's total control over foreign policy and security issues, and its determination to maintain policies directly contradictory to Lebanese economic interests. Needless to say, the prime example was Syria's continued support for Hizbollah activities against Israel in the South. The continuing conflict led to two large-scale Israeli military operations against Lebanon, one in 1993 and another in 1996. These incursions caused enormous damage to Lebanon's infrastructure and to the economy more generally. According to one of Lebanon's leading economists, Marwan Iskandar, Israel's sixteen-day "Grapes of Wrath" operation in April 1996 cost Lebanon some $500 million. The conflict may have cost Lebanon's tourist industry alone approximately $150 million.[19]

Of course, the overall damage caused by the South Lebanon conflict with respect to the Lebanese economic recovery is practically incalculable. It is highly likely that many potential investors and private-sector interests, both Lebanese and foreign, were put off by the general atmosphere of instability bred by the conflict. The constant possibility that there might be an escalation of the violence would obviously be detrimental to most kinds of business activity.

Hariri's efforts to seek even a very limited independent Lebanese foreign policy were met with extreme concern by Syria, and Damascus responded, in each case, by attempting to weaken his position. To cite just one example of how this interfered with Lebanon's economic welfare: Syria was opposed to Hariri's visit to Washington during the Friends of Lebanon conference in Washington in December 1996. Hariri's aim in attending was primarily economic. He was simply trying to secure aid that was promised in compensation for Israel's Grapes of Wrath operation. Syria, however, was worried that Washington and Hariri would form closer ties, thereby lessening Syrian power in Lebanon.

Finally, the controversy surrounding Syria's continuing presence in Lebanon and the marginalisation of the Maronite Christian community cost the economy the crucial support of the country's substantial expatriate communities. The number of potential investors, their enormous reserves of available capital and their natural interest in the welfare of the country meant that these were precisely the kind of private-sector actors upon whom the ultimate fate of the economic recovery was contingent. The political situation, however, meant that the participation of this whole class of possibly key contributors could be ruled out for all practical intents and purposes before the implementation of the Horizon 2000 programme even began.

An assessment of the programme based on its objectives

As noted elsewhere, the central aims of Hariri's recovery programme involved establishing an atmosphere conducive to private-sector activity, and stimulating such activity. Ultimately, the prime objective was to recapture Lebanon's traditional role as a major centre of international trade and banking. In terms of these objectives, it is impossible to avoid the conclusion that the Horizon 2000 programme, and other government policies running along these lines, were a substantial failure. However, before I proceed to consider the aspects of Hariri's policies that failed, I think it should be noted that, even if they did not live up to the planners' high expectations, they did result in a number of important positive developments.

First, Hariri's government did succeed in establishing and maintaining a considerable degree of macro-economic stability. In particular, the Lebanese pound was stabilised and inflation was brought under control.

In addition, although the Horizon 2000 programme was not fully implemented, most segments of the plan dealing with the reconstruction of physical infrastructure were carried out to a significant degree, resulting in a vast improvement in terms of quality of life for the Lebanese people. In vital areas such as electricity, tele-communications, water, roads and transport, services were greatly restored. At the very least, this constituted a foundation on which Lebanon could continue to build. In short, some of the crucial structural prerequisites for recovery were put in place.

Finally, after an extended period in which the country had been a pariah state, Hariri's policies enabled Lebanon once again to engage positively with the international community. International companies returned to Lebanon. Western governments and international organisations demonstrated support for the country and its economic recovery in the form of monetary aid and diplomatic relations. And, even during the late 1990s, when economic performance was poor, foreign aid donors and investors continued to show some confidence in Lebanon's long-term prospects by providing further aid, subscribing to new Eurobond issues, etc.

However, as noted above, the Horizon 2000 plan was never fully implemented. While many of the projects designed to restore physical infrastructure were completed, some of the more ambitious infrastructure development projects designed to market the country as a dynamic business environment with state-of-the-art facilities had to be suspended or cancelled due to lack of finance, political infighting, bureaucratic obstacles and a host of other problems. By the time of Hariri's resignation in December 1998, the further implementation of the programme seemed to be indef-initely postponed. The aspects of the plan dealing with the restoration of vital social infrastructure and stimulation of the industry, agriculture and tourism sectors were almost completely abandoned for all practical intents and purposes.[20]

Furthermore, Hariri ultimately had neither the political will, nor the power, to carry out a substantive reform of the Lebanese public sector. Since a major proportion of the completed infrastructure projects were administered by the public sector, its continuing corruption and inefficiency raised serious questions about the long-term value even of those parts of the Horizon 2000 programme that were successfully implemented.

Perhaps the most significant point of all is that the private-sector investment and involvement in the Lebanese economy that the programme was supposed to encourage never really materialised. Crucial areas such as the stock market, tourism and industry were essentially neglected, and most investor interest was centred on the banking and property development/real estate sectors.[21]

Even this interest was problematic. Much of the money put into the banking sector was short-term, and in some cases contributed to the growing national debt problem, as it involved investment in high-interest government treasury bills. Furthermore, the interest in property development was concentrated at the high end of the market and entailed only a short-term boost for the Lebanese economy, contributing nothing to the productive sectors, long-term job creation, etc. This criticism could certainly be applied, to some extent, even to Hariri's most treasured private-sector initiatives such as the Beirut Central District project.

To a very great extent, I think the failure of the private sector to respond to the recovery process must be attributed to the problems introduced by Syrian penetration of the Lebanese system. The conflict in the South, the marginalisation of the Maronite and large expatriate communities, and Syrian interference in Lebanese foreign policy initiatives designed to attract international involvement in the recovery process would all seem to be particularly relevant here.

It should also be recognised, however, that even under much better conditions, it might have been difficult to get the international business community excited about the Lebanese recovery. Prior to the civil war, Lebanon occupied an almost unique role as a financial and cultural bridge between the Middle East and the West. During the war years, the world economy moved on. New regional centres of trade and banking were established, and the increasing momentum of the globalisation process established all kinds of new economic links. In short, even according to the best possible interpretation of post-war global realities, Lebanon faced a number of competitors, and must offer something new and exciting to re-establish itself in the market. At worst, Lebanon's traditional economic role was obsolete, or was in the process of becoming so, in which case the government would have been better advised to consider finding a new role instead of trying to recapture the old one.

One must conclude, on the basis of all these observations, that the Horizon 2000 programme failed in its primary goals. It certainly did not prompt Lebanon's re-emergence as a major regional centre of finance and trade. If such a recovery is even possible, it may take at least a generation. In the meantime, in the years immediately following the Horizon 2000 programme, the economy was in a severe recession. Although the recovery programme did go some way towards rebuilding the country's shattered infrastructure, its legacy also included an array of chronic structural problems. I have already commented on the scale of the national debt and its fiscal consequences. The government's policies also tended to increase the gap between rich and poor, continuing the progressive decimation of an already thin middle class. Corruption and its attendant problems in the public sector became more ingrained than ever. Finally, the country had not even begun to address the disenfranchisement of many of its citizens.

4.3 The Lebanese economy since 1998

The Hoss interlude (December 1998–autumn 2000)

By 1998, the growing debt problem and the collapse of the real estate sector had brought the economic recovery programme to a halt and ushered in a serious recession. Since Hariri's political *raison d'être* was to improve the economic situation, this left him in an untenable position *vis-à-vis* both his political rivals in Lebanon and the Syrians. As discussed in Chapter 3, new stress on the corruption issue and Emile Lahoud's election as President in September of 1998 further weakened Hariri's influence, and ultimately led to his resignation later in the year.

While Hariri began using his financial resources and patronage network to prepare for a political comeback in the 2000 elections, the Syrians turned to the "safe hands" of the technocratic several-times-former Prime Minister Salim Hoss to form a new government. Although respected, Hoss's political influence was extremely limited, and he was in no position to pursue a serious economic reform programme. While Lahoud tended to be the dominant figure in Lebanese politics during his government, Hoss effectively limited his efforts to introducing some degree of fiscal responsibility and attempting, largely unsuccessfully, to reduce the budget deficit.

The Hariri government (2000–04)

Hariri's extremely impressive showing in the 2000 elections provided him with a mandate to return as Prime Minister and attempt to resolve the continuing economic and, in particular, fiscal and financial crisis. Upon his returning to office, Hariri outlined and began to pursue his intended policies for turning the economy around.[22] These policies were eventually presented to major donors (including the World Bank and IMF) at the so-called Paris II meetings held in November 2002. The Hariri government asked for grants and concessionary loans to deal with its substantial debt load, as well as to assist with macro-economic adjustments and economic programme development. A combination of external and internal (central bank, private banks) sources provided the Lebanese government with over $10 billion, and helped the country, at least in the short term, deal with the immediate financial crisis.[23] The Paris II meetings also cemented a worrying trend (which began in 1997[24]) that saw subsequent Lebanese governments become dependent on foreign aid to stabilise Lebanon's macro-economic situation (in particular, financial and currency crises), a policy that largely continues to this day.

With respect to Hariri's programme, I would argue that, in essence, it did not differ very substantially from his previous policies or address the problems that critically undermined them. Therefore one must question the extent to which Hariri's return during this period provided real grounds for optimism about Lebanon's future prospects.

Hariri's primary emphasis on building infrastructure and encouraging private-sector activity remained largely unchanged. One of the first initiatives of the new government was to introduce an "open skies" policy and to cut customs duties significantly in order to promote trade. However, it should be noted that roughly 44 per cent of the Lebanese government's annual revenue was drawn from customs duties. Therefore the need to develop a reliable alternative source of public revenue was critical. Hariri's solution involved the introduction of value added tax (VAT) and the stricter enforcement of existing taxation statutes.

Additional sources of revenue were expected to be provided by new economic growth and the privatisation of several major public companies. With respect to the former, Hariri's financial experts were confidently predicting that the economy would emerge from its recession within the near future. This obviously would have been beneficial, but there were no guarantees that it would actually happen.

With respect to the privatisations, sources close to Hariri estimated that nearly $10 billion worth of revenue could be realised from the sales of EDL, Middle East Airlines (MEA) and other public service industries such as telecommunications. In addition, selling off some of the loss-making concerns would cut costs and free up public funds for other initiatives. Consequently, the privatisations were one of the central pillars of Hariri's reform agenda.

The other major segment of Hariri's recovery agenda basically involved continuing the infrastructure works and large private-sector projects he had initiated during his first period in office. To this end, the government's five-year development plan was estimated to cost in excess of $5 billion. Why this plan should be implemented more successfully, or do more to stimulate the private sector, than the Horizon 2000 plan was unclear.

Funding for the plan was problematic. The financial situation had only got worse, and the proposed cuts in customs revenue would not help. It might have been possible to spend some revenue from privatisations, once this materialised, and there was foreign aid promised during Paris II, although much of it was tied to substantial structural reforms being carried out.

Furthermore, the plan seemed no less likely than previous efforts to succumb to problems associated with Lebanon's public sector and government infighting. The government attempted to allay concerns about this by making a few changes to give the CDR more power, but in the absence of more substantive reform, these were of questionable benefit.

Finally, it should be pointed out that, if anything, Hariri was in a much weaker position to safeguard and carry forward his chosen policies than he was in the mid-1990s. With the national debt problem, increasing Arab–Israeli tensions, and the US government's new focus on the country as a breeding ground for international terrorism, Lebanon was hardly a more attractive prospect for private-sector investors than it had been previously. Moreover, with Syria facing increasing pressure to withdraw from Lebanon, it seemed likely that Damascus would do everything possible to tighten its control of the Lebanese government and to play off internal rivals against each other. In fact, much of the reforms proposed by Hariri and presented at the Paris II meetings failed to materialise because of the infighting among Lebanon's political leaders. In particular, the conflict between President Lahoud and his Syrian backers on one hand, and Hariri on the other, was particularly acrimonious and led to political stalemate and a largely dysfunctional political programme. In fact, the government was even unable to agree on the project to submit to the Paris II donors, meaning much of the money was not utilised.[25] Unable to pursue his political or economic programme, Hariri ultimately resigned. In the end, it was probably naive to assume that the prospects for economic recovery and promised structural and administrative reforms would not suffer significantly as a result of such destabilising political tensions.

The post-2005 governments of Fouad Siniora and Saad Hariri

The sudden and unexpected withdrawal of Syrian troops from Lebanon in April 2005, followed by the victory of the pro-Western March 14 movement in parliamentary elections later that summer, raised hopes that the country's economy would benefit after years of war and military occupation. The euphoria, however, was short-lived as it became quite clear that political realities ensured that Lebanon would continue to be subject to the same sorts of constraint that affected economic development prior to 2005, primarily the inability of Lebanese governments to stabilise the security situation or to pursue key public sector and administrative reforms.

With respect to the first point, the Siniora government not only failed to normalise the security situation by disarming Hizbollah, securing the Lebanese border with Israel (and Syria), and preventing violence between various groups, but the country's security situation actually deteriorated considerably for most of the government's tenure. According to estimates, Hizbollah's war with Israel in 2006 cost the economy hundreds of millions of dollars, although its actual cost may be considerably more.[26]

The likelihood of another conflict between Hizbollah and Israel remains a very real possibility, given the massive arms build-up that Hizbollah has undertaken in the years following the 2006 conflict, and the continuing tense regional situation between Israel and Iran (Hizbollah's patron). The continuing effects on the Lebanese economy will be great, and the hopes of many that the country can realise its true economic potential will have to wait for perhaps many years to come.[27]

In January of 2007, the international donor community met at the so-called Paris III conference to discuss aid to Lebanon, particularly in light of the recent conflict. The Siniora government presented to donors a new programme promising significant economic and structural reforms, including labour law and social security reforms, changes to the tax regime and further privatisation. The international community pledged over US$7 billion, although it is unclear how much of this is actually tied to genuine reforms, and how much the Lebanese government has actually received. It is also unclear how the Siniora government planned to pursue structural reforms in the context of a bitterly divided political situation, where the opposition held a veto over government decisions.

In fact, with respect to my second point, it is highly unlikely that any Lebanese government, even one operating under a more conducive political environment, could truly pursue the types of public sector and administrative reforms needed to improve economic development against entrenched political and bureaucratic interests. In the current political situation, a weak Lebanese government is in no position to do so, and that economic programme will continue to operate within the context of the normal bargaining process between the various sectarian elites inherent in the neo-patrimonial Lebanese political system.

I conclude this chapter with a few observations on the performance of the Lebanese economy during the 2007–09 period. The economy did see growth during these years, which is rather impressive, given the global recession. Three major reasons account for this, all of which are largely immune to the global economic situation, but which are not a sign of sustained economic development. First, the country saw record numbers of tourists, particularly in 2009, consisting mostly of Lebanese expatriates returning to Lebanon to visit family and friends. This type of tourism, which is somewhat less vulnerable to economic recession, accounted for over a quarter of Lebanon's GDP. Second, the construction industry saw important growth, but this was tied, in part, to the rebuilding after the 2006 war with Israel. Foreign aid, from the West, the Arab World and Iran (through its client Hizbollah), meant that resources were available. The construction industry also benefited from tourist-related projects, including hotels, private vacation homes and luxury resorts. And third, the fact that the Lebanese banking system was not tied significantly to the global financial sector, especially in the mortgage back securities industry, meant that it weathered the global economic crisis better than the banking sectors in most other countries. As a result, billions of dollars continued to be invested in Lebanon's banks, which have prospered.[28] However, while all three of these were somewhat immune to the global economic downturn, they remain highly vulnerable to either political instability or a deterioration of the security situation. Another war between Israel and Hizbollah, for example, would have a significantly negative impact on the economy, and in particular the tourist industry.

5

POST-WAR FOREIGN POLICY: SYRIAN PENETRATION AND LEBANESE INTERESTS[1]

In this chapter, I examine the foreign policy of Lebanon in the post-civil war context. The chapter is divided into two parts. Part I deals with Lebanese foreign policy during Syria's occupation (1990–2005). Part II focuses on the period following Syria's withdrawal (2005–10).

Part I is divided into two sections. In the first I identify, and examine in some detail, the major determinants of Lebanese foreign policy. The purpose of this section is to consider the interplay of Syrian and Lebanese national interests in order to understand how the dynamic relationship between the two has shaped Lebanese foreign policy since the end of the civil war. In the second section, I apply the observations and conclusions established in the first to a more specific examination of Lebanon's relations with key international actors from 1990 to 2005.

Part II explains Lebanese foreign policy decision-making since 2005, a period that could have transformed the country's foreign policy as it had developed under Syrian tutelage, but did not. Part II re-examines the determinants of Lebanese foreign policy, and addresses Lebanon's relations with key players in the international period since 2005.

PART I: UNDERSTANDING LEBANESE FOREIGN POLICY DURING SYRIA'S OCCUPATION, 1990–2005

With respect to Lebanon's foreign policy in the post-war context, a crucial problem is that many scholars and policy makers look at the dominant role that Damascus played in Lebanese politics and tend to assume that Lebanon really had no authentic foreign policy of its own.[2] In short, it was assumed that, if one wished to understand the reasoning and processes that underlay Lebanon's actions on the regional and international stages, one simply needed to understand Syria's national interests.[3]

As I have explained in the past few chapters, it must be acknowledged that Syria has undoubtedly been the dominant player in Lebanese politics during this period. Moreover, at the time, it seemed likely that effective Syrian hegemony in Lebanon would continue for years to come. Hence there is considerable merit in an approach to examining Lebanese foreign policy during this period that stresses Syrian involvement and Syrian interests.

However, such an approach does have significant limitations in the sense that it ignores: 1) the fact that the internal forces that have historically shaped Lebanese foreign policy were still present, and strongly relevant, in Lebanese society; 2) the desire of the vast majority of the Lebanese people to pursue a foreign policy based on Lebanese interests; and 3) contemporary political and economic circumstances which had generated Lebanese foreign policy imperatives that were separate from, and in some cases contrary to, Syria's interests.

I propose that it is very important to consider in detail not only Syria's influence, but also these three areas, in order to arrive at a more developed understanding of Lebanon's post-war foreign policy. This chapter then argues that, although Lebanon was a heavily penetrated state from 1990 to 2005, with a limited capacity to define and pursue its own foreign policy, it would be a serious overstatement to suggest that Lebanon had no authentic foreign policy of its own. Indeed, I suggest that, even among elements that tended to support Syria's position in Lebanon, there were indications of a desire to pursue policies that accorded more with Lebanon's independent interests than with Syria's interests. For example, quite a few Lebanese policy makers clearly would have welcomed an increase in Western, and particularly European, influence in Lebanon. On one hand, this would have counter-balanced Syrian influence to some extent; on the other, it would have helped the country to address some of its pressing economic concerns.[4]

5.1 The determinants of Lebanese foreign policy

Lebanese foreign policy in historical context

Before proceeding to consider the various interests and circumstances that trace their genesis to developments during the civil war, it is crucially important briefly to re-examine some key factors that have had an extremely significant bearing on Lebanese foreign policy since the foundation of the modern state in 1943. Although Syrian hegemony in post-war Lebanon has tended to blunt the influence of these factors to some extent, I argue that they remain largely unchanged and continue to constitute the basic imperatives and restraints that give rise to an authentic Lebanese foreign policy. Four factors are particularly significant.

The first is the relative weakness of the Lebanese state throughout the country's history. The political order created by the combination of the 1926 Constitution and the 1943 National Pact was not designed to impose a well-defined national vision or any kind of ideological or religious/cultural uniformity on Lebanon's sharply divided confessional communities. On the contrary, the political order evolved in such a way that it embraced Lebanon's religious/cultural diversity and enabled the various sectarian *zu'ama* to come together, to negotiate with each other and to resolve disputes, while at the same time maintaining effectively autonomous control within their traditional spheres of influence. Whenever the power of the state threatened to infringe on the power and prerogatives of the *zu'ama*, the leaders of the various sects worked together to undermine its strength.

In short, the fundamental pillar of the Lebanese state was compromise among the sectarian elites, and its function was simply to provide a forum for the representatives of the different confessions to resolve disputes arising in the sphere of national politics. Consequently, the state was never really in a position to dictate policy to the *zu'ama* and/or the sectarian interests they represented. Rather, national policy was consistently dictated by the need to ensure that none of the major elites or sects was alienated to the extent that it would opt out of the system and disrupt the national compromise.

Naturally, the nature of the state had major implications with respect to defining the parameters of Lebanon's foreign policy. This is strongly related to the second major factor that has historically characterised Lebanese foreign policy: the necessity of maintaining a neutral orientation *vis-à-vis* the West on the one hand and the Arab/Islamic world on the other.

As explained in Chapter 1, this imperative is the consequence of a long-standing rift between the Christian and Muslim sects concerning what Lebanon's basic international alignment should be. While Christian elements, particularly the Maronite community, have historically tended to favour strong ties to the West, the Muslim elements have favoured close ties with the Arab/Islamic world. The National Pact sought to defuse potential conflict over this issue once and for all by committing the nation to a neutral foreign policy orientation. Ostensibly, Lebanon would remain somewhat detached politically and ideologically, while at the same time retaining functional relations with both the West and its Arab/Muslim neighbours. Hence, during the 1950s and 1960s, Lebanese leaders worked hard to avoid engagement in the pan-Arab movement and limited the country's participation in the Arab–Israeli conflict to the extent that it was possible to do so.[5]

The need to maintain non-alignment accounts, to a very great extent, for the third key factor: the traditional primacy of economic interests with respect to defining Lebanon's foreign relations, at least inasmuch as these relations were conducted within the formal state context. Since issues of political and cultural relations were extremely sensitive, and generally downplayed, the overwhelming preoccupation of formal Lebanese foreign policy for most of the period prior to the civil war was economic relations, especially the promotion and maintenance of Lebanon's status as the key financial and commercial centre of the Eastern Mediterranean. Obviously, the health of Lebanon's economy has always been a common interest that transcended confessional divisions, and it may be no exaggeration to say that many Lebanese have historically viewed it as the one truly national interest that the state exists to serve.[6]

However, the relative weakness of the state, coupled with the continuing importance of sectarian divisions, also accounts for the fourth factor that has historically characterised the Lebanese system and had a significant impact on its foreign relations: a high level of susceptibility to penetration by external actors. As the course of Lebanese history demonstrates all too clearly, the fact that the Lebanese as a nation officially adopted a neutral foreign policy did not mean that the different sectarian communities completely abandoned their traditional aspirations with respect to shaping the future direction of Lebanese society as a whole.[7]

Furthermore, although policy in the state context remained neutral for the most part, it should be remembered that the sectarian *zu'ama* continued to be effectively autonomous actors and to wield most of the real power in Lebanese society. This meant that the different communities historically tended to continue developing informal relations with their preferred international partners in the West and in the Arab world. Consequently, foreign elements probably always had a greater influence on the Lebanese system than the officially neutral foreign policy of the state would have suggested.[8]

Certainly, the actual or perceived existence of sectarian foreign agendas generated considerable inter-communal mistrust and greatly increased tensions in Lebanese society. Undoubtedly, this became a critical problem in the years leading up to the civil war. Lebanese Muslim support for the PLO presence in Lebanon during the early 1970s had two catastrophically destabilising consequences: 1) it dramatically inflamed internal tensions between the Christian and Muslim communities; and 2) it opened Lebanon to much more extensive, and more visible, penetration by the international actors engaged in the Arab–Israeli conflict.

Syrian penetration of the Lebanese system: 1990–2005

Because the focus of this chapter is on contemporary Lebanese foreign policy, I will not reiterate in detail the significance of various developments during the civil war period. At this point, it will suffice to state once again that the most important lasting development, not just in terms of Lebanon's foreign policy, but with respect to the political order as a whole, was that the country became exposed to overwhelming penetration by Syria, to the extent that Lebanon's existence as a truly independent national entity was legitimately questioned during this period.[9]

As noted in Chapter 3, Syria's primary interest with respect to maintaining control of Lebanon has always been firmly based on its own foreign policy imperatives, particularly its desire to maintain effective leverage in its negotiations with Israel concerning the return of the Golan Heights and other security arrangements. And, of course, the key source of Syrian leverage throughout the post-war period has been the continuation of the South Lebanon conflict. Thus, during the implementation of the Ta'if Accord, Damascus adopted measures designed to ensure that: 1) the South Lebanon conflict would be extended indefinitely; and 2) Syria, rather than any other actor, would be (and would be perceived to be) the decisive influence with respect to moderating and ultimately resolving the conflict.

First, Syria used its position as external guarantor of the Ta'if Accord to protect Hizbollah from the disarmament process that was successfully applied to the other sectarian militias. The explicit purpose of this was to enable Hizbollah to continue its efforts to liberate the Southern "security zone" from Israel. Hence it was clear from this point forward that the border conflict would continue. It was also fairly clear that Hizbollah had become a proxy combatant. The point of this observation is not to question the militia's genuine ideological commitment to the cause, or the fact that it was acting in accordance with its own interests. Rather, it calls attention to the fact that other interests were involved.[10]

One might argue that the interests of the Lebanese government and the Lebanese nation were being served by the war of liberation. However, this is highly questionable given: 1) the outrage expressed by other sects that had been forced to cooperate with the disarmament process;[11] 2) the general desire of the Lebanese people to put the war behind them and rebuild the country; and 3) the negative impact the conflict would have on the country's efforts to rehabilitate its image, attract aid and investment for the recovery process, and shield itself from Israeli reprisal attacks.

Syria, on the other hand, could benefit from the conflict without jeopardising any of its vital interests. Because it was not directly involved, and because none of the attacks on Israeli targets emanated from Syrian territory, there would be no reprisal attacks on Syria. Furthermore, since the Syrian forces were still the strongest military element on the ground in Lebanon, and since Syria had some influence due to its patronage of the Hizbollah movement, Damascus was in a good potential position to intervene, either to moderate or even to end the conflict. Whether or not they would do so was clearly to be determined by the incentive the Israelis provided for them on the negotiating table.

Damascus was also able to use the Ta'if process to establish the Treaty of Brotherhood and a range of coordination committees and other institutions designed to ensure its long-term control of Lebanese foreign and security policy.[12] The principal result of this was that it prevented the Lebanese government from entering into independent negotiations with Israel either to conclude a comprehensive peace agreement or to resolve the South Lebanon conflict. Since "coordination" of Lebanese and Syrian foreign policy really meant subordination of Lebanese to Syrian foreign policy, outstanding issues between Syria and Israel would have to be resolved before Lebanese–Israeli issues could be addressed.

As events developed throughout the 1990s and early 2000s, sporadic Syrian–Israeli negotiations yielded no substantive results, perhaps largely due to the fact that the more fundamental Israeli–Palestinian negotiations stalled and then collapsed. In the meantime, the intensity of the South Lebanon conflict has ebbed and flowed, generally with consequences detrimental to authentic Lebanese interests, especially in the economic sphere. Of course, Hizbollah's military campaign did succeed in eroding Israeli resolve, and the resulting withdrawal of Israeli forces from the security zone in May 2000 was welcomed by the vast majority of Lebanese. Of course, one must question whether or not a stronger and more independent Lebanese government would have been able to achieve the same result through diplomacy, possibly more quickly and without the same negative consequences.

Furthermore, Hizbollah's subsequent use of the relatively minor Shiba Farms dispute as justification for continuing anti-Israeli activities was almost certainly more in Syria's interest (as well as Hizbollah's) than Lebanon's. In short, Syria had come to rely on Hizbollah activism as a bargaining chip *vis-à-vis* Israel. When the unilateral Israeli withdrawal from South Lebanon removed the ostensible *raison d'être* for Hizbollah's continuing armed status, a new pretext had to be found.

As also noted in Chapter 3, Syria's economic interests in Lebanon increased steadily over time. These interests were not really compatible with the confrontational orientation of Syrian foreign and security interests in the country, a point considered in more detail below. On the other hand, protecting these economic interests, which were strongly resented by many Lebanese, gave Damascus another compelling reason to attempt to maintain its military presence indefinitely.

The residuum of authentic Lebanese foreign policy: 1990–2005

Clearly, it is impossible to establish firmly what Lebanese foreign policy would have looked like in the absence of overwhelming Syrian influence. However, I would suggest that it is possible to make some very defensible educated guesses. For example, it seems likely that an independent Lebanese government would have made a concerted attempt to disarm Hizbollah along with the other sectarian militias in the early 1990s, and in all likelihood would have disengaged from the Arab–Israeli conflict while it focused on the economic reconstruction of the country.[13]

With respect to the disarmament issue, it is not clear during the early post-war period that any of the sectarian communities really would have supported continuing Hizbollah military operations, including elements within the Shiite community. On the contrary, there was a fairly apparent consensus across the confessions that it was time to end hostilities and concentrate on rebuilding the country. Moreover, it is probable that strong Maronite feelings about the issue, and the specific disarmament provisions of the Ta'if Accord, would have forced the state to take action even if the other sects were not broadly supportive concerning the disarmament of Hizbollah.

Having carried out the complete disarmament of the militias, the next compelling priority would have been the resolution of other security issues, including securing the Southern border with Israel by preventing any paramilitary groups from using it as a theatre of operation. The stability that would have followed from this was, after all, viewed by most Lebanese and outside observers at the time as critically important because it would have created the most favourable environment for carrying out the reconstruction of the country's shattered infrastructure and economy. In the sphere of foreign policy, it would have advanced two important objectives related to the recovery process: 1) attracting foreign aid and investment to support the recovery process; and 2) facilitating the positive involvement, and even partial reintegration, of Lebanon's significant expatriate communities.

In the absence of Syrian involvement, and assuming that Lebanon and Israel could have come to an understanding (official or otherwise), these two priorities would almost certainly have become the fundamental basis of Lebanese foreign relations throughout most of the 1990s. Even as events actually developed, the Lebanese government attempted to pursue these two objectives. However, their efforts to do so were severely hampered by the continuing conflict in the South and by Syrian interference whenever they attempted to engage any foreign actor that Syria feared might pose a challenge to its interests in Lebanon.

This last point is particularly significant, because the purpose of all my speculation about what the shape of a truly independent Lebanese foreign policy might have been like during this period is to clarify the nature of the relationship between Lebanon and Syria with respect to defining the country's foreign policy. I would suggest that the key fact one needs to bear in mind is that Syria did not control Lebanon to the extent that authentic Lebanese interests had been effectively subsumed by Syrian interests.

On the contrary, a clear distinction can still be made between the two, and it seems likely that the nature of Lebanese interests throughout the 1990s would have been virtually identical, irrespective of Syrian involvement. That is to say, the settlement of the South Lebanon conflict, the attraction of foreign aid and investment for the recovery process, and the establishment of closer relations with Lebanese expatriate communities would have been Lebanon's key foreign policy objectives, one way or the other. Syria's influence in Lebanon, in the pursuit of Syrian foreign policy objectives such as the continuation of the South Lebanon conflict, compromised the Lebanese government's ability to pursue these objectives effectively. However, at least to the extent that the government attempted to pursue them, the residuum of an authentic Lebanese foreign policy existed.

In order to understand fully the imperatives and constraints that have shaped authentic Lebanese foreign policy initiatives since the end of the civil war, it is necessary to assess the continuing influence of the four major factors that have historically helped to shape Lebanese foreign policy. Although Syrian dominance of the Lebanese political order affected all of these factors to some extent, it can be argued that they were all still present, and still strongly relevant in Lebanese society.

With respect to the first factor – the traditional weakness of the Lebanese state – the post-Ta'if political order was intended to create a more even balance of power between the Christian and Muslim sects, but otherwise did not envisage major changes with respect to the role and/or power of the state institutions. The Lebanese state was still fairly weak and its function was still, at least ostensibly, dependent on the voluntary cooperation of the sectarian elites. The *zu'ama* continued to wield much of the real political power and influence within Lebanese society through their control of communal patronage networks.

An extremely important point that must be remembered with respect to this observation, however, is that Syrian hegemony actually disrupted the sectarian balance and led to the effective marginalisation of the Maronite community from the formal political process. This severely undermined the legitimacy of the restored state institutions and made it almost impossible for the state to engage in constructive relations with expatriate Maronite elements. This was a fairly significant blow to economic reconstruction efforts, since the expatriate Maronite communities potentially had much to contribute.

Clearly, the Treaty of Brotherhood, Cooperation and Coordination with Syria was a critical departure with respect to the second factor – the historical neutrality of

Lebanese foreign policy *vis-à-vis* the West and the Arab/Islamic world. One may certainly question, however, the extent to which the Lebanese people at the mass level have ever viewed such a close alignment with Syria as legitimate. It is not surprising that the Maronites have been strongly opposed from the beginning, but there is evidence to suggest that Lebanese Muslims, especially within the Sunni community, have also been deeply concerned about the nature and extent of Syria's continuing role in Lebanon throughout the past decade. Rhetorical support for greater Islamic solidarity and Arab brotherhood aside, elements within the Muslim communities have frequently joined with Christians in protests about: 1) Syria's continuing occupation of Lebanon; 2) Syrian penetration of the Lebanese labour market and other segments of the economy; 3) policies that have threatened the economic recovery or stability of the post-war political order; and 4) the great extent to which Syrian interference in the electoral process and the formation of governments has limited the public accountability of the state institutions. Of course, the situation was complicated particularly within the Shiite community, whose leaders (Amal and Hizbollah in particular) were clients of the Syrian regime and benefited greatly from the Syrian presence in the country.[14]

The third major historical factor – the primacy of Lebanese economic interests in the foreign policy sphere – continued to be crucially significant. In fact, the international climate of the 1990s helped to shift the balance of Lebanon's post-war foreign policy orientation back towards the West, despite the unprecedented alignment with the Arab world that Syrian influence had imposed. In short, since much of the Arab/Muslim world, including Syria to some extent, had been attempting to cultivate closer relations to the Western powers in order to attract aid, to improve trade relations, and to become more engaged in the economic globalisation process generally, Lebanon had also been free to some extent to attempt to cultivate closer relations.[15]

Furthermore, Syria was generally happy to allow the Lebanese government substantial autonomy in the economic sphere for much of the post-war period, provided that its basic foreign policy and security interests were not threatened. In due course, this created opportunities for the Lebanese government to pursue some more-or-less independent foreign policy initiatives designed to support the economic recovery. There were several reasons for Syria's willingness to cede control to the Lebanese government in the economic sphere.

First, it should be recalled that protests over worsening economic conditions brought down the first two post-war Lebanese governments. Syria had manipulated these governments to strongly secure its long-term dominance of the Lebanese system, but, by the second half of 1992, the pressing need to do something about the economy had begun to threaten the viability of the post-war order as a whole. As Syria did not have a particularly strong interest in becoming engaged in an economic recovery process that was bound to be fraught with difficulties, it was content to allow a new, primarily economically motivated, Lebanese government under Rafiq Hariri to direct the reconstruction efforts.

Second, allowing the Lebanese government substantial autonomy in the economic sphere reduced both international and internal Lebanese protests at Syria's dominance of the country, both of which had become very significant after the 1992 elections. Recognising the traditional importance accorded to economic matters in the Lebanese context, the Syrians clearly hoped that granting the Lebanese substantial autonomy in this area would placate many Lebanese opponents of the post-war order. And, indeed, in retrospect it must be conceded that this policy was fairly effective. It encouraged many Lebanese not so much to accept the legitimacy of the Syrian presence as to accept that, since the political situation could not be addressed effectively in the short term, they should make the best of things and start to re-engage in fairly normal economic and social relations.

Finally, by placing substantial control of the economy in Lebanese hands, it seemed likely that the Syrians were hoping to immunise themselves from ultimate responsibility in the case of economic crisis. In the 1992 protests, many Lebanese made little distinction between their discontent at economic conditions and their discontent at the Syrian presence, because the Lebanese governments up to that time were clearly perceived to be working for Syria's interests and neglecting the economy. A similar problem was rendered much less likely by the new arrangement in which the Lebanese government would be more directly responsible for economic affairs.

And, in fact, when the reconstruction process stalled and the economy went into recession in the late 1990s, Hariri and his government did take most of the blame, even though Syrian policies and priorities had caused some serious problems. One of these problems was related to Syria's tendency to play off major Lebanese political figures against each other to keep any one Lebanese leader from becoming too powerful – opposing Hariri to Speaker of the House Nabih Birri, bringing in Lahoud to further erode Hariri's influence, etc. This produced frequent political deadlock within the Lebanese state context, and certainly negatively affected the recovery process. Other problems were located more properly in the foreign policy sphere.

For example, Syria's need to maintain the conflict in South Lebanon had serious economic consequences. The periodic Israeli reprisal attacks against Hizbollah, particularly the two major operations in 1993 and 1996, not only inflicted substantial material damage but also had an incalculable negative impact on the Lebanese government's abilities to enlist much-needed foreign aid and investment to support the recovery process. Additional damage of the same kind was caused by Syria's constant efforts to limit Lebanese government contacts with major powers, such as France and the United States, that potentially could organise greater international pressure for a Syrian withdrawal from Lebanon, a resolution of the South Lebanon conflict, and so on.

The overriding point that must be stressed concerning Syria's foreign policy and security interests on one hand, and Lebanon's economic interests on the other, is that the two have never been particularly compatible. In fact, it is difficult to escape the conclusion that they were almost diametrically opposed.

Syria needed a certain amount of instability in the Lebanese context in order to: 1) justify its own military presence in the country; and 2) retain the Lebanese situation as a useful bargaining chip in its ongoing negotiations with Israel. Furthermore, in order to protect against Lebanese state challenges to its dominant role in Lebanon, it needed to continue to play off Lebanese government leaders against each other. By doing so, Syria was able to: 1) keep any one leader from becoming too strong; 2) ensure against the possibility of an inter-confessional anti-Syrian coalition in the Lebanese government; and 3) secure its own position as the arbiter through which individual Lebanese leaders must work if they wished to advance any kind of policy agenda.

Conversely, the long-term interests of the Lebanese economy either outright required, or would have been greatly facilitated by: 1) a greater level of systemic stability to secure the benefits of reconstruction and enhance the country's economic relations with external elements; 2) a higher level of consensus and cooperation within the government so that economic policy could be smoothly and effectively drawn up and implemented; 3) a more satisfactory resolution of internal sectarian tensions to achieve and safeguard both of the above; and 4) some effort to get the expatriate communities involved once again in the economic life of the country.

It is probably also worth noting, at this point, that the increasing intertwinement of the Syrian and Lebanese economies already began to generate a significant conflict of economic versus security interests for Syria. In short, if the Lebanese economy continued to perform poorly, it would not have been good for the Syrian economy, and furthermore it would almost certainly eventually have led to even greater public protest in Lebanon about Syria's continuing restrictions on Lebanese foreign policy. These considerations could have compelled the Syrians to allow the Lebanese government to pursue freer relations with major international economic powers, even if this held some risk that the major powers would become more closely involved in the politics of Syrian–Lebanese relations. Of course, it is also possible that, as Syria became more and more invested in the health of Lebanon's economy, the Syrian leadership could have rethought its willingness to let the Lebanese exercise so much autonomy in the economic sphere. The practical difficulties of reasserting economic control would, however, probably have been very significant. Lebanese public opposition would certainly have been difficult to manage, and Syria would also have had to consider its own need to cultivate closer relations with major Western actors, who would have been very likely to strongly oppose such a move.

As has already been indicated, a new complication in terms of Lebanon's international standing and the government's ability to promote better relations with potential trading partners and international aid donors was introduced by 9/11 and the ensuing war on terrorism. These events resulted in a considerable amount of negative world attention towards Lebanon as a breeding ground of international terrorism, and the major Western powers have urged the Lebanese government to do something about Hizbollah and Islamic radicalism within the Lebanese context. However, there was some awareness among Western policy makers that Syrian compliance would be required before the Lebanese government could take any effective action against Hizbollah.

This situation leads nicely into a consideration of the fourth factor that has historically played a crucial role in shaping Lebanon's foreign policy: the country's high level of susceptibility to penetration by foreign actors. With respect to the whole issue of foreign penetration, the post-war period has been the worst in Lebanese history, even if one only considers Syrian penetration of the Lebanese system. Israeli penetration has also been significant for much of the period, although this has been less of a factor since Israel's withdrawal from South Lebanon. Other foreign actors such as Iran have also continued to exert influence via ties with Hizbollah and other Shiite Lebanese elements. In fact, as we will see below, Iran's influence in Lebanon increased significantly post-2005. Other Arab countries, most especially Saudi Arabia, have significant influence with key Lebanese political actors, particularly within the Sunni community. Meanwhile, the Maronites, marginalised from the formal political process, have attempted to use their traditional connections and expatriate communities to raise Western awareness about the continuing disenfranchisement of the Lebanese people.

I would suggest that something very interesting, and basically unprecedented, was also happening with respect to the fourth factor. As noted above, the main reasons underlying Lebanon's traditional susceptibility to foreign penetration were the weakness of the state, and the existence of strong sectarian tensions about the country's political alignment *vis-à-vis* the West and the Arab/Muslim world. The weakness of the state continued to be significant, particularly since the critically important Maronite community had very little involvement in the formal institutions, and therefore must, to a very great extent, pursue its interests outside the state context.[16] However, there were some indications that sectarian tensions about the country's foreign policy alignment were somewhat defused by developing circumstances throughout the 1990s.

The important policy shift that led many Arab/Muslim states to pursue closer relations with the West has already been cited. This means that, for the time being at least, closer relations with the West and with Lebanon's Arab/Muslim neighbours were not mutually exclusive. A second, and probably even more significant, development was the emergence of a fairly stable consensus across confessional lines, and at both elite and popular levels, that Syria must eventually withdraw from Lebanon. It should be pointed out, however, that the level of anti-Syrian feeling varied considerably among the different sectarian groups. For example, the Maronites were fiercely anti-Syrian, whereas the Shiite community entertained a more complex relationship with Syria. Although Syria continued to exert almost complete dominance over the state institutions, it must be noted once again that Lebanon was a fairly weak state, and that the sectarian elites still exercised massive influence in Lebanese political life, even if much of this was informal and difficult to explore in detail.

It is probably no exaggeration to say that, for most Lebanese operating outside the formal state context, the most important foreign policy objective of the Lebanese nation at the time was to work for a Syrian withdrawal and a reassertion of Lebanese autonomy both domestically and with respect to foreign affairs. Popular opposition to the continuing Syrian presence increased steadily throughout this period and became particularly pronounced after Israel's withdrawal from South Lebanon in May of 2000. The Syrians' repressive response to this increasing pressure did not really help their cause as far as the Lebanese people were concerned, and it also raised some concerns internationally, leading the UN Security Council in September 2004 to demand Syria's withdrawal from Lebanon.[17]

5.2 Lebanon and the international community

The purpose of this section is to apply the observations and conclusions established in the previous section to a more specific examination of Lebanon's relations with key actors in the international community from 1990 to 2005. The crucial overriding conclusion one must draw here is that Lebanese foreign relations during this period have been rather limited.

Partly, this is attributable to the fact that Syria strongly opposed close Lebanese relations with any external actors who could potentially pose a challenge to its long-term interests in Lebanon. Needless to say, this certainly included the USA, other permanent UN Security Council members including Britain, France and Russia, and other influential Arab countries. It also included major economic powers, including all of the above, as well as other major EU countries.

Even in the absence of Syrian objections, however, it is not clear that Lebanese relations with the international community would have developed to a significantly greater degree. There are three major points that one must consider here.

The first is that Lebanon emerged from the civil war as a pariah state with very little to offer the international community in terms of vital political or economic interests. Prior to the war, Lebanon was widely seen as a stable state with a moderating regional influence, and it served an important function as a key centre for commerce and banking. By the end of the war, Lebanon had come to be seen as a potentially destabilising element in the regional balance of power, and had lost its traditionally important economic role to other regional competitors. Furthermore, it had a new and unenviable reputation as a dangerous place to do business. While the Lebanese reconstruction potentially represented substantial economic opportunities, it was unclear that the country would be able to reward its investors, pay its bills, honour its contracts, or guarantee the safety of foreign consultants and workers.

The second major point is that the continuation of the Arab–Israeli conflict led most major global actors to treat those states actively engaged in the conflict with a great deal of sensitivity. The common international interest in resolving the conflict and securing regional stability was generally perceived as a higher priority than individual countries' policy initiatives and preferences with respect to economic relations and issues such as political reform. In short, there was no desire potentially to antagonise any of the participants in the conflict by pressing them urgently to resolve what were perceived as lesser political and economic differences. With respect to the Lebanese situation, this meant that until the 2003–04 period most of the major global actors remained very wary about pressing for an immediate Syrian withdrawal, since the issue would presumably be addressed as part of a Syrian–Israeli and/or Lebanese–Israeli peace settlement. It is telling that Syria prior to 2003–04 was not even subjected to economic sanctions or other mild forms of practical coercion as a means of encouraging it to withdraw its forces from the country and/or to allow for greater Lebanese autonomy.[18]

A third, and to some extent related, point is that many international actors were also reluctant to press for a Syrian withdrawal due to fears about internal Lebanese stability in the absence of a strong external presence.[19] No one wanted to risk a new eruption of sectarian conflict in the country, particularly as this might escalate once again into a regional conflict and thereby critically destabilise an already precarious situation.[20]

Lebanon and the USA[21]

The USA is the major Western actor in the Middle East, but its interaction with Lebanon since the end of the civil war has been rather limited. To some extent this may be due to its active engagement as the primary moderator in the Middle East peace process. The issue of Lebanese–Israeli relations has long been regarded by the USA and most of the other actors involved in the Arab–Israeli conflict as a lower priority than Palestinian–Israeli and Syrian–Israeli relations, in that order. In the meantime, particularly as there has been little movement with respect to resolving the other two components of the conflict, the USA has had little desire to complicate matters by opening a third track of negotiations.

It should be remembered that the USA, along with Saudi Arabia, was one of the major sponsors of the Ta'if Accord, and therefore helped bring an end to the civil war. Apparently, the key objective was the restoration of relative regional stability that this engendered. The US response to Syria's manipulation of the Ta'if implementation process demonstrated that Washington would protest against Syrian violations of Lebanese sovereignty, but was not prepared, at least until 2003–04, to intervene actively or to take any measures that might: 1) risk a resurgence of the conflict and the regional implications that such would entail; or 2) alienate Syria and thereby limit US ability to encourage and mediate Syrian–Israeli peace negotiations.

Thus US officials occasionally made statements criticising Syrian interference in Lebanese politics, and after the 1992 elections helped to put pressure on Syria to allow a more independent Lebanese government. However, Washington never introduced sanctions or placed Syria under any kind of substantial pressure to withdraw from Lebanon. In fact, as the 1990s progressed, US opposition to Syria's presence in the country became increasingly muted. Only within the context of the post-9/11 period has Washington put any sort of real diplomatic pressure on Syria to quit Lebanon.

During the course of the economic reconstruction, the Lebanese government made a number of attempts to gain financial aid and investment from the US government and US private-sector interests. For example, Prime Minister Hariri made numerous trips to the USA, trying to win increased American support. However, these efforts were largely unsuccessful. Total US public and private contributions to the Lebanese recovery programme were minimal. A great part of the problem was the fact that the US State Department continued to impose a ban preventing US citizens from travelling to Lebanon. Even though the American government acknowledged that the Lebanese government was not hostile, it continued to view the country as unsafe for US citizens.

This line of policy was probably related, at least in part, to the continuation of the South Lebanon conflict, and what the USA perceived as Lebanon's tolerance for international Islamist and radical elements such as Hizbollah. Throughout the 1990s, the US government periodically made strenuous demands that the Lebanese government should disarm Hizbollah and take vigorous action to restrict other international extremist elements. These calls increased in frequency and intensity after 9/11.

On the other hand, it should be noted that the USA limited its response on this issue to rhetorical protest. It did not initiate sanctions or openly discuss the possibility of taking military action, measures it has taken against other nations it identified as sponsors of terrorism. This restraint probably suggests that there was considerable recognition in Washington that Syria, rather than the Lebanese government, was the critical actor with respect to Hizbollah disarmament and the final resolution of what remained of the South Lebanon border dispute.

Lebanon and the EU

It should be noted, first of all, that European influence in the Middle Eastern region as a whole was not particularly great. This is somewhat ironic, given that the EU is the region's largest trading partner and one of its main sources of financial assistance. However, Europe has never been able to translate these economic factors into particularly significant political influence. This fact is probably partly a result of great resistance to outside influences by many key regimes in the region. It is also partly explained by EU reluctance to impinge on an area where US influence is dominant. A final factor is the nature of inter-European relations. Although there is some policy coordination within the auspices of the EU, this does not generally extend into the political dimension of foreign policy. Furthermore, as the EU currently lacks a common security mechanism of its own, its ability to apply coercive force in the region is very limited.

Although Europe was greatly concerned by developments within Lebanon during the civil war, such as the violence of the conflict, intervention by regional powers such as Israel and Syria, the taking of Western hostages, and other terrorist activities, their actual involvement in attempting to end the civil war was quite limited. Ultimately, the European powers supported the Ta'if Accord, even if they did not actively promote it. This support became increasingly muted as it became clear that Syria was using its status as external guarantor of the accord in order to effectively take long-term control of the Lebanese political system. The European Commission and some individual countries, France particularly, were outspoken in their criticism of developments in the early 1990s, particularly the Treaty of Brotherhood and the controversial 1992 elections. There were additional sporadic protests throughout the balance of the decade about the extent of Syrian influence and the increasingly repressive policies used to secure it. Obviously, none of these had any real impact on Syrian policy. However, as noted elsewhere, France worked with the USA in 2004 to push for the UN Resolution calling for Syria's withdrawal from Lebanon.

With respect to funding for the Hariri government's ambitious economic reconstruction programme, European donors were very important. Of the $3.1 billion of foreign funding (including grants and loans) that the Lebanese government raised between 1992 and 1996, 13 per cent came from the European Investment Bank, 11 per cent from Italy, 9 per cent from France and 3 per cent from the Commission of European Communities. Additionally, around $800 million was raised from a series of very well-received Eurobond issues from 1994 to 1996. Of course, this funding did not meet Hariri's (somewhat unrealistic) external funding targets. Furthermore, it is clear that the European financing was not necessarily based on the most altruistic of motives. Only about 13 per cent of the money came from outright grants, and it has also been suggested that much of the aid supplied by Italy and France was tied to guarantees that lucrative infrastructure reconstruction projects would be awarded to Italian and French companies.[22]

Apart from financial aid earmarked specifically for the reconstruction programme, various EU actors have contributed funds for various purposes, including humanitarian aid and EU-funded projects designed to foster economic development and structural adjustment. Since 1995, Lebanon has been among the leading per capita beneficiaries of EU assistance to Euro–Mediterranean partners.

Lebanon's post-war efforts to restore traditionally good trade relations with Europe, and to achieve closer trade integration, generally met with greater success. Europe has long been Lebanon's leading trade partner, although it should be recognised that the balance of trade always heavily favoured Europe, with the value of Lebanese imports *vis-à-vis* Europe far outweighing that of their exports. Since 1978, Lebanese–European trade relations have been governed by a Cooperation Agreement under which Lebanese industrial goods enjoyed duty- and quota-free access to EC/EU markets.[23]

In January of 2002, as part of the Euro–Mediterranean Partnership Initiative (EMPI), the EU and Lebanon concluded a new Association Agreement, which provided for the further liberalisation of bilateral trade. European duties on most Lebanese agricultural products were immediately removed and, in turn, Lebanon committed itself to the reduction of tariff barriers on EU industrial and agricultural products over periods specified in the agreement. The agreement also entailed, at least in principle, intensified political dialogue and cooperation across a wide range of fields, from education and culture to international law enforcement and improvements in human rights and democratisation.[24]

Particularly given these final provisions calling for closer political relations, it may seem somewhat surprising that Syria actually allowed Lebanon to conclude the Association Agreement. In the past, the Syrian leadership tended to veto any agreement that raised even the possibility of greater European involvement in Lebanese affairs outside the strictly economic sphere. Their willingness to allow more latitude in this case may be partly explained by the agreement's economic importance, and Syria's own increasing stake in the Lebanese economy. Additionally, it should be noted that Syria itself was also involved in the EMPI and may have elected to enter into a similar agreement at some stage.

A final point concerning Lebanese–EU relations is that the types of mostly economic interaction examined above have generally helped Lebanon to greatly rehabilitate its image on the international stage. This improvement would have been much more difficult, if not impossible, if European actors had not welcomed and fostered Lebanon's return to the international fold. It may be a significant indicator of European support for Lebanon that the negotiations for the new EMPI Association Agreement were concluded some months after 9/11, at a time when some other Western actors, most notably the USA, were heavily criticising the Lebanese government for its failure to deal with Hizbollah and other alleged terrorist elements in the country.

Lebanon and the Arab/Muslim world

Lebanon has enjoyed functional relations with virtually all of the countries in the Arab/Muslim world throughout the post-war period. Naturally, the Western conception of the country as a pariah state never had much influence within the region, especially since a number of other Arab and Islamic countries fell within the same category. The end of sectarian violence and the introduction of a government closely linked with Syria were sufficient conditions for most Arab/Muslim countries to re-establish full working relations with Lebanon.

Of course, Lebanon was obliged by the Treaty of Brotherhood and other mechanisms to follow Syria's lead very closely in its relations with all the regional states. Since Syria had enjoyed reasonably good relations with the other regional powers since the Gulf War of 1991, Lebanon was able to maintain cordial relations with all of these states as well. However, its unilateral contacts with the same countries were relatively limited. That is to say, Lebanon was only really allowed to pursue initiatives approved by Syria in the first instance. It did not have much more of an independent foreign policy *vis-à-vis* the Arab/Muslim world than it had in its relations with the West.

Lebanon has had a special and rather complicated relationship with Shiite Iran. Since the 1980s, Iran has played an active role in encouraging and supporting Lebanon's large Shiite community, who drew their inspiration from the Iranian revolution. Iran has provided the community with material resources, and has been Hizbollah's patron, helping to build the organisation and providing it with the resources necessary to offer the Shiite community patronage, as well as to conduct a guerrilla campaign against Israel. Iran's influence within Lebanon, however, was greatly curtailed and controlled by Syria, which also had considerable influence within the Shiite community, including the Hizbollah movement. In other words, Iran's role was rather limited and was largely determined by its own dynamic relationship with its Syrian ally. Again, as we will see below, Iran's influence has greatly increased since 2005.

To some extent, Lebanon also has had a special relationship with Saudi Arabia, which some Lebanese observers hoped might eventually help to balance Syrian involvement in the country. After all, Saudi Arabia was one of the key sponsors of the Ta'if Accord, and also one of the driving forces behind Rafiq Hariri's political career. Furthermore, the Saudis were the most significant Arab financial contributors to the Lebanese recovery process. In addition, Saudi Arabia was also seen as a potential mediator between Lebanon and the USA, with hopes that they could be able to persuade the Americans to adopt a more supportive policy with respect to a number of issues. There is little evidence to suggest that Saudi efforts in this area, during this period, have borne much fruit. Indeed, I would contend that it is very important not to overstate the whole notion of Saudi Arabia as a major actor in the Lebanese context. Although its influence with the Sunni community has been strong, to all practical intents and purposes Saudi influence from 1990 to 2005 has been relatively limited, especially in relation to Syria's role in the country.

The economic recovery programme was one area where Lebanese relations with the Arab states were reasonably significant. The Gulf Arab states, particularly, were among the leading aid donors and sources of private-sector investment. To cite some examples: the Arab Fund for Economic and Social Development contributed 12 per cent of all foreign aid to the first phase of the reconstruction; the Kuwait Fund for Arab Economic Development contributed 6 per cent; and the Saudi government and a number of Saudi-based donors contributed approximately 15 per cent.[25]

Lebanese expatriate communities

A final point that merits some consideration in the context of Lebanese international relations is the country's dealings with its substantial expatriate communities.

Probably the most politically significant expatriate communities are based in the EU states. The expatriate Maronite community in France is probably the most important example in terms of influence. It included some of the most prominent Lebanese political exiles and opponents of the Syrian-dominated post-war order, such as General Michel Aoun, and worked tirelessly: 1) to call Western attention to Syrian abuses of Lebanese sovereignty; and 2) to lobby the French government and the EU to give more support to authentic Lebanese interests and to impose greater pressure on Syria to withdraw from the country.

Although these efforts certainly did the Lebanese cause no harm, and probably helped to raise the general level of French and Western awareness of, and sympathy for, continuing problems in Lebanon, they did not translate into much practical support from Western actors, at least until late 2003, when the political climate within the USA changed.

There are also a considerable number of (predominantly Christian) expatriate communities scattered throughout the rest of the world. The most significant numbers are located in North America and Latin America. Generally speaking, these communities were united in their opposition to the post-war political order in Lebanon, particularly Syria's continuing military occupation and its dominant role in the system. The North American community was especially politically active, and created a number of organisations to lobby the US government in support of authentic Lebanese national interests. Above all, they wanted to see America put some pressure on Syria to withdraw from Lebanon. They had some significant success in 2003–04, but this was largely connected to Washington's desire to put pressure on Syria to change its behaviour toward Iraq.

The Lebanese government took some steps in an attempt to establish some kind of relations with the expatriate communities. The primary motivation was to encourage them to invest in the country and facilitate the economic recovery. There was (and still is) a cabinet-level Minister for Expatriate Affairs, and Lebanese government ministers often made trips abroad to engage in dialogue with expatriate elements. However, the expatriate communities were generally resistant to government efforts, largely because they tended to see the post-war order as illegitimate. In view of the fact that the vast majority of expatriates are Christian, the continuing marginalisation of the Christians in Lebanese politics was obviously a factor. And it did not help matters that the Minister for Expatriate Affairs for much of the post-war period was not a Christian.

PART II: LEBANESE FOREIGN POLICY SINCE 2005

The purpose of Part II is to explain Lebanese foreign policy decision-making since 2005, a period that could have transformed the country's foreign policy as it had developed under Syrian tutelage, but did not. The determinants of Lebanese foreign policy that were at play prior to 2005 had remained in place even after Syria's with-drawal, and precluded any substantial change in policy. This is developed in some detail below. Another point to consider is that the post-2005 governments had very little time to achieve anything significant in this area, as they were hardly functional due to the political crises triggered by Hizbollah from 2006–08.[26]

5.3 Revisiting the determinants of Lebanese foreign policy

Syria's unexpected military withdrawal from Lebanon following the cedar revolution raised substantial hopes in Lebanon, the West and elsewhere that Syrian control over the Lebanese political system would end and, by extension, Lebanese foreign policy would be realigned toward the West. Those expectations were further raised by the fact that pro-Western prime ministers led Lebanon's two post-2005 governments.

However, significant changes to the political system never truly materialised. By extension, and even without the sort of overwhelming Syrian dominance of the political system that had been the case until 2005, Lebanese foreign policy did not see significant changes either.

The reasons for this are relatively straightforward, and should be understood within the context of the traditional determinants of Lebanese foreign policy, outlined in some detail in Part I. These include: 1) the sharp sectarian divisions within the country, with each of the dominant communities sharing a very different vision of Lebanon's international orientation; 2) the continued susceptibility of the country to foreign penetration; and 3) the weakness of the Lebanese state. All three of these factors were strongly present in the post-2005 period, to the degree that their inter-related dynamics account for the fact that the country's foreign policy shifted remarkably little after Syria's military withdrawal.

Lebanon's sectarian communities and their international orientation

It should be obvious by now that Lebanon's main political fault lines traditionally fall along sectarian lines. However, in 2005, Lebanese sectarian identity was more pronounced than at any time since the conclusion of the civil war in 1990. The cedar revolution simply served to exacerbate the long-standing sectarian divisions. The two political movements that came to dominate the Lebanese political scene post-Syria divided the country's two main Muslim communities, with the Christians split over both movements. Each political movement, March 14 and March 8, had very different and largely incompatible narratives regarding Lebanon's international orientation – with one sympathetic to the West and the conservative Sunni Arab world, and focused primarily on economic imperatives; while the other, fully anchored to Syria and Iran, prioritised armed resistance against Israel and a Western-dominated regional order.

The Sunni-led March 14 alliance, the political successor to the cedar revolution, considered its orientation toward the West and the conservative Sunni Arab world as essential to counter-balance Syrian and Iranian influence, and to advance the country's economic wellbeing. Ideally, the leaders of the March 14 movement preferred to end Syrian and Iranian influence in Lebanon, and to normalise the Lebanese security situation. With respect to the latter, this meant disarming Hizbollah and extending Lebanese state authority over Hizbollah-controlled parts of the country. By doing so, Lebanon would disengage itself militarily from the Arab–Israeli and Iranian–Israeli conflict. The existing situation was seen as untenable, as it exposed Lebanon to wider regional dynamics and put its political, security and economic interests at great risk.[27]

However, given the domestic and regional realities, the March 14 programme was difficult to pursue. As a consequence, the movement opted instead to re-orient Lebanese foreign policy towards its pre-civil war policy of neutrality.[28] This narrative holds that Lebanon would not identify strongly with any one camp, regionally or internationally. Rather, it would pursue functional and advantageous relations with all key regional and international actors. In practice, this would still entail renegotiating and correcting the pre-2005 pro-Syrian and pro-Iranian foreign policy, and pursuing the disarming of Hizbollah.

The March 8 Alliance was very much oriented toward Syria and Iran as the two dominant groups within the alliance, the Shiite parties Amal and Hizbollah, were long-time clients of Syria and, in Hizbollah's case, of Iran. Both Shiite parties share their patrons' ideological and international orientation. When Hizbollah emerged in control of the March 8 movement by late 2006, it set out to impose an even more radical narrative on Lebanon, one in line with that espoused by the very conservative leadership in Iran. The narrative was one of establishing Lebanon as a base of resistance against Israel and its Western allies. This differed from liberating Lebanon from Israel, the claim that Hizbollah had once used to retain its arms after the civil war ended and all other Lebanese militias were disarmed. According to the narrative of resistance, Hizbollah was to retain its arms indefinitely to fight Israel and its allies. The role of the Lebanese government was to offer the necessary support to facilitate the resistance. In other words, Lebanon would remain a theatre of conflict, tied to wider regional and international considerations.

A long-time observer of the Lebanese political scene summed up the two competing and incompatible narratives on Lebanon's international orientation as a choice between wanting the country to be the Hong Kong of the Middle East (the March 14 narrative) or the Hanoi of the Middle East (the Hizbollah-led March 8 narrative).[29]

Continuing susceptibility to external penetration

It should also be obvious by now that Lebanon's sectarian groups have historically tended to develop informal relations with their preferred international partners and, as a consequence, foreign elements have always had influence on the Lebanese system. However, it is the degree and nature of these relationships that one needs to appreciate to understand fully the depth of external penetration of the Lebanese political system. Since 2005, the highly intricate and interdependent relationship between Syria and Iran on one hand, and their Lebanese clients within the March 8 Alliance on the other, ensured that developments in Lebanon, most significantly the issue of Hizbollah's arms and its ongoing conflict with Israel, remained heavily tied to, and influenced by, decisions emanating from Damascus and Tehran.[30]

Syria has continued to see advantage in its support of Hizbollah in its strategic calculations with respect to Israel, Iran, other Arab states, the West and most obviously in Lebanon itself, and has sought to retain control of the Hizbollah–Israel conflict. Syria provides Hizbollah with much of its arms (which emanate from Iran), and the two continue to share key intelligence and strategic planning both in Lebanon and in wider regional affairs. According to some analysts, this included the planning and execution with Iran of the 2006 Hizbollah war with Israel.[31] Of critical note here is that the Lebanese government and the Lebanese security establishment are simply bypassed in these relationships, undermining Lebanese sovereignty and demonstrating a clear-cut example of the type of external penetration that the post-2005 Lebanese government has had to face.

Syria worked through its Lebanese clients to ensure that Lebanese foreign policy stayed largely in line with its own, particularly on critical regional issues related to the Arab–Israeli conflict and the Iranian–American rivalry. Obviously, the Syrians and their Lebanese allies would veto any Lebanese government attempt to align fully with the West or to sign a peace treaty with Israel that was independent of any deal Syria might first reach with the Jewish state.

While the Syrian–Hizbollah relationship was based largely on strategic calculations (the two need each other), rather than any strongly shared ideological affinity, the same cannot be said of the Iranian–Hizbollah relationship, which was far more intricate and included strong ideological, religious and even familial linkages. It should be remembered that Iran's revolutionary guards created Hizbollah in the early 1980s among Lebanon's Shiite community to help spread the Iranian revolution and to work towards establishing an Islamic state in Lebanon along the lines of that set up in Iran. Iran provided the organisation with arms, training and intelligence. In addition, many of the men in Hizbollah's top leadership positions, including its spiritual leaders, were tied to Iran through family or bloodlines. In some cases, these men were Iranian rather than Lebanese. Further, Iran provided Hizbollah with hundreds of millions of dollars in aid to facilitate the organisation's development of an effective patronage network within the Lebanese Shiite community.

Although Hizbollah had always served a useful role for Tehran, its importance increased substantially in the years after 9/11 as Iran found itself in an intense conflict with the international community, led by the United States and Israel. The main point of the conflict was Iran's attempt to build a nuclear deterrence capability. If successful, this nuclear programme could alter the strategic balance in the region away from Israel and in favour of Iran and its allies. Under the constant threat of sanctions, and with the possibility of a military strike from Israel and the United States, Iran has initiated a number of strategic steps to deter an attack. This included threatening to turn the Lebanese–Israeli front into a theatre of war by ensuring that its client, Hizbollah, retains the capabilities to strike effectively at Israel in case of an attack on Iranian territory.

Hizbollah's proven success against Israel on the battlefield (it forced Israel to withdraw from Lebanon in 2000 and fought it to a standstill in 2006), and Israel's inability to defeat Hizbollah or to even stop it from striking at its cities,[32] made Hizbollah that much more critical to Iranian strategic planning. It is hardly a surprise that, following the 2006 war, Iran provided billions of additional dollars in aid to Hizbollah in order to shore up the organisation's support within the Lebanese Shiite community, and to secure its overall political influence in Lebanon.[33] Further, with Syria's assistance, Iran re-armed Hizbollah, including purportedly providing advanced missiles capable of striking deep inside Israel. The latter was done in violation of UN Security Council Resolution 1701.

The possibility of conflict between Israel and Hizbollah remains very real, and is linked to dynamics emanating from Iran, Syria, Israel and the USA, as well as from the non-state actor Hizbollah. Given the advanced level of weaponry that Hizbollah has managed to secure, the risk of a war far more devastating than any other that Lebanon has seen in many years cannot be discounted in this context. The impact of such a conflict on the Lebanese political, security and economic environment would be severe. Unfortunately, such developments fall outside the control of the Lebanese government, which has retained very little influence over security matters in Hizbollah-controlled Southern Lebanon. Suffice it to say that Iran has a stranglehold over developments in Lebanon, and will work closely with its Lebanese clients to ensure the Lebanese government does not undertake initiatives that are contrary to Iran's foreign policy interests.

The weakness of the Lebanese state

The third traditional determinant of Lebanese foreign policy, the weakness of the Lebanese state, is also very relevant in this context. As we recall, prior to the civil war in 1975, the Lebanese state was generally weak, and simply tried to find a compromise among the different sectarian forces that made up the government. This generally worked well in times when regional tensions were manageable, and domestic forces were willing to reach compromise on their international orientation because it served their political purposes. Further, the institutional set-up allowed for the office of the President to act as the final arbiter on critical issues, and thereby a mechanism was in place to break deadlocks should it be necessary. But the system also failed, with catastrophic consequences, during other periods, most especially in the few years leading up to the collapse of the Lebanese political system in 1975, when the regional and domestic climates were particularly unforgiving.

Unfortunately for Lebanon, the domestic and regional climate post-2005 appears to be more reminiscent of the years leading up to the civil war. This includes the intense sectarian divisions, the high level of external penetration, the presence of a heavily armed non-state actor operating without government sanction in Southern Lebanon, and the inability of the Lebanese state to use coercive force to maintain order. Moreover, the institutional arrangements set up by the Ta'if Accord have, albeit unintentionally, actually weakened even further the Lebanese state's ability to act effectively in the realm of international relations.

In particular, the Ta'if Accord is generally interpreted to have designed the post-war Lebanese political system in a manner that gives all three major sectarian communities representation in the government and a veto over government decisions. It follows then that the Shiite-dominated March 8 opposition was within its rights to demand a role in governing the country, even though they had lost both parliamentary elections held after Syria's withdrawal from Lebanon. It is within this context that one could also place March 8's demands for the requisite number of cabinet seats that would give them a veto over major government decisions, however unsettling the means they used during the 2006–08 period to reinforce this point. Finally, by attributing equal powers to the Christian-held Presidency, the Sunni-held Prime Ministership and the Shiite-held Speaker of the House, the Ta'if Accord inadvertently removed the role of domestic arbiter formerly assumed by the all-powerful Presidency. This defect in the system became all too apparent after the cedar revolution, when Syria was no longer in a position to play the role of arbiter. Perhaps ironically, the former system may have been more apt at breaking the political deadlock that was so prevalent in the post-2005 Lebanese system.

5.4 Lebanese foreign policy from 2005 – compromise versus deadlock

On the heels of the cedar revolution and an electoral victory in Lebanon's first post-Syrian controlled parliamentary elections, the March 14-led Siniora government (2005–09) felt that it had secured a mandate to attempt to deal with a range of issues that would have an impact on its relations with key regional and international players. In particular, this included the two thorny issues of disarming Hizbollah, and renegotiating Lebanese–Syrian relations.

The Siniora government enjoyed initially strong backing and close relations with a number of key regional and international actors including, significantly, Saudi Arabia, France and the United States. The international community's strong diplomatic support also included economic and financial aid, which was important for helping to stabilise Lebanon's economy. Further, the international community, particularly the United States, provided assistance in helping to rebuild the Lebanese military and security infrastructure.[34] The fact that a number of high-level American government officials visited Lebanon, including then Secretary of State Condoleezza Rice, raised expectations in Lebanon and elsewhere that genuine changes were possible.

In return for supporting the Siniora government, the international community, and in particular the United States, expected the Lebanese government to initiate steps leading to the disarmament of Hizbollah and stabilisation of the security situation in Southern Lebanon. Pressure on the Lebanese government to pursue the disarmament in line with UN security resolutions continued throughout this period. As noted in Chapter 3, both issues were raised within the context of the National Dialogue process, but little progress was made. The political crises orchestrated by Hizbollah for most of the remainder of the Siniora government ended any real hopes that these two key issues could be dealt with. A resolution was reached only after the Siniora government agreed to form a national unity government during the final year of its term, thereby giving the March 8 opposition an effective veto over government decisions, a move the Siniora government had previously avoided. The pattern of forming a national unity government to govern Lebanon with opposition veto privileges was repeated following the 2010 parliamentary elections. In effect, unless the political climate changes dramatically in Lebanon in the foreseeable future, Lebanon will be governed by unity governments composed of the various sectarian parties that make up the March 14 and March 8 movements, two movements that share largely incompatible views of Lebanon's international orientation.

With respect to the issue of Syrian–Lebanese relations, some progress was made, particularly in terms of setting up official diplomatic relations, something Syria had avoided since Lebanese independence in the 1940s. However, the fact that so many anti-Syrian politicians and other public figures were murdered during this period sent a very clear message to the Siniora government that Damascus would not tolerate any moves to alter Lebanese–Syrian relations or policies that it considered anathema to its interests. Suffice to say, the message was understood, and by 2009 the March 14 movement was making amends with Syria, a policy that continues under the new government of Saad Hariri in 2010.[35]

Finally, Lebanon's relations with Iran remain centred around the issue of Hizbollah. In particular, this includes Iran's continuing support of Hizbollah's military wing, and the Lebanese government's wish to find a way either to disarm Hizbollah, or at the very least to integrate it into the Lebanese security apparatus under the full control of the Lebanese government. Given the critical importance of Hizbollah to Iran's strategic calculations *vis-à-vis* Israel, it has taken a strong interest in any initiative undertaken in this regard by the Lebanese government. Therefore the Lebanese government would need to tread very carefully on this issue, which is central to its internal politics but greatly affects its foreign relations with Iran or, for that matter, with Syria, Saudi Arabia, Israel and the West.

CONCLUSION

It has been twenty-one years since Lebanon's civil war ended, and just six since Syria withdrew its troops. Much euphoria followed Syria's departure from Lebanon, as many Lebanese believed that the country would finally enter a period of sustained peace, security and economic prosperity, putting the long years of the civil war and Syrian occupation behind them. Unfortunately, that has not been the case thus far. The underlying conditions that led to the collapse of the Lebanese political system in 1975 remain to this day. In particular, the political system continues to suffer from the three systemic weaknesses that have plagued it since the country's independence in 1943: 1) sectarian tensions, which continue to permeate nearly all facets of Lebanese society; 2) external penetration, which has continued to tie the fortunes of the country to regional and international conflicts and dynamics; and 3) the weakness of the Lebanese state, which continues to lack even the basic coercive capacity to assert its authority.

I argue throughout this book that these three systemic weaknesses are now worse than at any time in Lebanon's modern history, including even the period leading up to the civil war. This does not bode well for Lebanon's political future, although, as of this writing, it appears that none of the major sectarian players believes that it is in their interest to see the system collapse, since this would probably lead to a return to civil war. Through the existing political arrangements, including the formation of a unity government, the sectarian leaders have struck a precarious balance allowing them access to state patronage and power, without having to tackle issues that are very difficult, if not nearly impossible, to resolve, including the disarming of Hizbollah, the status of Lebanon's Palestinian refugees, the fate of the UN-backed Special Tribunal for Lebanon investigating the murder of Rafiq Hariri, or even the restructuring of the political system away from a sectarian consociational model to a majoritarian model.

Even the current leadership in Hizbollah sees benefits in the system and may not wish to jeopardise its favourable position within the Shiite community, or its domestic alliances with other non-Shiite Lebanese groups, by pursuing policies that would cause the system to collapse. However, Hizbollah's future actions may depend on the internal balances of power within the organisation between its more pragmatic leaders, who see its future within a multi-sectarian Lebanese system, and its more ideological forces, which will pursue policies completely in line with those of Iran, even if such policies risk weakening Hizbollah's position within Lebanon.

In short, the survival of the Lebanese political system hinges, at the very least, on: 1) a great deal of very careful negotiating and compromise among the various sectarian leaders and their respective external patrons; 2) the avoidance of a major regional war between Israel and Iran that would, in all likelihood, bring Lebanon into the conflict; and 3) perhaps some good fortune as the country's leaders find their way through the myriad of possible destabilising scenarios that they are likely to face in the years ahead.

Postscript

Since completing this manuscript in the summer of 2010, another political crisis has emerged, paralysing Lebanese politics and bringing the country once again to the brink of sectarian violence. In this case, the conflict stems from the work of the UN-backed Special Tribunal for Lebanon (STL), which was set up by the UN Security Council in May 2007 to investigate the murder of former Prime Minister Rafiq Hariri and try those suspects charged with carrying out the assassination. By March of 2009 the Tribunal's work officially began, and within a year startling information emerged that members of Hizbollah were being investigated for the crime. The implications of this development cannot be overstated. In short, Lebanon is faced with a scenario in which Hizbollah, the most influential and best armed group in the country, main representative of the Shiite community and key member of the government, might be formally accused by international investigators of murdering the pre-eminent leader of the Sunni community. Given that tensions between the Shiite and Sunni communities have been high for years, and reached dangerous levels in 2008, it would not be difficult to conclude that, if the situation is not managed carefully, relations between the two communities could implode. After all, it was Hariri's assassination, initially blamed on Syria, which triggered the unprecedented uprisings in 2005 and the Syrian military's subsequent departure from the country. Not surprisingly, then, this divisive issue dominated the political arena for much of 2010 and 2011 and ultimately led to the unity government's collapse in January 2011.

Prime Minister Saad Hariri and his allies in the March 14 movement were of the strong view that the STL should be allowed to continue its work and ultimately to prosecute those behind Rafiq Hariri's murder, viewing the issue as a legal and criminal matter. For Saad Hariri, the matter was also personal. Furthermore, the fact that Hizbollah might be implicated had the additional political advantage of damaging the credibility of a major political rival.

The possibility that Hizbollah, or at least members of the party, might be charged for the 2005 assassination of Rafiq Hariri could indeed prove damaging to the organisation's credibility, not only within Lebanon, where it has, with success, broadened its appeal, but across the Arab world, where for the past few years it has tried to raise its profile and extend its influence. Therefore it would appear that Hizbollah's leaders were determined to derail the STL investigation at all costs, using all the resources at their disposal to do so.

Hizbollah's approach was twofold. First, it worked to weaken the credibility of the STL by politicising the tribunal, claiming that the United States and its allies, especially Israel, were using the STL to destroy Hizbollah. For example, among the numerous allegations made against the STL is the claim that evidence collected by the tribunal was linked to Israeli intelligence agencies. Second, Hizbollah attempted to force the Lebanese government to abandon the STL, or at least to distance itself from it. In this regard, Hizbollah and its allies in the unity government linked their cooperation on government matters, including budgetary issues, to a successful resolution of the STL. Further, Hizbollah's leaders used a range of muscle-flexing exercises, reminiscent of earlier periods, aimed at intimidating their opponents.

Unable to get the Lebanese government to distance itself from the tribunal, and following the failure of Saudi–Syrian mediation efforts aimed at resolving the dispute, Hizbollah precipitated the collapse of Saad Hariri's unity government. In January 2011, cabinet ministers linked to Hizbollah, and an additional cabinet minister linked to President Suleiman, resigned from cabinet, bringing down the government.[1]

Reflecting a continuing and clear shift of political power in Lebanon, Hizbollah announced that it would attempt to form the next government. Walid Jumblatt, a former member of March 14 and the astute political leader of the Druze community, announced that he would back Hizbollah's efforts in this regard, while at the same time denouncing the STL as divisive at a time when Lebanon needed unity. Hizbollah backed the Sunni politician Najib Mikati to lead the government, and despite lacking any kind of significant support within his own Sunni community, Parliament asked Mikati in January to become Prime Minister and lead the next government.

After several months of significant negotiations, Mikati formed a thirty-member cabinet led by the March 8 movement. He was unsuccessful in bringing all of the key political players and their respective constituents into government. Saad Hariri, for example, announced early on that he would not join a unity government, but would instead lead the opposition to what he claimed would be a Hizbollah-dominated government. The failure to include the March 14 movement will probably deny the Mikati government legitimacy both within the Sunni community and in elements of the Christian community. It is clear, therefore, that he will need to take measures sensitive to Sunni and Christian concerns should he hope to gain the full support of both communities.

Mikati will probably try to govern from the middle, carefully balancing the interests of the various sectarian communities, political blocs, and their respective external patrons. His ability to manage the issue of the STL, however, will severely test his government, particularly as Hariri and his allies, free from the shackles of government, will strongly press him on an issue that continues to be of some concern to the Sunni community. In June 2011, four members of Hizbollah were formally charged by the STL with Rafiq Hariri's murder. How Mikati handles this crisis is likely to determine the longevity of his government. However, he is unlikely to take strong measures related to the STL that would be seen to be damaging to Hizbollah, which, as I have demonstrated throughout this book, is the dominant political force in the country and a key supporter of his government.

Finally, it would be worthwhile to explore briefly the implications for Lebanon – a penetrated state *par excellence* – of the recent and unprecedented developments that have occurred across the Arab world, and that have seen the downfall of long-standing authoritarian regimes in Tunisia and Egypt (and possibly Libya). Further uprisings are occurring throughout the Arab world.

While there is significant support in Lebanon for the uprisings, Lebanon is unlikely to face similar events, beyond perhaps small-scale rallies by relatively marginal groups wishing to end the sectarian consociational system.[2] The Lebanese political system is not an authoritarian one, and however ineffectual, does represent the diverse communities and dominant political views found in Lebanese society. Further, while the Lebanese can agree that their system is deeply flawed, there is no commonality on how to fix it, or what alternative political model to put forth. In fact, it could be said that Lebanon had its uprising in 2005 when, with the cedar revolution, an end was brought to Syrian military occupation.

The uprisings have recently spread to Syria, but, as of this writing in July 2011, have not led to regime change in Damascus. The implications for Lebanon of such an outcome could be significant. A number of possible scenarios could emerge that could shift the internal balance of power among the various Lebanese groups away from Hizbollah. For example, a new regime in Damascus could alter Syria's foreign relations by moving away from Shiite-dominated Hizbollah and Iran, and moving closer to the Sunni Arab world. If this were to materialise, what would this mean for Lebanon?

Obviously, I am simply speculating, but the point I would like to stress here is that developments in Lebanon, including the political balance of power, continue to rest, to a considerable extent, on external developments, a reality that Lebanon has faced since independence. The Lebanese therefore will continue to watch developments in the region very carefully, but most especially those in neighbouring Syria.

NOTES

Introduction

1 Arend Lijphart, "Consociational Democracy", *World Politics* 21, no. 2 (1969), 216.

1 The formation of the modern Lebanese state

1 For an examination of this period, see Albert Hourani, *A History of the Arab Peoples* (Cambridge, MA: Belknap Press of Harvard University Press, 1991), 207–314.

2 For an excellent account of events during this period, see Leila Fawaz, *An Occasion for War: Civil Conflict in Lebanon and Damascus in 1860* (London: I.B. Tauris, 1995).

3 Several books provide useful accounts of this period. In particular, see Meir Zamir, *The Formation of Modern Lebanon* (London: Croom Helm, 1985); Kamal Salibi, *A House of Many Mansions: The History of Lebanon Reconsidered* (London: I.B. Tauris, 1988).

4 For discussions of Maronite ideology during this period, see Salibi (*op. cit.*); and Asher Kaufman, "Phoenicianism: The Formation of an Identity in Lebanon in 1920", *Middle Eastern Studies* 37, no. 1 (January, 2001), 173–194.

5 The primary reason was political. The Maronite community (as well as others) objected to any further population census because of concerns that new data would reflect changes in the population make-up, revealing a Muslim majority in Lebanon, with all that entails.

6 For a particularly good account of this rivalry, see Eyal Zisser, *Lebanon: The Challenges of Independence* (London: I.B. Tauris, 2000).

7 A.B. Gaunson, *The Anglo–French Clash in Lebanon and Syria, 1940–45* (London: Macmillan, 1987).

8 The classic English language study of this period is Michael Hudson's *The Precarious Republic* (New York: Random House, 1968).

9 An excellent body of literature deals with these issues. See, in particular, Lijphart's (1968, 1969) work on democratic consociationalism.

10 An extensive body of literature exists on the role of patron–client systems in the political systems of developing countries.

11 In particular, see Albert Hourani, *Political Society in Lebanon: A Historical Introduction* (London: Centre for Lebanese Studies, 1986).

12 For an interesting insight into his thinking, see Kamal Jumblatt's *I Speak for Lebanon* (London: Zed Press, 1982).

13 Attributed to the contemporary Lebanese political commentator Michael Young.
14 For two of the few studies of political parties in Lebanon, see Nazih Richani, *Dilemmas of Democracy and Political Parties in Sectarian Societies: The Case of the Progressive Socialist Party of Lebanon 1949–1996* (New York: St Martin's Press, 1997); Michael Suleiman, *Political Parties in Lebanon* (Ithaca, NY: Cornell University Press, 1967).
15 See his two early works on consociational democracy: Arend Lijphart, "Consociational Democracy", *(op. cit.)*; Typologies of Democratic Systems", *Comparative Political Studies* 1, no. 1 (1968).
16 For a detailed analysis of the country's political economy, see Carolyn Gates, *The Merchant Republic of Lebanon* (London: I.B. Tauris, 1998).
17 For a detailed examination of this period, see Eyal Zisser's *Lebanon: The Challenges of Independence (op. cit.)*, and "The Downfall of the Khuri Administration: A Dubious Revolution", *Middle Eastern Studies* 30 (July, 1994), 486–511.
18 For analyses of the 1958 conflict, see Nasser Kalawoun, *The Struggle for Lebanon* (London: I.B. Tauris, 2000); Michael Bishku, "The 1958 American Intervention in Lebanon: A Historical Assessment", *American–Arab Affairs* no. 31 (Winter, 1989–90), 106–119; and Arnold Hottinger, "Zu'ama and Parties in the Lebanese Crisis of 1958", *Middle East Journal* 15, no. 2 (Spring, 1961), 127–140.
19 For a recent analysis of Western intervention in the Levant, see N. Lee, "More Like Korea than Suez: British and American Intervention in the Levant in 1958", *Small Wars and Insurgencies* 8, no. 3 (Winter, 1997), 1–24.
20 For a succinct analysis of this period, see Kamal Salibi, "Lebanon under Fouad Chehab – 1958–1964", *Middle Eastern Studies* 2, no. 3 (April, 1966), 211–226.
21 Meir Zamir, "The Lebanese Presidential Elections of 1970 and their Impact on the Civil War of 1975–1976", *Middle Eastern Studies* 16, no. 1 (January, 1980), 49–69.
22 Numerous studies have accounted for this period. See, in particular, Farid El Khazen, *The Breakdown of the State in Lebanon, 1967–1976* (Reading, UK: I.B. Tauris, 1999); Walid Khalidi, *Conflict and Violence in Lebanon: Confrontation in the Middle East* (Cambridge, MA: Center for International Affairs, Harvard University, 1979); and Kamal Salibi, *Crossroads to Civil War: Lebanon 1958–1976* (Reading, UK: Ithaca Press, 1976).
23 Michael Johnson, *Class & Client in Beirut: The Sunni Muslim Community and the Lebanese State 1840–1985* (Reading, UK: Ithaca Press, 1986).
24 Tewfik Khalaf, "The Phalange and the Maronite Community", in Roger Owen (ed.), *Essays on the Crisis in Lebanon* (Reading, UK: Ithaca Press, 1976), 43–56.
25 Georges Corm, "Myths and Realities of the Lebanese Conflict", in Nadim Shehadi and Dana Haffar Mills (eds), *Lebanon: A History of Conflict and Consensus* (London: I.B. Tauris, 1988), 240–259.
26 Walid Khalidi, *Conflict and Violence in Lebanon, op. cit.*, 101.
27 For a detailed argument of this, see Farid El Khazen, *The Breakdown of the State in Lebanon, 1967–1976, op. cit.*

2 The civil war: 1975–90

1 The bibliography includes a sample of the very extensive literature on the Lebanese conflict. In particular, see Robert Fisk, *Pity the Nation: Lebanon at War* (Oxford: Oxford University Press, 1990); Noam Chomsky, *The Fateful Triangle: The United States, Israel and the Palestinians* (Boston, MA: South End Press, 1983); Samir Khalaf, *Civil and Uncivil Violence in Lebanon: A History of the Internationalization of Communal Conflict* (New York: Columbia University Press, 2002); and Itamar Rabinovich, *The War for Lebanon, 1970–1985* (Ithaca, NY: Cornell University Press, 1985).
2 For details of these events, see Robert Fisk, *Pity the Nation, op. cit.*
3 For an excellent, if somewhat sympathetic, view of Syria's intervention and subsequent role in Lebanon, see Patrick Seale, *Asad: The Struggle for the Middle East* (Berkeley, CA: University of California Press, 1989), 267–289.

4 For a succinct analysis of the Christian community during this period, see Lewis Snider, "The Lebanese Forces: Their Origins and Role in Lebanon's Politics", *Middle East Journal* 38, no. 1 (Winter, 1984), 1–32.

5 For detailed studies of Lebanon's Shiite community during this period, see Majed Halawi, *A Lebanon Defied: Musa al-Sadr and the Shi'a Community* (Boulder, CO: Westview Press, 1992); Richard Augustus Norton, *Amal, and the Shi'a Struggle for the Soul of Lebanon* (Austin, TX: University of Texas Press, 1987).

6 For an analysis of this relationship, see As'ad AbuKhalil, "Syria and the Shiites: al-Asad's Policy in Lebanon", *Third World Quarterly* 12, no. 2 (April, 1989), 1–19.

7 Lewis Snider, "The Lebanese Forces", *op. cit.*

8 For a succinct analysis of the invasion, see David Gilmour, *Lebanon: The Fractured Country* (London: Sphere Books, 1987), 146–157.

9 A lucid account of developments leading to the conflict can be found in Itamar Rabinovich, *The War for Lebanon, 1970–1985, op. cit.*

10 For an explanation of Israeli policy, see Ze'ev Schiff and Ehud Ya'ari, *Israel's Lebanon War* (New York: Simon & Schuster, 1984).

11 For a discussion of PLO decision-making, see Rashid Khalidi, *Under Siege: PLO Decisionmaking During the 1982 War* (New York: Columbia University Press, 1986).

12 Developments between 1982 and 1988 are vividly covered by Robert Fisk, *Pity the Nation, op. cit.*

13 Again, see *ibid.* for a description of events during this period.

14 For a look at the politics of the Druze community during this period of the conflict, see J. Harik, "Change and Continuity among the Lebanese Druze Community: The Civil Administration of the Mountains, 1983–1990", *Middle Eastern Studies* 29, no. 3 (July 1993), 377–398.

15 For a good account of *Hizbollah* by a leading student of the party, see Magnus Ranstorp, *Hizb'Allah in Lebanon* (London: Palgrave Macmillan, 1996).

16 Patrick Seale, *Asad: The Struggle for the Middle East, op. cit.*

17 For a detailed examination of the Aoun era, see Carole Dagher, *Les Paris du General* (Beirut: FMA, 1992); Sarkis Naoum, *Michel Aoun, Reve ou Illusion?* (Beirut: Mediterranean Press, 1992).

18 Issam Fares, a Greek Orthodox from North Lebanon, made his billions in the Gulf.

19 For some statistics on the state of the Lebanese economy, see Tom Pierre Najem, *Lebanon's Renaissance: The Political Economy of Reconstruction* (Reading, UK: Ithaca Press, 2000), chapters 2 and 3.

3 The post-war political system

1 A copy of the text can be found in Deirdre Collings and Jill Tansley, *Peace for Lebanon? Obstacles, Challenges, and Prospects*, Working Paper 43 (Canadian Institute for International Peace and Security, 1992).

2 Several students of the Lebanese political system have weighed into the debate on Ta'if. They include Richard Augustus Norton, "Lebanon After Ta'if: Is the Civil War Over?" *Middle East Journal* 45, no. 3 (1991), 457–473; Simon Haddad, "Christian–Muslim Relations and Attitudes towards the Lebanese State", *Journal of Muslim Minority Affairs* 21, no. 1 (April, 2001), 131–148; and Samir Khalaf, *Civil and Uncivil Violence in Lebanon: A History of the Internationalization of Communal Conflict* (New York: Columbia University Press, 2002), 289–303.

3 Richard Augustus Norton, "Lebanon After Ta'if: Is the Civil War Over", *op. cit.*; Ronald McLaurin, "Lebanon: Into or Out of Oblivion?" *Current History* (January 1992), 29–33.

4 For a succinct discussion of the South Lebanon issue, see T.P. Najem, "Palestinian–Israeli Conflict and South Lebanon", *Economic and Political Weekly* XXXV, no. 46 (November 11, 2000), 4006–4009.

5 A text of the Treaty can be found in *Arab Press Service*, Diplomat 22, Recorder Covering (18/25 Mat 1991), SP 386. For a succinct analysis see Jim Muir, 'The Syrian–Lebanese Treaty: Grounds for Concern or Hope?" *Middle East International* no. 401 (31 May 1991), 3–4.

6 A particularly strong critique can be found in Habib Malik, "Lebanon in the 1990s: Stability without Freedom?" *Global Affairs*, part 7 (Winter, 1992).

7 Peretz Kidron and Donald Neff, "Euphoria and Alarm", *Middle East International* no. 401 (31 May 1991), 5.

8 A discussion of the elections can be found in Richard Augustus Norton and Jillian Schwedler, "Swiss Soldiers, Ta'if Clocks, and Early Elections: Toward a Happy Ending in Lebanon", *Middle East Insight* 10, no. 1 (1993), 45–54.

9 This included the establishment of a "Supreme Council" chaired by the two heads of state, the Foreign Affairs Committee, and the Defence and Security Affairs Committee.

10 For an examination of Syrian foreign policy, see Patrick Seale, *Asad: The Struggle for the Middle East* (Berkeley, CA: University of California Press, 1989); Neil Quilliam, *Syria and the New World Order* (Reading, UK: Ithaca Press, 1999); Raymond Hinnebusch, "The Foreign Policy of Syria", in Raymond Hinnebusch and Anoushiravan Ehteshami (eds) *The Foreign Policies of Middle East States* (London: Lynne Rienner, 2002), 91–114.

11 Neil Quilliam, *Syria and the New World Order, op. cit.*, chapters 5 and 6.

12 T.P. Najem, "Palestinian–Israeli Conflict and South Lebanon", *op. cit.*, 4006–4009.

13 For an examination of succession in Syria, see Volker Perthes, "The Political Economy of Syrian Succession", *Survival* 43, no. 1 (September, 2001), 143–154.

14 For a discussion of the situation in South Lebanon, see Hussein Sirriyeh, "Lebanon in Search of a Viable Settlement", *Israel Affairs* 4, no. 2 (Winter, 1997), 112–129.

15 Eric Thompson, "Will Syria Have to Withdraw from Lebanon?" *Middle East Journal* 56, no. 1 (Winter, 2002), 72–93.

16 Of course, the situation may change if hard-liners within the US government decide to expand the "war on terrorism" to include Damascus.

17 Very little academic work has actually been done on the intricate relationship between Syria and Lebanon.

18 For a recent study of Lebanon's confessional politics, see Andrew Rigby, "Lebanon: Patterns of Confessional Politics", *Parliamentary Affairs* 53, no. 1 (January 2000), 169–180.

19 Paul Salem, "Skirting Democracy: Lebanon's 1996 Elections and Beyond", *Middle East Report* 27, no. 2 (Spring, 1997), 26–29; Andrew Rigby, "Lebanon: Patterns of Confessional Politics", *op. cit.*, 169–180; Steven Simon and Jonathan Stevenson, "Declawing the 'Party of God': Toward Normalization in Lebanon", *World Policy Journal* 18, no. 2 (Summer, 2001), 31–42.

20 Perhaps the leading observer of the troika system is Michael Young, whose columns on the subject can be found in the *Lebanon Report* and the Beirut daily, *The Daily Star*.

21 A further examination of the troika system can be found in Tom Pierre Najem, *Lebanon's Renaissance: The Political Economy of Reconstruction (op. cit.)*, 213–237.

22 A more detailed assessment of this period can be found in *ibid.*, 25–37.

23 *ibid.*, 37–49.

24 *ibid.*, 49.

25 This included some notable journalists, including editorials in the leading paper, *Al-Nahar*, as well as by leading politicians who have participated in the post-Ta'if political order.

26 The most accessible account of the cedar revolution published to date is Michael Young, *The Ghosts of Martyrs Square: An Eyewitness Account of Lebanon's Life Struggle* (New York: Simon & Schuster, 2010).

27 In addition to Young's work, see Nicolas Blanford, *Killing Mr Lebanon: The Assassination of Rafik Hariri and its Impact on the Middle East* (London: I.B. Tauris, 2006).

28 A good deal of literature has been published on Hizbollah and its relations with Iran. For different accounts, see Magnus Ranstorp, *Hizb'Allah in Lebanon* (London: Palgrave

Macmillan, 1996); Joseph Alagha, *The Shifts in Hizbullah's Ideology: Religious Ideology, Political Ideology, and Political Program* (Amsterdam: Amsterdam University Press, 2007); Amal Saad-Ghorayeb and Marina Ottaway, *Hizbollah and its Changing Identities* (Washington, DC: Carnegie Endowment for International Peace, 2007); Anthony Cordesman, *Iran's Support of the Hezbollah in Lebanon* (Washington, DC: Center for Strategic and International Studies, 2006); Barbara Slavin, *Mullahs, Money, and Militias: How Iran Exerts its Influence in the Middle East* (Washington, DC: United Institute of Peace, 2008); and Matthew Levitt, *Hezballah Finances: Funding the Party of God.* (Washington, DC: Washington Institute for Near East Policy, 2005).

29 For an account of the National Dialogue process, see V.E. Shields, "Political Reform in Lebanon: Has the Cedar Revolution Failed?" *Journal of Legislative Studies* 14, no. 4 (2008), 474–487.

30 Several works have been published on the 2006 conflict between Israel and Hizbollah. See Gilbert Achcar and Michel Warschawski, *The 33-day War: Israel's War on Hezbollah in Lebanon and its Consequences* (Boulder, CO: Paradigm, 2007); Amos Harel and Avi Isacharoff, *34 Days: Israel, Hezbollah and the War in Lebanon* (London: Palgrave Macmillan, 2008); Shlomo Brom, *The Confrontation with Hizbullah* (Tel Aviv: Tel Aviv University, Jaffee Center for Strategic Studies, 2006); and Anthony Cordesman, *The Lessons of the Israeli–Lebanon War* (Washington, DC: Center for Strategic and International Studies, 2008).

31 For an account of the 2006–08 crisis, see International Crisis Group, *Hizbollah's Weapons Turn Inward* (Brussels: International Crisis Group, 2008) and International Crisis Group, *Hizbollah and the Lebanese Crisis* (Brussels: International Crisis Group, 2007).

32 See, for example, Paul Salem, *Hizbollah Attempts a Coup d'État* (Washington, DC: Carnegie Endowment for International Peace, 2008).

33 For a discussion of the 2009 elections, see Michael Young, *The Ghosts of Martyrs Square: An Eyewitness Account of Lebanon's Life Struggle, op. cit.*; and International Crisis Group, *Lebanon's Elections: Avoiding a New Cycle of Confrontation* (Brussels: International Crisis Group, 2009).

4 Post-war reconstruction and the economy

1 A handful of academic books have been published on the Lebanese economy, including Marwan Iskandar, *Rafiq Hariri and the Fate of Lebanon* (London: Saqi, 2006); Samir Makdisi, *The Lessons of Lebanon: The Economics of War and Development* (London: I.B. Tauris, 2004); Kamal Dib, *Warlords and Merchants: The Lebanese Business and Political Establishment* (Reading, UK: Ithaca Press, 2004); and Tom Pierre Najem, *Lebanon's Renaissance: The Political Economy of Lebanon's Reconstruction (op. cit.)*.

   A number of useful academic articles have been published on the economy during this period, including G. Denoeux and R. Springborg, "Hariri's Lebanon: Singapore of the Middle East or Sanaa of the Levant?" *Middle East Policy* 6, no. 2 (2008), 158–173; Ghassan Dibeh, *Foreign Aid and Economic Development in Postwar Lebanon*, Research Paper No. 2007/37 (Helsinki: United Nations University, World Institute for Development Economics Research, 2007); T. Nizameddin, "The Political Economy of Lebanon under Rafiq Hariri: An Interpretation", *Middle East Journal* 60, no. 1 (January, 2006), 95–114; and Volker Perthes, "Myths and Money: Four Years of Hariri and Lebanon's Preparation for a New Middle East", *Middle East Report* 27, no. 2 (Spring, 1997), 16–21.

2 For an extensive survey of the Lebanese economy, see World Bank, *Memorandum and Recommendation of the President of the International Bank for Reconstruction and Development to the Executive Directors on a Proposed Loan to the Lebanese Republic for an Emergency Reconstruction and Rehabilitation Project* – Report #P-5982-LE (Washington, DC: World Bank, 9 February 1993).

3 *ibid.*

4 A comprehensive treatment of Hariri's reconstruction programme is found in Najem, *Lebanon's Renaissance, op. cit.*

5 Council for Development and Reconstruction, *Horizon 2000 for Reconstruction and Development: Main Report* (Beirut: Council for Development and Reconstruction, 1993), 2.

6 For a detailed account, see Najem, *Lebanon's Renaissance, op. cit.*, 63–80.

7 Council for Development and Reconstruction, *Horizon 2000, op. cit.*, 14–15.

8 *ibid.*, 2.

9 Najem, *Lebanon's Renaissance, op. cit.*, 163–175.

10 Council for Development and Reconstruction, *The Reconstruction Project* (Beirut: Council for Development and Reconstruction, April 1983).

11 Najem, *Lebanon's Renaissance, op. cit.*, 85–90.

12 *ibid.*, 90–92.

13 For a succinct study of the Lebanese bureaucracy, see Maroun Kisirwani, "The Lebanese Bureaucracy under Stress: How did it Survive?" *The Beirut Review* no. 4 (Fall, 1992), 29–42.

14 Najem, *Lebanon's Renaissance, op. cit.*, 58.

15 Economist Intelligence Unit, *Country Reports – Lebanon 1996/97; The Lebanon Report* no. 2 (Summer 1996), 24–25.

16 Najem, *Lebanon's Renaissance, op. cit.*, 143–148.

17 All examples taken from *ibid.*, chapter 6.

18 *ibid.*, 216–217.

19 Economist Intelligence Unit, *The Lebanon Report* no. 2, *op. cit.*, 26.

20 According to one author, only around 60 per cent of the planned projects between 1992 and 1997 were realised or were in the process of being completed. See Ghassan Dibeh, *Foreign Aid and Economic Development in Postwar Lebanon, op. cit.*, 5.

21 For a comprehensive examination of this point, see Najem, *Lebanon's Renaissance, op. cit.*, chapter 5.

22 The information in this section was taken from a number of editions of the English language Beirut daily, *The Daily Star.*

23 Ghassan Dibeh, *Foreign Aid and Economic Development in Postwar Lebanon, op. cit.*, 9.

24 *ibid.*, 7.

25 *ibid.*, 11; and T. Nizameddin, "The Political Economy of Lebanon under Rafiq Hariri: An Interpretation", *Middle East Journal* (2006), 95–114.

26 Lebanon's tourism industry, which consists mostly of expatriates returning home for their summer holidays, makes up a considerable portion of Lebanon's GDP, and is highly vulnerable to conflict and more general political instability.

27 Estimating the true cost of the South Lebanon conflict to the Lebanese economy would be very difficult, and in all likelihood one would obtain widely different numbers depending on source, method, etc.

28 Many Lebanese bankers attribute the success of their industry to the head of Lebanon's Central Bank, Riad Salamé. For more on this, see Borzou Daragahi, "Lebanon Central Bank Chief got it Right", *Los Angeles Times* 21 February, 2009.

5 Post-war foreign policy: Syrian penetration and Lebanese interests

1 An earlier version of the theoretical portion of this chapter can be found in T.P. Najem, "Lebanon and Europe: the Foreign Policy of a Penetrated State", in Gerd Nonneman (ed.) *Analyzing Middle East Foreign Policies And the Relationship with Europe* (Abingdon, UK: Routledge, 2005), 100–121.

2 Very little has actually been published on Lebanese foreign policy. Even studies that focus on the foreign policies of Middle East states tend simply to ignore Lebanon. This includes the otherwise excellent volume by Raymond Hinnebusch and Anoushiravan Ehteshami (eds), *The Foreign Policies of Middle East States* (London: Lynne Rienner, 2002). Rather, studies that look at Lebanon's external relations tend to focus on Lebanon's domination by foreign powers. The exceptions include a few works that have focused

on Lebanese relations with Palestinians living within Lebanon's borders. See, for example, a collection of articles recently published in the *Journal of Refugee Studies*: Michael
Hudson, "Palestinians and Lebanon: The Common Story", *Journal of Refugee Studies* 10,
no. 3 (1997), 243–260; Farid Khazen, "Permanent Settlement of Palestinians in Lebanon: A Recipe for Conflict", *Journal of Refugee Studies* 10, no. 3 (1997), 275–293; Fida
Nasrallah, "Lebanese Perceptions of the Palestinians in Lebanon: Case Studies", *Journal of
Refugee Studies* 10, no. 3 (1997), 349–359.
3 This is the dominant view of academics, policy makers and the media.
4 This point, which is discussed in detail below, includes Lebanon's recent free-trade
negotiations with the EU.
5 The Lebanese government stayed out of the 1967 and the 1973 Arab–Israeli wars,
despite some internal pressure to do so.
6 During much of the pre-civil war period, Lebanon served as both a regional banking and
trading centre, as well as the regional headquarters for many Western firms.
7 For example, Egyptian leader Nasser had extensive influence within the Lebanese
Muslim community.
8 Syria, Iraq, Egypt, Saudi Arabia, Libya all had clients within the Lebanese system.
9 See, in particular, Najem, *Lebanon's Renaissance: The Political Economy of Lebanon's Reconstruction (op. cit.,* 2000); Habib Malik, *Between Damascus and Jerusalem: Lebanon and the Middle
East Peace Process* (Washington, DC: Washington Institute for Near East Policy, 1997);
Habib Malik, "Lebanon in the 1990s: Stability Without Freedom?" *Global Affairs*, part 7
(Winter, 1992), 79–109.
10 For a developed examination of Hizbollah, see Magnus Ranstorp, *Hizb'Allah in Lebanon
(op. cit.,* 1996).
11 Especially the Maronites.
12 For a text of the treaty, see *Arab Press Service*, Diplomat 14, Recorder Covering (16/23
March 1991), SP 252.
13 J. Harik, "Syrian Foreign Policy and State/Resistance Dynamics in Lebanon", *Studies in
Conflict and Terrorism* 20, no. 3 (1997), 249–265.
14 Although clearly restricted in covering/discussing events critical of Syria, the Lebanese
press has nevertheless reported such events over the years. This includes the English
language paper, *The Daily Star*.
15 For a detailed discussion of Western/international involvement in Lebanon, see Najem,
Lebanon Renaissance, op. cit., chapters 3–5.
16 For example, the Maronite religious establishment, most notably the Patriarch, is
probably the major articulator of Maronite concerns. Other Maronite political leaders are
outside the mainstream political process. Also, the Maronite community has found a
voice in the diaspora located in several countries throughout the world.
17 Eric Thompson, "Will Syria Have to Withdraw from Lebanon?" *Middle East Journal* 56,
no. 1 (Winter, 2002), 72–93.
18 France may have been the only major country openly to state its concerns over Syrian
dominance of Lebanon.
19 In fact, this very point probably drives US reluctance to oppose Syria's presence in Lebanon.
20 Eric Thompson, "Will Syria Have to Withdraw from Lebanon?", *op. cit.*
21 Very little has actually been written on contemporary Lebanese–US relations. For a historical
overview, see Noam Chomsky, *The Fateful Triangle: The United States, Israel and the
Palestinians* (Boston, MA: South End Press, 1983); Barbara Gregory, "U.S. relations with
Lebanon: A Troubled Course", *American–Arab Affairs* no. 35 (Winter, 1990–91), 62–93.
22 Najem, *Lebanon's Renaissance, op. cit.,* 133–141.
23 *ibid.*
24 Although not particularly well covered, the Beirut broadsheet *The Daily Star* carried
several articles on the agreement.
25 Najem, *Lebanon's Renaissance, op. cit.,* 133–141.

26 The most recent account of this period is found in Michael Young, *The Ghosts of Martyrs Square: An Eyewitness Account of Lebanon's Life Struggle* (New York: Simon & Schuster, 2010).
27 For a discussion on security-sector reform, see Emile el-Hokayem and Elena McGovern, *Towards a More Secure and Stable Lebanon: Prospects for Security Sector Reform* (Washington, DC: Henry L. Stimson Center, 2008).
28 This was a theme constantly promoted at the National Dialogue meetings by leaders within the movement, including former president Amin Gemayel.
29 Michael Young, *The Ghosts of Martyrs Square, op. cit.*
30 For a discussion of this dynamic alliance, see Sune Haugbolle, *The Alliance Between Iran, Syria and Hizbollah and its Implications for the Political Development in Lebanon and the Middle East* (Copenhagen: Danish Institute for International Studies, 2006); Esther Pan, *Syria, Iran, and the Mideast Conflict* (New York: Council on Foreign Relations, 2006).
31 See, for example, Michael Bell, "Get Real, Get Smart on Lebanon", *The Globe and Mail* 10 August 2006.
32 For a human rights perspective on Hizbollah's rocket attacks into Israel, see Human Rights Watch, *Civilians under Assault: Hezbollah's Rocket Attacks on Israel in the 2006 War* (New York: Human Rights Watch, 2007).
33 Anthony Cordesman, *Iran's Support of the Hezbollah in Lebanon* (Washington, DC: Center for Strategic and International Studies, 2006).
34 For an account of the state of the Lebanese armed forces, see Aram Nerguizian and Anthony Cordesman, *The Lebanese Armed Forces: Challenges and Opportunities in Post-Syria Lebanon* (Washington, DC: Center for Strategic and International Studies, 2009).
35 See Michael Young, *The Ghosts of Martyrs Square, op. cit.*

Conclusion

1 For the most recent and detailed account of the STL controversy, see International Crisis Group, *Trial by Fire: The Politics of the Special Tribunal for Lebanon*, Middle East Report N100 (Brussels: International Crisis Group, 2010).
2 Asraf Monzar, "Secular Activists Plan Protest in Bid to Topple Sectarian Regime", *The Daily Star* 26 February 2011.

BIBLIOGRAPHY

AbuKhalil, As'ad. *Historical Dictionary of Lebanon*. Lanham, MD: Scarecrow Press, 1998.

Achcar, Gilbert and Michel Warschawski. *The 33-Day War: Israel's War on Hezbollah in Lebanon and its Consequences*. Boulder, CO: Paradigm, 2007.

Alagha, Joseph. *The Shifts in Hizbullah's Ideology: Religious Ideology, Political Ideology, and Political Program*. Amsterdam: University Press Amsterdam, 2007.

Arnson, Cynthia J. and I. William Zartman. *Rethinking the Economics of War: The Intersection of Need, Creed, and Greed*. Baltimore, MD: Johns Hopkins University Press, 2005.

Barakat, Halim. *Lebanon in Strife: Student Prelude to the Civil War*. Austin: University of Texas Press, 1977.

——(ed.) *Toward a Viable Lebanon*. London: Croom Helm, 1988.

Betts, Robert Brenton. *The Druze*. New Haven, CT: Yale University Press, 1988.

Binder, Leonard (ed.) *Politics in Lebanon*. New York: John Wiley and Sons, 1966.

Blanford, N. *Killing Mr Lebanon: The Assassination of Rafik Hariri and its Impact on the Middle East*. London: IB Tauris, 2006.

Brynen, Rex. *Sanctuary and Survival: The PLO in Lebanon*. Boulder, CO: Westview Press, 1990.

Chomsky, Noam. *The Fateful Triangle: The United States, Israel and the Palestinians*. Boston, MA: South End Press, 1983.

Cobban, Helena. *The Making of Modern Lebanon*. London: Hutchinson, 1985.

Cobham, David and Ghassan Dibeh. *Monetary Policy and Central Banking in the Middle East and North Africa*. London: Routledge, 2009.

Collings, Deirdre (ed.) *Peace for Lebanon? From War to Reconstruction*. London: Lynne Rienner, 1994.

Council for Development and Reconstruction. *Progress Reports (1994–96)*. Beirut: Mediterranean Press (1994–96).

Dagher, Carole. *Les Paris du General*. Beirut: FMA, 1992.

——*Bring Down the Walls*. London: Palgrave Macmillan, 2000.

Dawisha, Adeed. *Syria and the Lebanese Crisis*. New York: St Martin's Press, 1980.

Dib, Kamal. *Warlords and Merchants: The Lebanese Business and Political Establishment*. Reading, UK: Ithaca Press, 2004.

El Khazen, Farid. *The Breakdown of the State in Lebanon, 1967–1976*. London: I.B. Tauris, 1999.

Evron, Yair. *War and Intervention in Lebanon: The Israeli–Syrian Deterrence Dialogue*. London: Croom Helm, 1987.

Fawaz, Leila. *An Occasion for War: Civil Conflict in Lebanon and Damascus in 1860*. London: I.B. Tauris, 1995.

Fisk, Robert. *Pity the Nation: Lebanon at War*. Oxford: Oxford University Press, 1990.

Gates, Carolyn. *The Merchant Republic of Lebanon*. London: I.B. Tauris, 1998.

Gaunson, A.B. *The Anglo–French Clash in Lebanon and Syria, 1940–45*. London: Macmillan, 1987.

Gemayel, Amin. *Rebuilding Lebanon*. Lanham, MD: University Press of America, 1992.

Gilmour, David. *Lebanon: The Fractured Country*. London: Sphere Books, 1987.

Gilsenan, Michael. *Lords of the Lebanese Marches: Violence and Narrative in an Arab Society*. Berkeley, CA: University of California Press, 1996.

Goria, Wade. *Sovereignty and Leadership in Lebanon 1943–1976*. Reading, UK: Ithaca Press, 1985.

Halawi, Majed. *A Lebanon Defied: Musa al-Sadr and the Shi'a Community*. Boulder, CO: Westview Press, 1992.

Haley, Edward P. and Lewis W. Snider (eds) *Lebanon in Crisis: Participants and Issues*. Syracuse, NY: Syracuse University Press, 1979.

Hanf, Theodor. *Coexistence in Wartime Lebanon: Decline of a State and Rise of a Nation*. I.B. Tauris, 1994.

Harel, Amos and Avi Isacharoff. *34 days: Israel, Hezbollah, and the War in Lebanon*. London: Palgrave Macmillan, 2008.

Harris, William. *Many Faces of Lebanon*. Princeton, NJ: Markus Wiener, 1997.

Hinnebusch, Raymond and Anoushiravan Ehteshami (eds) *The Foreign Policies of Middle East States*. London: Lynne Rienner, 2002.

Hitti, Philip. *A Short History of Lebanon*. New York: St Martin's Press, 1965.

Hof, Frederic. *Galilee Divided: The Israel–Lebanon Frontier, 1916–1984*. Boulder, CO: Westview Press, 1985.

Hourani, Albert. *A History of the Arab Peoples*. Cambridge, MA: Harvard University Press, 1991.

Hudson, Michael. *The Precarious Republic*. New York: Random House, 1968.

Iskandar, Marwan. *Rafiq Hariri and the Fate of Lebanon*. London: Saqi, 2006.

Johnson, Michael. *Class & Client in Beirut: The Sunni Muslim Community and the Lebanese State 1840–1985*. London: Ithaca Press, 1986.

——*All Honourable Men*. London: I.B. Tauris, 2001.

Jumblatt, Kamal. *I Speak for Lebanon*. London: Zed Press, 1982.

Kalawoun, Nasser. *The Struggle for Lebanon*. London: I.B. Tauris, 2000.

Kerr, M. *Imposing Power-sharing: Conflict and Coexistence in Northern Ireland and Lebanon*. Dublin: Irish Academic Press, 2006.

Khalaf, Samir. *Lebanon's Predicament*. New York: Columbia University Press, 1987.

——*Civil and Uncivil Violence in Lebanon: A History of the Internationalization of Communal Conflict*. New York: Columbia University Press, 2002.

Khalidi, Rashid. *Under Siege: PLO Decisionmaking during the 1982 War*. New York: Columbia University Press, 1986.

Khalidi, Walid. *Conflict and Violence in Lebanon: Confrontation in the Middle East*. Cambridge, MA: Center for International Affairs, Harvard University, 1979.

Makdisi, Samir A. *The Lessons of Lebanon: The Economics of War and Development*. London: I.B. Tauris, 2004.

Makdisi, Ussama. *The Culture of Sectarianism*. Berkeley, CA: University of California Press, 2000.

Najem, Tom Pierre. *Lebanon's Renaissance: The Political Economy of Reconstruction*. Reading, UK: Ithaca Press, 2000.

Naoum, Sarkis. *Michel Aoun, Reve ou Illusion?* Beirut: Mediterranean Press, 1992.

Norton, Richard Augustus. *Amal, and the Shi'a Struggle for the Soul of Lebanon*. Austin, TX: University of Texas Press, 1987.

Odeh, B.J. *Lebanon: Dynamics of Conflict*. London: Zed Press, 1983.

Owen, Roger (ed.) *Essays on the Crisis in Lebanon*. Reading, UK: Ithaca Press, 1976.

Phares, Walid. *Lebanese Christian Nationalism*. London: Lynne Rienner, 1995.

Quilliam, Neil. *Syria and the New World Order*. Reading, UK: Ithaca Press, 1999.

Rabinovich, Itamar. *The War for Lebanon, 1970–1985*. Ithaca, NY: Cornell University Press, 1985.

Ranstorp, Magnus. *Hizb'Allah in Lebanon*. London: Palgrave Macmillan, 1996.

Richani, Nazih. *Dilemmas of Democracy and Political Parties in Sectarian Societies: The Case of the Progressive Socialist Party of Lebanon 1949–1996*. New York: St Martin's Press, 1997.

Roeder, Philip G. and Donald Rothchild. *Sustainable Peace: Power and Democracy After Civil Wars*. Ithaca, NY: Cornell University Press, 2005.

Rubin, Barry. (ed.) *Lebanon: Liberation, Conflict, and Crisis*. London: Palgrave Macmillan, 2009.

Salem, Elie. *Modernization Without Revolution: Lebanon's Experience*. Bloomington, IN: Indiana University Press, 1973.

Salibi, Kamal. *Crossroads to Civil War: Lebanon 1958–1976*. Reading, UK: Ithaca Press, 1976.

——*A House of Many Mansions: The History of Lebanon Reconsidered*. London: I.B. Tauris, 1988.

Schiff, Ze'ev and Ehud Ya'ari. *Israel's Lebanon War*. New York: Simon & Schuster, 1984.

Seale, Patrick. *Asad: The Struggle for the Middle East*. Berkeley, CA: University of California Press, 1989.

Sirriyeh, Hussein. *Lebanon: Dimensions of Conflict*. Oxford: Nuffield Press, 1989.

Shahin, Wassim N. and Ghassan Dibeh. *Earnings Inequality, Unemployment, and Poverty in the Middle East and North Africa*. Westport, CT: Greenwood, 2000.

Shanahan, Rodger. *The Shi'a of Lebanon: Clans, Parties and Clerics*. London: I.B.Tauris, 2005.

Shay, Shaul. *The Axis of Evil: Iran, Hizballah, and the Palestinian Terror*. Piscataway, NJ: Transaction Publishers, 2005.

Shehadi, Nadim and Dana Haffar Mills (eds) *Lebanon: A History of Conflict and Consensus*. London: I.B. Tauris, 1988.

Suleiman, Michael. *Political Parties in Lebanon*. Ithaca, NY: Cornell University Press, 1967.

Sulh, Raghïd. *Lebanon and Arabism: National Identity and State Formation*. London: I.B.Tauris, 2004.

Weinberger, Naomi Joy. *Syrian Intervention in Lebanon: The 1975–76 Civil War*. Oxford: Oxford University Press, 1986.

Winslow, Charles. *Lebanon: War and Politics in a Fragmented Society*. London: Routledge, 1996.

Young, Michael. *The Ghosts of Martyrs Square: An Eyewitness Account of Lebanon's Life Struggle*. New York: Simon & Schuster, 2010.

Zamir, Meir. *The Formation of Modern Lebanon*. London: Croom Helm, 1985.

——*Lebanon's Quest*. London: I.B. Tauris, 1997.

Zisser, Eyal. *Lebanon: The Challenges of Independence*. London: I.B. Tauris, 2000.

Journal articles

Abraham, A.J. "The Lebanon War, in Retrospect and Prospect", *Journal of Third World Studies* 11 (Fall, 1994), 117–150.

AbuKhalïl, As'ad. "Syria and the Shiites: Al-Asad's Policy in Lebanon", *Third World Quarterly* 12, no. 2 (April, 1989), 1–19.

Abu Hamad, Aziz. "Communal Strife in Lebanon: Ancient Animosities or State Intervention", *Journal of International Affairs* 49 (Summer, 1995), 231–254.

Aruri, Naseer. "The United States Intervention in Lebanon", *Arab Studies Quarterly* 7, no. 4 (Fall, 1985), 59–74.

Baroudi, Sami. "Conflict and Co-operation within Lebanon's Business Community: Relations between Merchants' and Industrialists' Associations", *Middle Eastern Studies* 37, no. 4 (October, 2001), 71–100.

Bieber, Florian. "Bosnia-Herzegovina and Lebanon: Historical Lessons of Two Multireligious States", *Third World Quarterly* 21, no. 2 (April, 2000), 269–281.

Bishku, Michael. "The 1958 American Intervention in Lebanon: A Historical Assessment", *American–Arab Affairs* no. 31 (Winter, 1989–90), 106–119.

Chami, Saade. "Economic Performance in a War-Economy: The Case of Lebanon", *Canadian Journal of Development Studies* 13, no. 3 (1992), 325–336.

Crighton, Elizabeth and Martha Abele MacIver. "The Evolution of Protracted Ethnic Conflict: Group Dominance and Political Underdevelopment in Northern Ireland and Lebanon", *Comparative Politics* 23 (January, 1991), 127–142.

Deeb, Marius. "The External Dimension of the Conflict in Lebanon: The Role of Syria", *Journal of South Asian and Middle Eastern Studies* XII, no. 3 (Spring, 1989), 37–52.

Deeb, Mary-Jane and Marius Deeb. "Regional Conflict and Regional Solutions: Lebanon", *Annals of the American Academy of Political and Social Science* 518, (November, 1991), 82–94.

Denoeux, G. and R. Springborg. "Hariri's Lebanon: Singapore of the Middle East or Sanaa of the Levant?", *Middle East Policy* 6, no. 2 (2008), 158–173.

Goglio, Silvio. "Lebanon: From Development to Civil War", *Mediterranean Quarterly* 8, no. 3 (Summer, 1997), 76.

Gregory, Barbara. "U.S. Relations with Lebanon: A Troubled Course", *American–Arab Affairs* no. 35 (Winter, 1990–91), 62–93.

Haddad, Simon. "The Christians of Lebanon in the Context of Syrian–Israeli Political Relations", *Journal of Social, Political and Economic Studies* 26, no. 3 (Fall, 2001), 589–624.

——"Christian–Muslim Relations and Attitudes towards the Lebanese State", *Journal of Muslim Minority Affairs* 21, no. 1 (April, 2001), 131–148.

Hamzeh, Nizar. "Clientalism, Lebanon: Roots and Trends", *Middle Eastern Studies* 37, no. 3 (July, 2001), 167–178.

Harik, Iliya. "Voting Participation and Political Integration in Lebanon 1943–1974", *Middle Eastern Studies* 16, no. 1 (January, 1980), 27–47.

——"The Economic and Social Factors in the Lebanese Crisis", *Journal of Arab Affairs* 1, no. 2 (April, 1982), 209–244.

Harik, J. "Change and Continuity Among the Lebanese Druze Community: The Civil Administration of the Mountains, 1983–1990", *Middle Eastern Studies* 29, no. 3 (July, 1993), 377–398.

——"Syrian Foreign Policy and State/Resistance Dynamics in Lebanon", *Studies in Conflict and Terrorism* 20, no. 3 (1997), 249–265.

Hottinger, Arnold. "Zu'ama and Parties in the Lebanese Crisis of 1958", *Middle East Journal* 15, no. 2 (Spring, 1961), 127–140.

Hudson, Michael. "The Lebanese Crisis: The Limits of Consociational Democracy", *Journal of Palestine Studies* 5, no. 3–4 (Spring–Summer, 1976), 109–122.

——"The Palestinian Factor in the Lebanese Civil War", *Middle East Journal* 32, no. 3 (Summer, 1978), 261–277.

——"Palestinians and Lebanon: The Common Story", *Journal of Refugee Studies* 10, no. 3 (1997), 243–260.

Johnson, Michael. "Factional Politics in Lebanon: The Case of the Islamic Society of Benevolent Intentions (al-Maqasids) of Beirut", *Middle Eastern Studies* 14, no. 1 (Janaury, 1978), 56–75.

Kaufman, Asher. "Phoenicianism: The Formation of an Identity in Lebanon in 1920", *Middle Eastern Studies* 37, no. 1 (January, 2001), 173–194.

Khalaf, Samir. "Primordial Ties and Politics in Lebanon", *Middle Eastern Studies* 4, no. 2 (1968).

Khalidi, Walid. "Lebanon: Yesterday and Tomorrow", *Middle East Journal* 43, no. 3 (Summer, 1989), 375–387.

Khazen, F. "Permanent Settlement of Palestinians in Lebanon: A Recipe for Conflict", *Journal of Refugee Studies* 10, no. 3 (1997), 275–293.

Kisirwani, Maroun. "The Lebanese Bureaucracy under Stress: How Did It Survive?" *Beirut Review* no. 4 (Fall, 1992), 29–42.

Knight, Caroline. "Traditional Influences upon Lebanese Politics", *Journal of Social, Political and Economic Studies* 17 (Fall/Winter, 1992), 327–343.

Lee, N. "More Like Korea than Suez: British and American Intervention in the Levant in 1958", *Small Wars and Insurgencies* 8, no. 3 (Winter, 1997), 1–24.

Lijphart, Arend. "Typologies of Democratic Systems", *Comparative Political Studies* 1, no. 1 (1968), 3–44.

——"Consociational Democracy", *World Politics* 21, no. 2 (1969), 207–225.

Malik, Habib. "Lebanon in the 1990s: Stability Without Freedom?" *Global Affairs*, part 7 (Winter, 1992), 79–109.

McLaurin, Ronald. "Lebanon: Into or Out of Oblivion?" *Current History* (January, 1992), 29–33.

Nasrallah, F. "Lebanese Perceptions of the Palestinians in Lebanon: Case Studies", *Journal of Refugee Studies* 10, no. 3 (1997), 349–359.

Nehme, Michel. "Lebanon: Open Arena for Regional Feuds", *Journal of Third World Studies* 12 (Spring, 1995), 120–149.

Nizameddin, T. "The Political Economy of Lebanon under Rafiq Hariri: An Interpretation", *Middle East Journal* 60, no. 1 (January, 2006): 95–114.

Norton, Augustus Richard. "Lebanon After Ta'if: Is the Civil War Over?" *Middle East Journal* 45, no. 3 (1991), 457–473.

——"Lebanon: With Friends Like These", *Current History* 96, no. 606 (January, 1997), 6–12.

——"Lebanon's Malaise", *Survival* 42, no. 4 (Winter, 2000/2001), 35–50.

Perthes, Volker. "Myths and Money: Four Years of Hariri and Lebanon's Preparation for a New Middle East", *Middle East Report* 27, no. 2 (Spring, 1997), 16–21.

——"The Political Economy of the Syrian Succession", *Survival* 43, no. 1 (September, 2001), 143–154.

Rigby, Andrew. "Lebanon: Patterns of Confessional Politics", *Parliamentary Affairs* 53, no. 1 (January, 2000), 169–180.

Road, Mansour. "Everyone Misunderstood the Depth of the Movement Identifying with Aoun", *MERIP Reports* 20, no. 1 (1990), 11–14.

Salem, Paul. "Skirting Democracy: Lebanon's 1996 Elections and Beyond", *Middle East Report* 27, no. 2 (Spring, 1997) 26–29.

Salibi, Kamal. "Lebanon under Fouad Chehab – 1958–1964", *Middle Eastern Studies* 2, no. 3 (April, 1966), 211–226.

Seaver, Brenda. "The Regional Sources of Power-sharing Failure: The Case of Lebanon", *Political Science Quarterly* 115, no. 2 (Summer, 2000), 247–271.

Shiblak, A. "Palestinians in Lebanon and the PLO", *Journal of Refugee Studies* 10, no. 3 (1997), 261–274.

Shields, V. E. "Political Reform in Lebanon: Has the Cedar Revolution Failed?", *Journal of Legislative Studies* 14, no. 4 (2008): 474–487.

Simon, Steven N. and Jonathan Stevenson. "Declawing the 'Party of God': Toward Normalization in Lebanon", *World Policy Journal* 18, no. 2 (Summer, 2001), 31–42.

Sirriyeh, H. "Lebanon in Search of a Viable Settlement", *Israel Affairs* 4, no. 2 (Winter, 1997), 112–129.

Snider, Lewis. "The Lebanese Forces: Their Origins and Role in Lebanon's Politics", *Middle East Journal* 38, no. 1 (Winter, 1984), 1–32.

Suleiman, J. "Palestinians in Lebanon and the Role of Non-Governmental Organizations", *Journal of Refugee Studies* 10, no. 3 (1997), 397–410.

Thompson, Eric. "Will Syria Have to Withdraw from Lebanon?" *Middle East Journal* 56, no. 1 (Winter, 2002), 72–93.

Weighill, M. "Palestinians in Lebanon: The Politics of Assistance", *Journal of Refugee Studies* 10, no. 3 (1997), 294–313.

Zamir, Meir. "The Lebanese Presidential Elections of 1970 and their Impact on the Civil War of 1975–1976", *Middle Eastern Studies* 16, no. 1 (January, 1980), 49–69.

Zisser, Eyal. "The Downfall of the Khuri Administration: A Dubious Revolution", *Middle Eastern Studies* 30 (July, 1994), 486–511.

Reports

Abdel-Latif, Omayma. *Lebanon's Sunni Islamists: A Growing Force*. Washington, DC: Carnegie Endowment for International Peace, 2008.

Addis, Casey L. *Lebanon: Background and U.S. Relations*. Congressional Research Service Reports for the People, 2008. http://opencrs.com
——*U.S. Security Assistance to Lebanon*. Congressional Research Service Reports for the People, 2009. http://opencrs.com
Amnesty International *Israel/Lebanon: Deliberate Destruction or "Collateral Damage"? Israeli Attacks on Civilian Infrastructure*. London: Amnesty International Publications, 2006.
——*Israel/Lebanon: Out of All Proportion – Civilians Bear the Brunt of the War*. London: Amnesty International Publications, 2006.
——*Israel/Lebanon: Under Fire; Hizbullah's Attacks on Northern Israel*. London: Amnesty International Publications, 2006.
——*Lebanon: A Human Rights Agenda for the Elections*. London: Amnesty International Publications, 2009.
Aspen Institute. *Lebanon: The Swing State of a New Levant*. Washington, DC: Aspen Institute, 2008.
Avraham, Hanna. *Disarming Hizbullah: The Public Debate in Lebanon*. Washington, DC: Middle East Media Research Institute, 2005.
Azani, Eitan. *Hizballah: A Pragmatic Terror Organization of Global Reach*. Herzliya, Israel: International Policy Institute for Counter-Terrorism, 2005.
Berkovich, Dani. *The Report of the Commission of Investigation into the Murder of Hariri: Implications for Syria*. Tel Aviv: Tel Aviv University, Jaffee Center for Strategic Studies, 2006.
Beyhum, Nabil, Assem Salam and Jad Tabet (eds) *Beyrouth: construire l'avenir, reconstruire le passe?* Paris: l'Urban Research Institute, 1995.
Brom, Shlomo. *The Confrontation with Hizbullah*. Tel Aviv: Tel Aviv University, Jaffee Center for Strategic Studies, 2006.
Chaitou, Kamal, Thaer Ghandour, Rima Merhi and Lynn Zovighian. *Lebanon is Not Two Camps*. Zurich: Swiss Federal Institute of Technology, Center for Security Studies and Conflict Research, 2008.
Chernitsky, B. and Y. Carmon. *The Lebanon Crisis: Hizbullah's Victory and its Regional Implications*. Washington, DC: Middle East Media Research Institute, 2008.
Clawson, Patrick and Robert G. Rabil. *The Role of International Monitors and Observers in the Lebanese Elections*. Washington, DC: Washington Institute for Near East Policy, 2005.
Cordesman, Anthony H. *Iran's Support of the Hezbollah in Lebanon*. Washington, DC: Center for Strategic and International Studies, 2006.
——*Israel's Uncertain Military Performance and Strategic Goals in Lebanon*. Washington, DC: Center for Strategic and International Studies, 2006.
——*The Road to Nowhere: Everyone's Strategic Failures in Lebanon*. Washington, DC: Center for Strategic and International Studies, 2006.
——*Summer Wars in Lebanon?* Washington, DC: Center for Strategic and International Studies, 2007.
——*The Lessons of the Israeli–Lebanon War*. Washington, DC: Center for Strategic and International Studies, 2008.
Council for Development and Reconstruction. *Horizon 2000 for Reconstruction and Development: Main Report*. Beirut: Council for Development and Reconstruction, 1993.
Coyne, A. Heather and Patricia Karam. *Prospects for Mediation of the Lebanon Crisis*. Washington, DC: United States Institute of Peace, 2006.
Davis, Ian. *The Transatlantic Dimension to the Conflict in Lebanon: Whatever Happened to the Responsibility to Protect?* London and Washington, DC: British American Security Information Council, 2006.
Dibeh, Ghassan. *Foreign Aid and Economic Development in Postwar Lebanon*. Research Paper No. 2007/37. Helsinki: United Nations University, World Institute for Development Economics Research, 2007.
Eken, S. *Economic Dislocation and Recovery in Lebanon*. Occasional Paper. Washington, DC: International Monetary Fund, 1995.
El-Hokayem, Emile. *The Middle East After the Lebanon War*. Washington, DC: Henry L. Stimson Center, 2006.

El-Hokayem, Emile and Elena McGovern. *Towards a More Secure and Stable Lebanon: Prospects for Security Sector Reform*. Washington, DC: Henry L. Stimson Center, 2008.

Eytan, Freddy. *Europe and the War in Lebanon*. Jerusalem: Jerusalem Center for Public Affairs, 2006.

Feltman, Jeffrey, Tony Badran and David Schenker. *Elections in Lebanon: Implications for Washington, Beirut, and Damascus*. Washington, DC: Washington Institute for Near East Policy, 2007.

FitzGerald, Peter. *Report of the Fact-finding Mission to Lebanon Inquiring into the Causes, Circumstances and Consequences of the Assassination of Former Prime Minister Rafik Hariri*. New York: Council on Foreign Relations, 2005.

Ganji, Babak. *Iran and Israel: Asymmetric Warfare and Regional Strategy*. Zurich: Swiss Federal Institute of Technology, Center for Security Studies and Conflict Research, 2006.

Ghobril, Nassib. *The Effects of Government Policies on Lebanon's Banking Sector*. Vancouver: Fraser Institute, 2006.

Gissin, Raanan. *The Critical Importance of Israeli Public Diplomacy in the War against the Iran–Hizballah Axis of Terror*. Jerusalem: Jerusalem Center for Public Affairs, 2006.

Guitta, Olivier. *France and Hizbullah: The End of the Affair*. Washington, DC: Brookings Institution, 2005.

Haugbolle, Sune. *The Alliance Between Iran, Syria and Hizbollah and its Implications for the Political Development in Lebanon and the Middle East*. Copenhagen: Danish Institute for International Studies, 2006.

Herzog, Michael. *The Hizballah Conundrum*. Washington, DC: Washington Institute for Near East Policy, 2005.

Hourani, Albert. *Political Society in Lebanon: A Historical Introduction*. London: Centre for Lebanese Studies, 1986.

Human Rights Watch. *Fatal Strikes: Israel's Indiscriminate Attacks against Civilians in Lebanon*. New York: Human Rights Watch, 2006.

——*Civilians Under Assault: Hezbollah's Rocket Attacks on Israel in the 2006 War*. New York: Human Rights Watch, 2007.

——*Why They Died: Civilian Casualties in Lebanon During the 2006 War*. New York: Human Rights Watch, 2007.

International Crisis Group. *Lebanon: Managing the Gathering Storm*. Brussels: International Crisis Group, 2005.

——*Syria After Lebanon, Lebanon After Syria*. Brussels: International Crisis Group, 2005.

——*Israel/Hizbollah/Lebanon: Avoiding Renewed Conflict*. Brussels: International Crisis Group, 2006.

——*Israel/Palestine/Lebanon: Climbing Out of the Abyss*. Brussels: International Crisis Group, 2006.

——*Hizbollah and the Lebanese Crisis*. Brussels: International Crisis Group, 2007.

——*Lebanon: Hizbollah's Weapons Turn Inward*. Brussels: International Crisis Group, 2008.

——*The New Lebanese Equation: The Christians' Central Role*. Brussels: International Crisis Group, 2008.

——*Lebanon's Elections: Avoiding a New Cycle of Confrontation*. Brussels: International Crisis Group, 2009.

Irani, George Emile. *Irregular Warfare and Non-State Combatants: Israel and Hezbollah*. Madrid: Fundacion para las Relaciones Internacionales y el Dialogo Exterior, 2007.

——*The Lebanese Predicament: Stability or Civil War in 2007?* Madrid: Real Instituto Elcano de Estudios Internacionales y Estrategicos, 2007.

Jacob, C. *Reactions to Former Lebanese PM al-Hariri's Assassination*. Washington, DC: Middle East Media Research Institute, 2005.

Jacoby, Tami Amanda. *Conflict in Lebanon: On the Perpetual Threshold*. Calgary, Alberta: Canadian Defence & Foreign Affairs Institute, 2007.

Jaulin, Thibaut. *Lebanese Politics of Nationality and Emigration*. Florence, Italy: European University Institute, 2006.

Kagan, Kimberly. *Iran's Proxy War Against the United States and Iraq.* Washington, DC: Institute for the Study of War, 2007.

Kattouf, Theodore and Walid Phares. *After the Hariri Assassination: Syria, Lebanon, and U.S. Policy.* Washington, DC: Washington Institute for Near East Policy, 2005.

Koekenbier, Peter. *Balancing Lebanon.* Zurich: Swiss Federal Institute of Technology, Center for Security Studies and Conflict Research, 2007.

Levitt, Matthew. *Hezballah Finances: Funding the Party of God.* Washington, DC: Washington Institute for Near East Policy, 2005.

——*Shutting Hizballah's "Construction Jihad".* Washington, DC: Washington Institute for Near East Policy, 2007.

——*Hizballah's Military Wing under Pressure Despite Political Gains.* Washington, DC: Washington Institute for Near East Policy, 2008.

Levitt, Matthew and Jake Lipton. *Dangerous Partners: Targeting the Iran–Hizballah Alliance.* Washington, DC: Washington Institute for Near East Policy, 2007.

Malik, Habib. *Between Damascus and Jerusalem: Lebanon and the Middle East Peace Process.* Washington, DC: Washington Institute for Near East Policy, 1997.

McDowell, David. *Lebanon: A Conflict of Minorities.* London: Minority Rights Group, 1986.

Muehlbacher, Tamirace Fakhoury. *Lebanon's Versatile Nationalism.* Florence, Italy: European University Institute, 2008.

Nerguizian, Aram and Anthony H. Cordesman. *The Lebanese Armed Forces: Challenges and Opportunities in Post-Syria Lebanon.* Washington, DC: Center for Strategic and International Studies, 2009.

Pan, Esther. *Syria, Iran, and the Mideast Conflict.* New York: Council on Foreign Relations, 2006.

Pascual, Carlos. *Restoring Confidence in Lebanon's Future.* Washington, DC: Brookings Institution, 2006.

Pew Global Attitudes Project. *Mixed Views of Hamas and Hezbollah in Largely Muslim Nations: Little Enthusiasm for Many Muslim Leaders.* Washington, DC: Pew Global Attitudes Project, 2010.

Rabil, Robert. *Lebanon's Presidential Crisis.* Washington, DC: Washington Institute for Near East Policy, 2007.

Raphaeli, Nimrod. *The Iranian Roots of Hizbullah.* Washington, DC: Middle East Media Research Institute, 2008.

Saad-Ghorayeb, Amal and Marina Ottaway. *Hizbollah and its Changing Identities.* Washington, DC: Carnegie Endowment for International Peace, 2007.

Salem, Paul. *Hizbollah Attempts a Coup d'État.* Washington, DC: Carnegie Endowment for International Peace, 2008.

Salame, Ghassen. *Lebanon's Injured Identities: Who Represents Whom During a Civil War?* Oxford, UK: Centre for Lebanese Studies, 1986.

Slavin, Barbara. *Mullahs, Money, and Militias: How Iran Exerts its Influence in the Middle East.* Washington, DC: United States Institute of Peace, 2008.

Tocci, Nathalie. *What Went Wrong? The Impact of Western Policies Towards Hamas and Hizbollah.* Brussels: Centre for European Policy Studies, 2007.

Tov, Imri. *The Budget Debate after the Lebanon War: A Chance to Change.* Tel Aviv: Tel Aviv University, Jaffee Center for Strategic Studies, 2006.

Zelnick, Robert. *How Iran Could Help End the Israeli–Palestinian Conflict.* Philadelphia, PA: Foreign Policy Research Institute, 2007.

Other sources

The Daily Star (daily) – Beirut

Lebanon Report (monthly) – Beirut

The Economist (weekly) – London

INDEX

March 8 Alliance seats in 75; members term of office 60; Muslim representation in 13, 32, 60, 75; sectarian parity in 50, 60; *see also* parliamentary elections; Speaker of the House
Chamoun, Camille 16, 23
Chatilla refugee camp massacre 39
Chehab, Fouad 23–4
Christian militias 37–8; and Amin Gemayel government 39; and Aoun government 43; dominance in East Beirut 36; and Druze conflict 39, 40; formation of 25, 28; and Leftist/PLO fighting 35; Palestinian massacres 35, 39; *see also* Kata'eb; Lebanese Forces
Christians 5, 6, 8, 26; and Cairo Agreement (1969) 25; and cedar revolution 72, 75; and deconfessionalisation 29; disenfranchisement of, Leftist/PLO demand for 36; and Israel alliance 38, 39; and Lebanese Left, perception of 29; and March 14 Alliance 73, 74; and Mikati government 124; and *mutasarrifiyya* 7; and national office 9, 10, 13; nationalist elements among 11; and Palestinian presence, opposition to 28, 30; and Palestinian refugees 25; and power-sharing arrangements 32; as pro-Western 12, 29, 101; and Saad Hariri government 81–2; and secular system 9; and Syrian presence, opposition to 72, 73; *see also* Maronite Christians
civil service *see* bureaucracy
civil war (spring 1958) 23
civil war (1975–90) 2, 3, 27, 34–47; Beirut as focal point 35, 36; causal factors, differing schools of thought 28–33; "dual government" (1988–90) 42–3, 44; end of 43, 49; EU and 112; Israeli invasion and occupation (1982–85) 38–40, 42; Lebanese army and 35; Lebanese state and 35, 37, 41; Leftists/PLO alliance and 35, 36, 37; massacres and revenge killings 35, 39, 40; militia rule (1985–88) 41–5; multinational peacekeeping force 38, 40–1; outbreak 35; PLO and 35, 36, 37–8; sectarian entrenchment and shifting alliances (1976–81) 37–8; Syrian intervention 36–7, 38, 39, 40, 41; systemic implications of 44–7
class-related tensions 6, 31
Clinton, Bill 56

Cold War, end of 43
collapse of Lebanese state 28–33
colonialism 5
commerce, Lebanon as regional centre for 85, 101, 110
Communist parties 17
confessionalism 1, 5, 8, 14, 15–17, 18, 21, 50, 88; and constitution (1926) 9; elimination of 26, 29
consociational democracy 1, 5, 15, 17–19, 50, 125
Constitution 14, 15, 100; and abolition of French mandate 11; French suspension of 11; law/legal relations and 9; and National Pact (1943) 13; as reflection of confessional divisions 9; Syrian push to amend 70, 71; Ta'if Accord reforms 43, 50, 51, 60
construction industry 98
Corm, Georges 30
corruption 68, 69, 94; public sector 87, 88, 89, 93, 94; and reconstruction process 87, 90–1, 93
Council for Development and Reconstruction (CDR) 87, 89, 96
Council of Ministers 9, 13, 42–3
Council of the South 90
cultural neutrality 12–13, 19
culture 7, 113
currency crises 85, 95
customs duties 95

debt 68, 89, 93, 94, 95, 96
Defence and Security Affairs Committee 53
democracy: consociational 1, 5, 15, 17–19, 50, 125; liberal 1, 9, 14, 15, 17, 19
democratisation 113
demographic shifts 28, 29, 31–2, 49, 50, 54–5
Deuxieme Bureau 24, 25–6
disarmament of militias 43, 51, 52, 65, 70, 78, 104; Hizbollah 52, 70, 72, 73, 78, 79, 80, 97, 102–3, 104, 112, 117, 120, 121, 122
Doha Agreement (2008) 80, 81
Druze 5, 16, 60; and cedar revolution 72, 73, 75; conflict with Christian militias 39, 40; and March 14 Alliance 74; and Maronite hostility 6; militias 41; and political crisis (2006–08) 81

economic crisis: (1991–92) 65, 84–5; (1997) and (1998) 68, 107; global 98
economic inequality 28, 31